For many years Bill Dembski has been the pacesetter in philosophical discussions of Intelligent Design. In this volume he applies his talents once again, suggesting an exceptionally creative, honest, and thought-provoking theodicy that analyzes the presence of evil prior to the Fall. Whatever your position, this work will stretch and challenge you to think carefully through a variety of crucial issues in an attempt to avoid the perennial problems that confront each major interpretation of the biblical data.

— *Gary R. Habermas,* Distinguished Research Professor, Liberty University

William Dembski seeks to uphold the traditional view that natural evil is the result of human sin, in the face of the massive scientific evidence that suffering and death were prevalent in nature long before the advent of humankind. His answer to the problem is embedded in far-reaching theological and philosophical speculations. In spite of his sometimes harsh dismissal of opposing views, Dembski's proposals are ingenious and thought-provoking, and deserving of careful consideration.

— *William Hasker,* Professor Emeritus of Philosophy, Huntington University

William Dembski is a first-rate scholar who has focused his attention on the perennial challenge to Christianity: Why does God allow such evil and cruelty in the world? While staying well within the bounds of Christian orthodoxy, Dembski offers fresh insights that can truly be described as groundbreaking. Whether you end up embracing his solution or not, *The End of Christianity* is a book all Christians—and even non-Christians—need to wrestle with. We enthusiastically recommend it.

— *Josh and Sean McDowell,* coauthors of
Evidence for the Resurrection and *More Than A Carpenter*

This is a thought-provoking and well-worth-reading book by a brilliant evangelical thinker on the perennial and puzzling problem of how to explain physical evil in the world before the Fall. I could not put it down. It has so much intellectually stimulating material in it.

— *Norman Geisler,* Distinguished Professor of Theology and Apologetics,
Veritas Evangelical Seminary, and author of many books on Christian apologetics

By brilliantly wrestling with a range of scientific, theological, and philosophical challenges to the conservative Christian worldview, William Dembski is establishing himself as the C. S. Lewis of this generation. Dembski blazes a new trail of thought through the morass of the problem of evil and leads us to a powerful and inspiring view of God, His Creation, and of our purpose in God's kingdom. This is a must-read book for everyone who has wondered how a good God fits with an evil world, be they conservative, liberal, or atheist.

— *John A. Bloom,* Professor of Physics,
Academic Director of the Science and Religion Program, Biola University

When Bill Dembski employs his characteristic brilliance and boldness to illuminate one of theology's thorniest problems, as he does in *The End of Christianity*, the result is a book that deserves a wide readership and serious attention from the experts.

— Phillip E. Johnson, author of *Darwin on Trial*

The End of Christianity is very different from William Dembski's previous books, most notable of which were the academic classic *The Design Inference* and the popular best seller *Intelligent Design*. The present book deals with perhaps the most profound question to challenge humankind, the problem of evil. Like everything else Dr. Dembski has written, this book will be controversial. However, the readers of *The End of Christianity* will be greatly rewarded with a rich intellectual/philosophical/theological feast.

— Henry F. Schaefer III,
Graham Perdue Professor of Chemistry, University of Georgia

I am deeply grateful for Dr. Dembski and his work. Theologians have long known that the problem of evil is one of the biggest threats to traditional Christianity. Here Dembski boldly tackles the problem and offers a thoughtful and clearly written approach to it. His overall argument, that all evil can be traced to the fall of man (even in a trans-temporal way), deserves serious consideration. Even if you might find particular points on which to differ with his judgments, you will do well to incorporate his insights into your own thinking. And the final two chapters, on thankfulness and purpose, show that this book supports a vigorous love for God in daily life. Thank you, Dr. Dembski, for using your talents so well!

—C. John ("Jack") Collins,
Professor of Old Testament, Covenant Theological Seminary

The most telling argument presented by non-Christians against the existence of the God of the Bible is the claim that the evils in our world are incompatible with the existence of a good, all-powerful, and loving God. This "argument from evil" turns up again and again, for example, in the writings of English atheist John Mortimer, author of the *Rumpole* stories. Believers have badly needed the kind of compelling case for biblical theodicy provided in Dr Dembski's new book.

—John Warwick Montgomery, author of many books and
Director of the International Academy of Apologetics,
Evangelism and Human Rights in Strasbourg, France

This book is an example of philosophical theology at its best. It contains fascinating and even exciting new perspectives on the problem of evil. While I am not convinced of every point that the author makes, *The End of Christianity* should be read by anyone who is interested in a Christian approach to natural and moral evil.

—Stephen T. Davis,
Russell K. Pitzer Professor of Philosophy, Claremont McKenna College

William Dembski's latest book, *The End of Christianity: Finding a Good God in an Evil World*, shows how the traditional Christian doctrine that sin entered the world through humans is not refuted by the evidence that natural evils (earthquakes, storms, disease, death, etc.) are chronologically much older than humans within the universe. Because time within the created universe need not follow the same order as the logical process of God's creation of the universe, human sin could have caused earlier evil. There are many aspects of the problem of evil left mysterious by this book (and indeed by all other attempts to solve the problem), but I strongly recommend *The End of Christianity* as a refreshing approach that maintains the traditional theistic doctrines of God's omniscience and omnipotence.

— *Don Page,* Professor of Physics, University of Alberta, Canada

For much too long, theodicy has been little more than a boutique topic in theology, a justification for the world's misery that lets God off the hook. William Dembski's new book goes a long way to restoring theodicy's original claim to be a master science of intelligent design. It is arguably the most worthy successor to Leibniz's own *Theodicy*, which artfully showed how a rational theology, properly understood, could retain its role of queen of the sciences in the modern world. No doubt the book will stir controversy among both the religious and the secular, as Dembski intertwines quite specific interpretations of Scriptures with equally specific interpretations of an array of physical and biological sciences, all in clear prose and with a deft philosophical touch. However, Dembski is no dogmatist, and all along he suggests alternative lines of thought that readers might pursue. Here we finally see in open view the full potential of intelligent design theory to put an end to the intellectual segregationism that has limited science-religion relations for much too long.

— *Steve Fuller,* Professor of Sociology, University of Warwick, UK, and author of *Dissent over Descent: Intelligent Design's Challenge to Darwinism*

Addressing the problem of a perfect God in an imperfect world, this book offers the most coherent answer to this question I've ever read. William A. Dembski has given us a bold and uncompromising theodicy that both confirms Christian orthodoxy *and* makes peace among our family of believers. Martin Luther King Jr. once said, "We will not build a peaceful world by following a negative path." This book eschews the "negative path" by launching a peace offensive offering a *positive* solution that meets the demands of natural and revealed theology. Reconciling the many points of an issue that has confounded generations, this is the most important contribution to the question of God and evil since Leibniz defined it nearly three hundred years ago.

— *Michael A. Flannery,* Professor and Associate Director for Historical Collections, University of Alabama, Birmingham

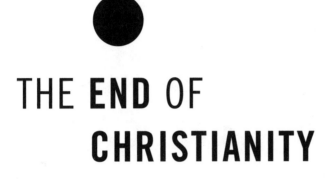

THE **END** OF **CHRISTIANITY**

THE **END** OF
CHRISTIANITY

FINDING A GOOD GOD IN AN EVIL WORLD

WILLIAM A. DEMBSKI

Published by B&H Publishing Group
Nashville, Tennessee

ISBN: 978-0-8054-2743-1

Dewey Decimal Classification: 231.8
Subject Heading: APOLOGETICS\CHRISTIANITY—
APOLOGETIC WORKS\PROVIDENCE AND GOVERNMENT OF GOD

Published in the UK by Paternoster
An imprint of Authentic Media
9 Holdom Avenue
Bletchley
Milton Keynes
Buckinghamshire
MK1 1QR, UK
www.loveauthentic.com/paternoster

British Library Cataloguing in Publication Data
A catalogue record for this book is available from the British Library
ISBN: 978-1-84227-682-2

In memory of

Ethel and Harry Cooper

John 13:35

---

*"What you believe to be true will control you,
whether it's true or not."*

—Jeremy LaBorde

CONTENTS

FOREWORD

F OR some years I have felt like a cork on a teeming sea tossed by the random nature of suffering. I was left holding on to the Christ who saves me and the Christ who will return, but with a heart that aches for meaning and purpose in the present and that too often is robbed of joy. I have felt like an actor on a stage and wondered whether anyone really is living a genuine life.

The week that I read this book I began to feel different. It has profoundly influenced my thinking. I am grateful to my friend Bill Dembski for writing it. I got to know Bill through his work on intelligent design (ID), for which he is well-known. Indeed, his contributions in this field have been seminal. And yet I suspect he will be remembered for the ideas in this book as much as for his shepherding of the intelligent design movement.

Bill is a brilliant man who speaks and writes without fear. It has been his life's work to know, love, and understand God as He is revealed in Jesus Christ and in creation. I am personally grateful that it isn't only a private matter for him. He has a consuming passion to help explain to others the mysteries he has come to grasp. The clear aim of all he does is to shine a brighter light on the One he loves, or rather to stand aside while the Light of the world shines into the lives of ordinary people like me.

On entering the Christian life, I devoured the Bible in frequent large portions and worked tirelessly to understand the history and purposes of God and to integrate them into a cogent whole. It was natural for me to opt for a plain reading of the Bible. And what could be plainer than the teaching of Genesis on creation? A young-earth perspective therefore seemed to me the only viable approach to anyone who took the Bible seriously.

To survive a medical education, I had a bubble into which I placed what I perceived to be theologically incompatible data. Surprisingly, not much in medical studies challenged a plain reading of the Bible. Yet there were times when the faculty insisted on enlightening us by inserting an evolutionary perspective on life and the human body. Uncomfortable as I was during these times, I felt inside that someday my beliefs in the Bible would trump the findings of science.

At the same time, in biochemistry, physiology, anatomy, and histology, I was studying complex systems that to me, as a former engineering student, looked obviously to be the product of intelligent design. I had to wait a long time for the birth of an articulated theory that confirmed my intuitions. I am thankful to Bill for his part in the development of such a theory.

In my 12 years in a rural hospital in Papua, New Guinea, I saw a lot of suffering. I saw the killing and maiming that resulted from tribal warfare—suffering inflicted by men. But I also saw innocent babies and mothers dying in childbirth, people dying in a flooded river, and the ravages of diseases such as malaria and tuberculosis—suffering inflicted by nature.

This is a broken world. We can all think of changes that we would make if we were God. Theologically, I understand all this evil and suffering to derive from rebellion against God. This understanding of evil and suffering can be more readily maintained when people are guilty of behaving badly. The tragic events of September 11, 2001 cannot be blamed on God. It is far more difficult, however, to maintain this understanding of evil and suffering where no guilty party is immediately evident.

I never intended to depart from a plain reading of Genesis. It was forced upon me with great pain and with tears. It tore me apart. I felt like an infidel. I kept it quiet, knowing how I myself would have responded earlier in my walk with God. To question a young-earth reading of Genesis was to question the entire Bible and to place one's faith in jeopardy.

I was not coaxed away from a plain reading of Genesis by theological arguments, by so-called liberals or higher critics. I was compelled by the scientific evidence: stars are a long way off and very old; the earth and its landforms seem clearly the result of millions of years of normal processes; the world presents strong evidence of suffering and death that occurred well before Adam and Eve opened their minds and closed their teeth on the forbidden fruit.

The principle of "double truth," in which reason teaches one thing and faith can teach the exact opposite, has always left me cold. Some people are comfortable with holding apparent contradictions in tension. One young-earth geologist I know is comfortable writing about millions of years of geological history in his doctoral dissertation. Yet you would never know from reading it that he believes the world to be less than 1 percent of a million years old! Unlike this geologist, I couldn't live in parallel universes, one old and one young.

Wallowing in this no-man's-land that pitted science against faith and without someone to whom I could confess my agony, I nonetheless approached with considerable skepticism Bill's undertaking to explain how the Fall of Adam and Eve could be held accountable for natural evils that were occurring hundreds of millions of years before them. How could the cause (the sin of Adam and Eve) come after the effect (millions of years of natural evil)? I expected that Bill would engage in rationalizations and verbal gymnastics that in the end would leave me unconvinced.

What I experienced was nothing short of an epiphany. In my mind, sealed compartments like bubbles were straining not to touch one another, lest one should swallow the other. I feared God's reputation would be hurt by any attempt to unify faith and reason. I now feel that that these two separated parts of my life are at peace, that head and heart are back together again.

The End of Christianity provides a remarkable theological framework that reveals God as He is in all His glory, that makes sense of the Cross in cosmic history, that shows us as we are in all our self-inflicted peril, and that accepts the physical world as it really is. It demonstrates that the power of the Fall, like the power of Christ's death and Resurrection, is not only prospective but also retrospective—it applies not only forward in time but also backward.

Every pastor needs to read this book. Once its ideas are grasped by God's people, it will free those who are chained to a young earth, fearing the Cross will be annulled if death and suffering are allowed to precede the Fall. This book won't force you to stop believing in a young earth. But it will force you to stop believing that a young earth is the only way to be biblically sound and theologically faithful.

I love God more for having read this book. Because of it, I am more eager to give my life in loving service of Jesus Christ and of those He loves. I now understand better the seriousness of my own sin and the incredible costly grace of God at work in my life. I also understand the cosmic consequences of human sin and that the redemption in Christ covers all of reality. I have a deeper respect for the Word of God revealed in the Bible. I have a fresh hope of an eternity delighting in the presence of God, my Creator and Redeemer.

Mark Fitzmaurice, M.D.
Sydney, Australia

ACKNOWLEDGMENTS

T HIS book is dedicated to Ethel and Harry Cooper, a precious African-American couple who meant so much to me growing up in Chicago. Harry worked at Garrett Theological Seminary in Evanston, Ethel at Marshall Field's in the Loop. In the late 1960s, during a very turbulent time in America, my family would spend Thanksgivings at their place on the south side of Chicago. Ethel's mother, who was living with them, died the fall of 1969. That December, weeks later, Harry died. My own mother had just been diagnosed with cancer, so Ethel hesitated at first to reveal to her that Harry had died—not until my mother shouted into the phone *"Ethel, what's wrong?"* In 1981, Ethel herself succumbed to pancreatic cancer. I was able to visit her and offer some comfort. I wish I had done more. Harry and Ethel's kindness and generosity continue to testify to me of the love of Christ. Without people like them, everything in this book would be hollow and straw.

The End of Christianity began as a paper posted on my Website (www.designinference.com). It was titled "Christian Theodicy in Light of Genesis and Modern Science." That paper touched a nerve, and many people offered useful insights as I was conceiving and revising it and then writing this book. Here I would like to thank Jake Akins, Barry Arrington, the ASA list (www.calvin .edu/archive/asa), Robert Bass, John Baumgardner, Chris Beling, Ray Bohlin, Joel Borofsky, Jon Buell, Jack Collins, Samuel Conner, Bryan Cross, Stephen Davis, Ted Davis, Edward Fackerell, Mark Fitzmaurice, Michael Flannery, Bruce Gordon, Jack Greenoe, Paul Hodge, Michael Keas, Mario Lopez, Robert Marks,

Donald McLaughlin, J. P. Moreland, Terry Mortenson, Bill Newby, Denyse O'Leary, Don Page, J. Brian Pitts, Fuz Rana, Brock Ratcliff, Geoff Robinson, Hugh Ross, Greg Smith, David Snoke, Southwestern Seminary's annual "Creation Conversation," Ide Trotter, Rick Wade, Mark Whorton, and Peter Zoeller-Greer. I'm especially grateful to Mark Fitzmaurice for writing the foreword and to Denyse O'Leary for superb editing of the final draft.

Research, reflection, and writing on this project have spanned the greater part of the decade. During that time I enjoyed some very helpful institutional support. Here I would like to thank the Templeton Foundation, which provided generous financial support for a project on the metaphysics of information (part III of this book derives from that project and will eventually become a book of its own titled *Being as Communion*). I would also like to thank Berkeley's Center for Theology and the Natural Sciences, which through the encouragement of Bob Russell and Ted Peters first got me writing on the topic of theodicy (in 2003 at the Graduate Theological Union they had me deliver a paper titled "Making the Task of Theodicy Impossible? Intelligent Design and the Problem of Evil"). Additionally, I want to thank Discovery Institute's Center for Science and Culture, whose moral, intellectual, and financial support has been indispensable over the years. Finally, I'm grateful to Southwestern Baptist Theological Seminary, which under the direction of President Paige Patterson and Provost Craig Blaising have provided me with an immensely fruitful environment in which to work.

Many people over the years have shaped my views about the goodness of God in creation. The most influential in this regard have been Diogenes Allen, Louise Cowan, William Lane Craig, Thomas Hopko, Steve Kreissl, John Stott, and above all my beloved wife Jana. My heartfelt thanks go to all of them. Jana and I met as students at Princeton Theological Seminary. I've found her theological instincts and literary sensibilities unsurpassed. Hers is the last chapter of this book, titled "Luminous with Purpose."

William A. Dembski
Southwestern Baptist Theological Seminary
Fort Worth, Texas

Postscript. Twenty percent of this book consists of explanatory and reference notes. A careful reading therefore requires attention to the notes.

INTRODUCTION:
OUR MENTAL ENVIRONMENT

W E inhabit not just a physical environment but also a moral environment. Cambridge philosopher Simon Blackburn defines our moral environment as "the surrounding climate of ideas about how to live."[1] Though we cannot help but be aware of our physical environment, we are often oblivious of our moral environment. Yet our moral environment is always deeply influential. As Blackburn notes,

> It determines what we find acceptable or unacceptable, admirable or contemptible. It determines our conception of when things are going well and when they are going badly. It determines our conception of what is due to us, and what is due from us, as we relate to others. It shapes our emotional responses, determining what is a cause of pride or shame, or anger or gratitude, or what can be forgiven and what cannot.[2]

Blackburn's moral environment belongs to a still larger environment—our *mental environment*. Our mental environment is the surrounding climate of ideas by which we make sense of the world. It includes our moral environment since our ideas about how to live are a prime way we make sense of the world. But our mental environment is broader still. It includes our ideas about what exists, what can be known, and what counts as evidence for our beliefs. It assigns value to our life and work. Above all, it determines our plausibility structures—what we find reasonable or unreasonable, credible or incredible, thinkable or unthinkable.[3]

I finished what I thought would be my last graduate degree in 1988, a doctorate in mathematics from the University of Chicago. On completing that degree, I began a postdoctoral fellowship at the Massachusetts Institute of Technology (MIT). There I was struck by how readily my colleagues regarded Christianity as passé. They did not think that Christianity was dangerous and had to be stamped out. They thought that Christianity lacked intellectual vitality and deserved to be ignored. Its stamping out was, in their minds, a long-accomplished fact—the war was over and Christianity had lost.

In the mental environment of my MIT colleagues, Christianity carried no weight. As a Christian who believed then (and still does now) that the revelation of God in Jesus Christ is humanity's chief truth, I found this light dismissal of Christianity troubling. How could my colleagues so easily reject the Christian faith? I had to get to the bottom of this question and therefore set aside a promising career as a research mathematician to pursue further studies in philosophy and theology.

Much has happened in our culture in the 20 years since my time at MIT. Notably, the intelligent design movement has grown internationally and pressed Western intellectuals to take seriously the claim that life and the cosmos are the product of intelligence. To be sure, many of them emphatically reject this claim. But their need to confront and refute it suggests that our mental environment is no longer stagnating in the atheistic materialism that for so long has dominated Western intellectual life. That atheistic worldview, supposedly buttressed by science, has constituted a major obstacle, at least in the West, to taking Christianity seriously.[4] With atheistic materialism now itself in question, Christianity is again on the table for discussion.

This is not to say that the discussion is friendly or that Christianity is about to find widespread acceptance at places like MIT. Instead of routinely ignoring Christianity as they did 20 years ago, many Western intellectuals now treat it with open contempt, expending a great many words to denounce it. But this is progress. The dead are ignored and forgotten. The living are scorned and reviled. I was therefore gratified to see the recent rash of books by the "neo-atheists" such as Richard Dawkins's *The God Delusion*, Christopher Hitchens's *god Is Not Great* (Hitchens insists on not capitalizing references to the deity), and Sam Harris's *The End of Faith*.[5]

These books would be unnecessary if Christianity, and theism generally, were not again a live issue.[6]

The neo-atheists' first line of attack in challenging religious belief, and Christianity in particular, is to invoke science as the principal debunker of religion. Science is supposed to show that any God or intelligence or purpose behind the universe is not merely superfluous but an impediment to reason. Yet evidence from science shows the opposite. The case for a designing intelligence producing life and the cosmos is now on solid ground, as can be seen from such books as *The Design of Life* and *The Privileged Planet*.[7] Indeed, the neo-atheists are not having a good time of it when they attempt to disprove Christian faith simply by appealing to science. True, their denunciations of Christianity contain many references to "science." But the denunciations are ritualistic, with "science" used as a conjuring word (like "abracadabra"). One finds little actual science in their denunciations.

Instead of presenting scientific evidence that shows atheism to be true (or probable), the neo-atheists moralize about how much better the world would be if only atheism *were* true. Far from demonstrating that God does not exist, the neo-atheists merely demonstrate how earnestly they desire that God not exist.[8] The God of Christianity is, in their view, the worst thing that could befall reality. According to Richard Dawkins, for instance, the Judeo-Christian God "is arguably the most unpleasant character in all of fiction. Jealous and proud of it; a petty, unjust unforgiving control-freak; a vindictive, bloodthirsty ethnic-cleanser; a misogynistic homophobic racist, infanticidal, genocidal, filicidal, pestilential, megalomaniacal, sadomasochistic, capriciously malevolent bully."[9]

Dawkins's obsession with the Christian God borders on the pathological. Yet he underscores what has always been the main reason people reject God: they cannot believe that God is good. Eve, in the Garden of Eden, rejected God because she thought he had denied her some benefit that she should have, namely, the fruit from the Tree of the Knowledge of Good and Evil.[10] Clearly, a God who denies creatures benefits that they think they deserve cannot be good. Indeed, a mark of our fallenness is that we fail to see the irony in thus faulting God. Should we not rather trust that the things God denies us are denied precisely for our benefit? Likewise, the neo-atheists find lots of faults with God, their list of denied benefits being much longer than Eve's—no surprise here since they've had a lot longer to compile such a list!

In an interview several years back, Princeton philosopher Cornel West was asked, "What is your overall philosophical project?"[11] He responded: "I think that fundamentally it has to do with wrestling with the problem of evil."[12] Wrestling with the problem of evil is a branch of philosophical theology known as *theodicy*. Theodicy attempts to resolve how a good God and an evil world can coexist. Like Cornel West, the neo-atheists are wrestling with the problem of evil. Unlike him, however, they demand a simplistic solution. For them, God does not exist, so belief in God is a delusion. But it is not just any old delusion. It is the worst of all possible delusions—one that, unchecked, will destroy humanity.

Dawkins, for instance, regards belief in a God who does not exist as the root of all evil. He even narrated a 2006 BBC documentary with that very title—*The Root of All Evil?*[13] Demonizing religious faith is nothing new for Dawkins. A decade earlier he remarked, "I think a case can be made that faith is one of the world's great evils, comparable to the small-pox virus but harder to eradicate."[14] Dawkins might be surprised to learn that he was here echoing Adolf Hitler: "The reason why the ancient world was so pure, light, and serene was that it knew nothing of the two great scourges: the pox and Christianity."[15] Given that belief in God is human-ity's greatest scourge, the only legitimate business of theodicy would be to eradicate it.

By contrast, the challenge of this book is to formulate a theodicy that is at once faithful to Christian orthodoxy (thereby underscoring the exis-tence, power, and goodness of God) and credible to our mental environ-ment (thereby challenging the neo-atheists at their own game).[16] But is developing such a theodicy worthwhile? Should we, as Christians, even care whether such a theodicy is credible? And credible to whom? Is not credibility vastly overrated? After all, Scripture teaches that the human heart is corrupt, that expedience rather than principle dictates many of our actions, and that too often we use our minds not to seek truth but to justify falsehoods that we wish were true (see Jer 17:9). It would follow that our mental environment is itself corrupt and that credible ideas may well be false. In fact, given a sufficiently corrupt mental environment, what would be the point of appearing credible? A proposition's credibility in that case might even constitute a positive reason for rejecting it!

As Christians, we must not confuse making our faith credible to the world with seeking its approval. Craving the world's approval is a sure road to perdition. Notwithstanding, Christianity refuses to abandon the world to itself but seeks instead to restore it to God. Now, such restoration, minimally, means changing the way people think.[17] And changing the way people think means entering and reshaping their mental environment. We need to start somewhere. Not everything in even the most corrupt mental environment is wrong. We must look for points of entry, which are often the points of greatest need or doubt in a culture.[18] At such points, by contending for the truth and relevance of the Christian faith, we can demonstrate its credibility. Moreover, we must do this without watering down the faith or selling it out to preserve a vain shine of respectability.

The theodicy formulated in this book attempts to combine credibility in the current mental environment with faithfulness to Christian orthodoxy. As such, it needs to be fairly elaborate. This elaborateness, however, raises a worry: what are we to make of people who in times past got by without elaborate theodicies, even though they faced many more evident sufferings than we do today? In the fourteenth century, for instance, plague killed a third of the population of Europe. Infant mortality in times past was much higher than it is now, touching virtually every family. Yet despite such afflictions and hardships, there was no call for elaborate theodicies. Why, then, do we need one now? Is it because pampered Western intellectuals simply have too much time on their hands and fret about minutiae that our more hardy ancestors would have ridiculed? Two brief responses:

1. Just because people didn't feel the need to construct elaborate theodicies in times past doesn't mean that they didn't feel the weight of the problem of evil. More likely, it just means that they thought they had an adequate theodicy. For instance, Augustine's theodicy, in which evil is mitigated by the ultimate good that God brings out of it, has satisfied many Christians over the centuries. In fact, I take this theodicy to heart as well, only I propose to build on it.

2. The need to construct more elaborate theodicies has arisen because science has raised a new set of issues about the goodness of God in creation. Young-earth creationism was historically the position of the Church up through the Reformation. With the rise of modern science, especially advances in geology and biology in the nineteenth century and in physics and cosmology in the twentieth century, the problem of natural evil prior to the Fall and, perhaps more significantly, the truth of Scripture in its depiction of Creation, came to the fore and needed addressing.

Simply put, we need more elaborate theodicies because people are now asking harder questions about divine benevolence. Answers that may have worked for past mental environments don't work any longer. What's needed are answers that make the goodness of God credible in the current mental environment. In setting the stage for a specifically Christian theodicy, let us therefore turn to the task of theodicy in general.

Theodicy is fundamentally about the benevolence of ultimate reality—whether what ultimately underlies the world is benevolent. A successful theodicy demonstrates that, despite evil, ultimate reality is benevolent. Though I use the terms interchangeably, I prefer *benevolence* to *goodness* because *goodness* often refers to impersonal things or abstractions, which can be indifferent to human welfare. Benevolence, on the other hand, suggests an interest in and active fostering of individual and corporate human welfare. Accordingly, I take theodicy's main task as convincing us that ultimate reality is benevolent and that we humans are an object (perhaps the chief object) of that benevolence.

Many contemporary thinkers have abandoned the task of theodicy. Materialists, who regard ultimate reality as consisting of material entities governed by unbroken natural laws, are a case in point. Take Richard Dawkins: "In a universe of blind physical forces and genetic replication, some people are going to get hurt, other people are going to get lucky, and you won't find any rhyme or reason in it, nor any justice. The universe we observe has precisely the properties we should expect if there is, at bottom, no design, no purpose, no evil and no good, nothing but blind pitiless indifference."[19] Clearly, for Dawkins and his fellow atheistic materialists, rock-bottom reality is not benevolent.

For Christians, on the other hand, God is the ultimate reality; and God's benevolence toward his creation is typically taken for granted. But on what basis are Christians entitled to believe that God is benevolent? According to John Milton, we need an argument: "What in me is dark / Illumine, what is low raise and support; / That, to the height of this great argument, / I may assert Eternal Providence, / And justify the ways of God to men."[20] Yet the idea that an argument can justify the ways of God and thereby convince us of God's benevolence will strike many of us as hollow. How do we preserve our confidence in divine benevolence given the world's evil and cruelty? This is the challenge ever before us. Life's circumstances do not always go our way. When they go against us, sometimes violently, our confidence in divine benevolence depends less on an argument than on an attitude.

Epictetus summarized this attitude as follows: "For everything that happens in the world it is easy to give thanks to Providence if a person has but these two qualities in himself: a habit of viewing broadly what happens to each individual and a grateful temper. Without the first he will not perceive the usefulness of things which happen; and without the second he will not be thankful for them."[21] The apostle Paul displayed this same attitude by noting that God works all things out for good (Rom 8:28) and that we are to thank God for all things (Eph 5:20). Such an attitude, however, is warranted only if what ultimately underlies the world is benevolent. And how do we know that? It seems, then, that we need some argument for divine benevolence after all, if only to justify this attitude.

Epictetus, a Stoic philosopher, looked to his philosophy to justify this attitude. Christians look to Christian theology to formulate a specifically Christian theodicy and thereby justify this attitude. According to Catholic theologian Edward Oakes, the task of a Christian theodicy is to "show that an omnipotent and benevolent God can coexist with evil in His finite creation."[22] The key to resolving the theodicy problem for Oakes is an insight of Augustine's. In his apologetics manual *The Enchiridion*, Augustine writes, "God judged it better to bring good out of evil than not to permit any evil to exist."[23] For Augustine, like Epictetus, theodicy requires a broad perspective. The triumph of good over evil cannot be seen from a narrow vantage. Instead, the infinitely broad vantage of God's ultimate purposes for the world is needed. Accordingly, for Oakes, Augustine's theodicy requires that the world be viewed "both as a totality and under the aegis of eschatology."[24]

All this is sound Christian theodicy as far as it goes. But a Christian theodicy needs to go further. It needs, additionally, to make peace with three claims:

1. God by wisdom created the world out of nothing.
2. God exercises particular providence in the world.
3. All evil in the world ultimately traces back to human sin.

Mainstream academic theology regards the first two of these as problematic and the third as, frankly, preposterous. By contrast, I'm going to argue that all three claims are true and can be situated within a coherent Christian theodicy.

Claim 1, creation out of nothing by an all-wise God, has of late fallen on hard times. In the interest of theodicy, mainline theologians now increasingly adopt a pared-down view of divine wisdom, knowledge, and power. We thus get a god who means well but can't quite overcome the evil in the world, a god who is good but in other ways deficient. The goodness of God is thus preserved, but at the cost of his other attributes. Process theology, in which the world is autonomous and God changes with the world, is a case in point.[25] Evolving gods constrained by natural laws are much the rage these days. Because creation out of nothing suggests a God to whom everything is subject, the diminished gods of these theologies tend not to be ultimate but rather depend on still deeper aspects of reality.[26]

Claim 2, concerning *particular providence*, refers to God's willingness and ability to act for the good of creation at particular places and times. Accordingly, God acts not just on the creation as a whole but on particular parts of it, the most important part being us—humans. God's particular providence includes miracles, answers to prayer, predictive prophecy, and, most significantly for the Christian faith, the redemption of humanity through Christ and his Cross. Particular providence contrasts with *general providence*, whereby God guides the course of the world as a whole (as by ordaining the seasons and their weather). A god of general but not particular providence may thus ordain a pattern of weather, but he takes no responsibility for the tornado that blew down your barn and pays no attention to your prayers for protection from such tornados. A god of particular providence knows your name and the number of hairs on your head; not so a god of general providence.

Claim 3, which ascribes to human sin the entrance of evil into the world, is the most difficult to square with our current mental environment. It is also the key to resolving the problem of a specifically Christian theodicy. If you're going to blame evil on something besides God, you've got two choices: conscious rebellion of creatures (as in humans or the devil disobeying God) or autonomy of the world (as in the world doing its thing and God, though wringing his hands, unable to make a difference). The current mental environment prefers an autonomous world. It seeks to contract the power of God at every point where God might do something to cast doubt on his goodness. Indeed, contemporary theology's resistance to claims 1 and 2 reflects its desperate need to preserve God's goodness even if that means contracting God's power. But if evil is not a consequence of the world's autonomy, then there is no need to contract God's power. It follows that once claim 3 is shown to be plausible, claims 1 and 2 become plausible as well.

Although I will address all three claims in this book, if there is any originality here, it is my analysis of claim 3. In asserting that all evil in the world ultimately traces back to human sin, claim 3 is not attributing to humanity an absolute origin of evil. Rather it is asserting that human sin is the immediate or proximate cause of evil in the world. In Genesis 3, humans are tempted by a serpent, who is traditionally understood as Satan, a fallen angel, and thus a creature that is not embodied in the material stuff out of which humans are made. Consequently, the fall of humanity presupposes the fall of angelic beings. And the fall of angelic beings may presuppose some still deeper features of reality that bring about evil.[27]

In any case, the crucial question is not the ultimate origin of evil but whether all evil in the world traces back to humanity and its sin. According to this view, humanity is the gatekeeper through which evil passes into the world. In this metaphor, the Fall becomes the failure of the gatekeeper to maintain proper control of the gate. This metaphor works regardless of the ultimate source of evil that lies outside the gate (be it something that crashes the gate or suborns the gatekeeper or both).

Much of my past work has been on intelligent design and the controversy over evolution. Nothing in this book, however, takes sides in that debate. In arguing that the Fall marks the entry of all evil into the world (both personal and natural evil), I make no assumptions about the age of the Earth, the extent of evolution, or the prevalence of design. The theodicy I develop here looks not to science but to the metaphysics of divine action and purpose. At the heart of this theodicy is the idea that the effects of the Fall can be retroactive as well as proactive (much as the saving effects of the Cross stretch not only forward in time but also backward, saving, for instance, the Old Testament saints).

The view that all evil in the world ultimately traces back to human sin used to be part and parcel of a Christian worldview—standard equipment in our mental environment. As the *Catholic Encyclopedia* notes:

> Christian philosophy has, like the Hebrew, uniformly attributed moral and physical evil to the action of created free will. Man has himself brought about the evil from which he suffers by transgressing the law of God, on obedience to which his happiness depended. . . . The errors of mankind, mistaking the true conditions of its own well-being, have been the cause of moral and physical evil.[28]

In arguing for this traditional understanding of how evil came into the world, I will in subsequent chapters need to review how our mental environment came to regard it as increasingly implausible.

The title of this book, *The End of Christianity*, requires some explanation. It can be interpreted in several ways. For those hostile to Christianity and religious belief, the phrase "end of Christianity" signifies Christianity's demise as an institutional religion and system of belief. To them, Christianity is an organism that no longer fills an ecological niche and is ready to go extinct. This view of Christianity's demise, however, displays wishful thinking. The best estimates indicate that among religious faiths worldwide, Christianity has the most adherents. Christianity shows no signs of going extinct. Quite the contrary, by some accounts it is thriving as never before. Hence, far from signifying its demise, the phrase "end of Christianity" could as well signify its ultimate triumph. Christians have many images to symbolize their faith's ultimate triumph. At the center of them all is Christ and the Cross.

In this book, I want to interpret the phrase "end of Christianity" in a third way. To be sure, as a Christian, I reject that Christianity is doomed (first interpretation) and accept that it will ultimately triumph (second interpretation). Nevertheless, Christianity's ultimate triumph remains for now unfulfilled. The question I therefore want to pose—and help answer—in this book is how we, as Christians, are to help bring about the ultimate triumph of Christ. According to 1 John 5:4, the victory that overcomes the world is our faith. Christian faith—a living faith whose author and finisher is Christ (Heb 12:2)—is thus described as the essential element for bringing about Christ's ultimate triumph. I want, therefore, to interpret the phrase "end of Christianity" as what our faith must become—in the here and now—to bring about that ultimate triumph.

What, then, must our faith become? The key mark of a faith that overcomes the world is the ability to discern God's goodness in the face of evil. Indeed, faith's role in bringing about Christ's ultimate triumph presupposes faith's ability to discern God's goodness. Just as humanity's Fall and the consequent rise of evil resulted from the *faulty belief* that divine goodness is imperfect (witness Eve in the Garden of Eden, where she rejects God's will and asserts her own), so humanity's restoration and Christ's ultimate triumph over evil results from the *sound belief* that divine goodness is perfect (witness Christ in the Garden of Gethsemane, where he surrenders his will to God's).

The end of Christianity, as envisioned in this book, is the radical realignment of our thinking so that we see God's goodness in creation despite the distorting effects of sin in our hearts and evil in the world.

PART I

DEALING WITH EVIL

ONE

THE REACH OF THE CROSS

G OD'S goodness in creation begins and ends with the Cross of Christ.
So Christians have always believed. In 1 Corinthians, Paul underscores the centrality of the Cross:

> I, brethren, when I came to you, came not with excellency of
> speech or of wisdom, declaring unto you the testimony of God.
> For I determined not to know any thing among you, save Jesus
> Christ, and him crucified. (1 Cor 2:1–2)

Why did Paul, in his ministry to the Corinthians, focus so exclusively on
the Cross? Why has the Cross played such a preeminent role in Christian
theology? Why, in the iconography of the Church, is the Cross absolutely
central? Why did George Bernard Shaw, himself a religious skeptic, think
that Christians ought to rename themselves "Crosstians"?[1]

In the Cross, the eternal Son of God enters fully into the human condition, takes on himself the totality of human sin and pain, and once and for
all extinguishes the power of evil over our lives. To accomplish so great a
salvation, Christ paid the ultimate cost, undergoing rejection, humiliation,
physical torture, psychic torment, and death. Out of love for humanity, he
laid down his life for ours, thereby securing our redemption. And then,
through his Resurrection, he defeated death and gave us eternal life. As the
ancient Easter hymn exults,

> Christ is risen from the dead,
> trampling down death by death,
> and upon those in the tombs
> bestowing life![2]

Truly, there is no greater suffering or triumph of love than Christ's sacrifice for us on the Cross.

The last paragraph is traditional orthodoxy. We've heard it before. Sermons repeat it endlessly. But do we really believe it? And if we do believe it, should we? Consider James Carroll, a former Catholic priest, who sees the Cross not as God's means of redemption but as an excuse for Christians to persecute Jews (for their complicity in Christ's crucifixion).[3] Granted, the history of anti-Semitism includes the persecution of Jews by persons claiming to represent Christianity. But persons claiming to represent Christianity have committed all manner of heinous crimes. The question, therefore, is not what people do in the name of Christianity, but what Christianity is essentially. Jesus himself was a Jew, as were the first Christians who spread the good news of God's redemptive work at the Cross. To fault the Cross because it has been misrepresented is therefore itself to misrepresent the Cross.

A more troubling worry about the Cross comes from a diary entry by Anna Williams, a medical researcher active in the early part of the twentieth century. The Cross gave her no comfort. As she saw it, Jesus knew that his anguish would be momentary and that in exchange he would save the world. As she wrote in her diary, "This knowledge . . . if we were sure, oh! what would we not be willing to undergo."[4] Williams implies that anybody would willingly endure the Cross once the costs and benefits are properly weighed—the costs being minimal compared to the huge benefits.

How should we respond to Williams? Is it relevant that Christ was sinless and thus, unlike all other persons in history, utterly undeserving of any punishment he received (see Heb 4:15)? Does it help to note that crucifixion was the ultimate form of torture in the ancient world? Was Anna Williams therefore taking the sufferings of our Lord too lightly? As a cosseted ivory-tower intellectual, what did she know about suffering anyway? Didn't Christ on the Cross suffer more than she ever did in her little bourgeois world? Instead of complaining about the Cross not being enough, shouldn't she have gratefully accepted the redemption that could be hers only through the Cross?

Such questions miss the point. Williams wasn't comparing her personal sufferings to those of Christ. Rather, she was asking about the *reach* of the Cross. Specifically, she was asking whether Christ's suffering on the Cross could adequately encompass the full extent of human suffering. Williams suggests that Christ got off cheap. Christ's passion, after all, lasted only a matter of hours. By the standards of the day, his time on the Cross was short, beginning in the morning and ending in the afternoon. Yes, his scourging must be factored in as well. But crucifixion was common in the Roman Empire, and most crucifixions lasted days rather than hours before the victim expired. The physical suffering of our Lord was no more than that of many others brutalized by Rome. Thus, for Williams, Christ's Cross seemed like a small price to pay in exchange for the redemption of the whole world.

I don't mean to make light of our Lord's physical suffering, but it seems that Williams has a point. She underscores why a movie like Mel Gibson's *The Passion of the Christ* does not convey the full measure of what Christ, in securing our redemption, endured on the Cross. Mel Gibson, a master of movie violence (going back to his early *Mad Max* days), was clearly in his element in portraying the cruelty that Jesus experienced at the hands of the Romans. But by focusing so one-sidedly on the physical violence surrounding Jesus' crucifixion, Gibson missed the far deeper suffering of our Lord, for which the Cross was but an outward expression.

Let's be frank. If the entirety of Christ's suffering was the physical pain he endured on the Cross, then Anna Williams is right: Christ's suffering on behalf of humanity has limited reach. Perhaps it can reach well-fed, heavily sedated, incessantly entertained Westerners whose main afflictions are stress and disillusionment. But can it reach the whole of humanity and the worst of its afflictions? Many forms of death, degradation, and torment seem far worse than the few hours that Christ suffered at the hands of the Romans. Off the top of my head, here are three:

1. Locked-in syndrome, in which the body is completely without ability to move or respond but the mind remains fully conscious. Imagine your body being in this state, a living coffin, for decades.

2. Being a long-term subject of Josef Mengele's medical experiments at the Nazi extermination camp of Auschwitz.

3. Being raped and tortured over a period of months by one of Saddam Hussein's sons for refusing his advances and then finally being torn apart by his Doberman pinschers.

Ask yourself, If faced with such horrors, what comfort you would find in the Cross if it meant only that Jesus suffered a few hours of scourging and crucifixion. What comfort would you find in his words "Lo, I am with you always, even unto the end of the world" (Matt 28:20) if, for all you could tell, his suffering was markedly less than yours? The Church father Gregory of Nazianzus stressed that Christ cannot redeem what he has not taken on himself. The usual theological formula for stating this is "That which is not assumed is not redeemed."[5] How can Christ overcome the sin of the world if his experience of the consequences of that sin are at best partial—if he has not fully drunk the cup of God's wrath against sin?

The brief time into which Christ's Passion was compressed is not the only problem we must consider. In anticipating the Passion, Jesus gives every impression of knowing exactly what is to happen and when it is to happen. Everything seems scripted. Everything seems to happen on cue. In John's Gospel we are told that Jesus knew that Judas would betray him from the start (John 6:64). On the Cross, Jesus exclaims that God has abandoned him (Matt 27:46). The terror of that abandonment, however, ends no more than six hours later when Jesus utters, "It is finished," and gives up the ghost (John 19:30). Moreover, leading up to the Cross, Jesus has been continually assuring his disciples that he would rise again from the dead on the third day (Mark 9:31)—a prophecy he fulfills, once again, right on cue (Mark 16:2–6).

Most of us, when in the throes of suffering, however, don't have the luxury of having our tribulation so neatly choreographed. We don't know exactly what to expect when, and when the suffering will be over, if at all. Often we see no end to the suffering, and we don't know how things will turn out. Uncertainty about the course of suffering makes suffering doubly hard. And yet, by his knowledge of the future, our Lord seems to have avoided this aspect of suffering. Statistician David Bartholomew even goes so far as to ask whether "Jesus was truly human" since he seems to have escaped the experience of uncertainty and risk that "is part of what it means to be human."[6]

What, then, is the reach of the Cross? Is it enough to embrace the totality of the human condition? I submit that it is. But to see this, we need to look beyond the physical agony of the Cross. The Cross points to a deeper reality of divine suffering that gets largely lost in films like *The Passion of the Christ*. How can we see that the reach of the Cross encompasses the full consequences of the Fall, including the full extent of human suffering? I'm not sure that our finite minds can fully comprehend the reach of the Cross. Nonetheless, we can catch glimpses of it.

Certain biblical images indicate that the suffering of the Cross cannot be confined merely to the few hours of Christ's earthly passion. After Jesus is resurrected, he appears to his doubting disciple Thomas and has him place his fingers in the wounds that were inflicted on the Cross. Ask yourself, Why would a resurrection body show marks of crucifixion? And why, in the book of Revelation, is Christ portrayed as a lamb that was slain? There's no indication in Scripture that in eternity the redeemed of Christ will exhibit any marks of suffering from their life on earth. And yet our Lord bears these marks in eternity, and is referred to, in Rev 13:8, as "the Lamb slain from the foundation of the world."[7] Clearly, then, the sufferings of Christ transcend his torture by the Romans.

Another factor to consider in probing the reach of the Cross is Christ's complete willingness to embrace it. Most of us, when in pain and sorrow, look for a way of escape. Indeed, if there were a button we could press to make our troubles disappear, most of us would press it. But seldom is such a button available. Yet, when Jesus gave himself up to be crucified, he could at any time have halted the proceedings. He makes that clear in the Scriptures. Thus, he informs the disciples that no one takes his life from him but that he lays it down freely (John 10:17–18). He adds that at any time he could call on more than 12 legions of angels to rescue him (Matt 26:53). According to a hymn sung on Good Friday, "He who hung the earth upon the waters is hung upon the Cross."[8] Instead of the Cross holding Jesus, in reality Jesus upheld the Cross. What does it say about our Lord that he chose, on our behalf, to experience the utmost agony even though at any time he could have called it off?

Still another way to see how the reach of the Cross exceeds our first impressions comes, perhaps surprisingly, from the doctrine of divine omniscience. God knows all things. But if God knows all things, does God know—really know from the inside out—the full conscious experience of human suffering? In particular, does he know what it feels like to experience the uncertainty of not knowing the outcome of suffering?

The philosopher Bertrand Russell, atheist though he was, offered a useful distinction when he differentiated two forms of knowledge: *knowledge by description* versus *knowledge by acquaintance.*[9] I have knowledge by description of what it is like to climb Mount Everest. I have that knowledge because the climb up Mount Everest has been described to me. But I have no knowledge by acquaintance of climbing Mount Everest. I've never actually climbed a mountain and have no plans to do so.

Now consider God and his knowledge of human experience. Does he know human experience simply by description? Or does he also know it by acquaintance? And if by acquaintance, how deep is his acquaintance? If God only knew human experience by description, he would be like a fabulously wealthy king gazing serenely on emaciated subjects who are dying of starvation. Even if this king eased the plight of his subjects and even if he assured them of how bad he felt on account of their pain, his role as comforter would be hopelessly compromised because he himself had never felt hunger.

That's why missionaries who live in mansions when the bulk of the local population lives in hovels are never very impressive. As human beings, we have a fundamental need to be known, and being known means being known by acquaintance and not merely by description. Knowledge by description is available from books. But knowledge by acquaintance means getting your hands dirty in the nitty-gritty of human experience. On the Cross, Christ has done exactly that. He has fully embraced the human condition. He knows it by acquaintance.

As a consequence, the doctrine of divine omniscience entails a paradox: to know everything, God must know by acquaintance the full measure of human experience and thus must know what it is not to know since not knowing (what we call "ignorance") is a basic feature of human finiteness. We know that Jesus himself experienced this limitation since the Scriptures teach that the boy Jesus grew not only physically but also mentally

(Luke 2:52). Moreover, we find the mature Jesus telling his disciples that there are things the Father knows that he doesn't (Mark 13:32).

Note that I am not here advocating openness theology, or open theism. On that view, the future is taken to be indefinite and therefore not knowable even by God. Openness theology flies in the face of Christian orthodoxy. Christianity's clear teaching throughout the ages has been that God fully knows the future.[10] Yes, this teaching is under dispute, and a growing literature disputes it. But the incompatibility of openness theology with Christian orthodoxy becomes evident on reflection. In particular, strict uncertainty about the future means that God cannot guarantee his promises because the autonomy of the world can always overrule God. Of course, we could try to get around this by saying that God can step in when things get out of hand, but that defeats the point of openness theology, which is to limit God and thereby absolve him of evil.

God's knowledge includes knowledge of the future. When God becomes man in Jesus Christ, however, he sets aside divine omniscience. The point of God's becoming man is for God to identify with the whole of human experience, and this is not possible if Christ retains all his divine privileges. Christ does not set aside every divine privilege. Quite the contrary, he retains the ability to heal people at command, raise the dead, expel demons, and calm storms. He refuses only those privileges that would prevent his subjection to our misfortunes. In particular, Christ on the Cross identifies with the whole of human suffering, and this includes the ignorance and uncertainty that intensify human suffering.

But how can this be? How can God in Christ so fully identify with humanity that he fully knows the full extent of human suffering (albeit without himself sinning)? Can Christ look each of us in the eye and honestly tell us that because of what he endured on the Cross, he knows what each of us is going through *even better than we do ourselves*? As Christians we want this to be true and, in our heart of hearts, we know it to be true. But how can it be true? A mystery exists here that our finite minds will never fully comprehend. Nonetheless, let me offer two considerations that may help.

First, we need to see the Cross as a window into a much deeper reality of divine suffering. For instance, the Scriptures teach that with God a day is as a thousand years. But if a day is as a thousand years, then each day in a thousand years is itself a thousand years. Thus, if you run the numbers, a day with God is also as 365 million years. Follow the math to its logical conclusion, and with God an instant is an eternity. For this reason the mere six hours that Jesus hung on the Cross is no obstacle for God's taking upon himself the full sufferings of humanity.

Second, in the Incarnation, and especially on the Cross, Jesus identifies with humanity at the deepest level. In Col 3:4, Paul teaches that Christ is our life. In Gal 2:20, Paul describes the believer as being crucified with Christ. In Philippians 3, Paul rejoices to share in the sufferings of Christ, so much so that our suffering becomes an expression of Christ's suffering. It's not that Christ vainly tries to imagine what we are suffering; when we suffer, Christ *is* suffering.

We see this in Matthew 25, where Jesus describes the final judgment as a separation of goats and sheep. The goats' crime is that they did not show mercy to Christ as he suffered hunger, sickness, and imprisonment. But when the goats ask how they could have missed ministering to his needs, Jesus replies that what they failed to do for others, they failed to do for him (Matt 25:45). Their failure is a failure to follow Jesus' command to love one's neighbor as oneself (Matt 22:39). This commandment does not mean that as one looks in the mirror, one should think about all the warm feelings one feels toward oneself and then consciously determine to project those warm feelings onto others (small comfort since warm feelings do not come easily to many of us). Rather, Jesus is talking about the bond that, as descendants of Adam and now of the second Adam, ought to hold humanity together.

We need to love our neighbor as our self because our neighbor *is* our self. In saying this, I'm not advocating an all-is-one pantheism of the sort popularized by the Beatles in their song "I Am the Walrus." There's a simple reason our self and the self of others constitute a unity: our life and their life are Christ's life (Col 3:4). Christ on the Cross sacrificed himself for the life of the world and thereby became the life of the world (John 6:51). In loving one another, we love Christ. In refusing to love one another, we refuse to love Christ.

Christ's identification with us in our limitation and weakness makes it possible for God to love us and to call us friends (John 15:13–15). In fact, it's not clear that any other religion or system of thought can account for

[21]

God's love for humanity. Aristotle, for instance, saw friendship as something possible only among equals. Consequently, his God, an "unmoved mover," was so far above and distant from humanity that he could never be our friend: "If the interval is great, as between a man and God, there can be no friendship at all."[11] Indeed, Aristotle's God thought only about himself since thinking about anything else would be degrading and therefore unworthy of God.[12]

But in the Incarnation and then upon the Cross, God in Christ did degrade himself. The word *degrade* comes from the Latin and means to "step down." God stepped down to save us. God's ultimate act of love is therefore the ultimate act of humility. Not only did the exalted God who fills the heavens and whom the heavens cannot contain step down to our level, but he went as low as it is possible to go. As Paul teaches in 2 Cor 5:21, God made Christ "to be sin for us, who knew no sin; that we might be made the righteousness of God in him." The suffering servant passage in Isaiah 53 makes the same point.

Aristotle's ethics is therefore radically incomplete. Among the vast catalogue of virtues that adorn Aristotle's ethics, humility is nowhere to be found. Yet humility is the only virtue that captures the love of God for humanity, a love fully expressed in the Cross. Only by humility does Christ—and those who share his life—defeat the sin of pride that led to the Fall. Without humility, as Martin Luther noted, all the other virtues become merely occasions for pride (as in, "See how well I'm doing").[13]

By the Cross, an infinite God forms a relationship of love and friendship with finite creatures. In mathematics there are two ways to go to infinity. One is to grow large without measure. The other is to form a fraction in which the denominator goes to zero. The Cross is a path of humility in which the infinite God becomes finite and then contracts to zero, only to resurrect and thereby unite a finite humanity within a newfound infinity.

This is why the Scriptures teach that God's strength is made perfect in weakness (2 Cor 12:9). In contrast to Aristotle's God, the Christian God does not meditate exclusively on himself. Rather, "the eyes of the LORD run to and fro throughout the whole earth, to show himself strong in the behalf of them whose heart is perfect toward him" (2 Chr 16:9). Far from finding human finiteness boring, God delights in it, finding creative possibilities that an unchangeable infinity cannot match.

At the Cross, divine infinity and human finiteness intersect. Hence "the death of Jesus," writes Timothy Keller, "was qualitatively different from any other death."[14] We see this difference underscored in the gospel narratives, which "all show that Jesus did not face his approaching death with anything like the aplomb and fearlessness that was widely expected in a spiritual hero. The well-known Maccabean martyrs, who suffered under the Syrian rule of Antiochus Epiphanes, were the paradigms for spiritual courage in the face of persecution. They were famous for speaking defiantly and confidently of God even as they were having limbs cut off."[15]

By contrast, Jesus, when confronted with his impending death in the Garden of Gethsemane, was deeply troubled (Mark 14:33–36 and Luke 22:42–44). Why? Not because of the physical pain. Keller explains:

> The physical pain was nothing compared to the spiritual experience of cosmic abandonment. Christianity alone among the world religions claims that God became uniquely and fully human in Jesus Christ and therefore knows firsthand despair, rejection, loneliness, poverty, bereavement, torture, and imprisonment. On the Cross he went beyond even the worst human suffering and experienced cosmic rejection and pain that exceeds ours as infinitely as his knowledge and power exceeds ours.[16]

But why was the Cross necessary at all? If there was a rift between God and humanity, why was suffering—Christ's suffering on the Cross—the key to healing it? *In a fallen world, the only currency of love is suffering.* Indeed, the only way to tell how much one person loves another is by what that person is willing to endure for the other. Without the cost incurred by suffering, love among fallen creatures becomes cheap and self-indulgent. Suffering removes the suspicion that the good we do for one another is for ulterior motives, with strings attached, a quid pro quo. Christ, by going to the Cross and there taking on himself the sin of the whole world, fully demonstrates the love of God. Moreover, only such a full demonstration of God's love enables us to love God with all our heart. The extent to which we can love God depends on the extent to which God has demonstrated his love for us, and that depends on the extent of evil that God has had to absorb, suffer, and overcome on our behalf.

But note, for us to love God also depends on our seeing the magnitude of our offense against God and gratefully receiving the forgiveness that God's suffering, in Christ on the Cross, has made possible. The principle at issue here is stated in Luke 7:47: those who realize that they have been forgiven much love much; those who think that they have only been forgiven little love little. It would seem that God has demonstrated a lot of love for celebrity atheists such as Oliver Sacks, Ted Turner, and Richard Dawkins.[17] In an interview with Dawkins for the movie *Expelled*, Ben Stein even noted that if God exists, he's been awfully good to Dawkins, giving him lucrative book contracts, a cush professorship, etc. Because Stein's criteria for what constitutes a divine blessing may be a bit off (lucrative book contracts are fine and well, but no biblical prophet would have regarded such monetary rewards as a sure sign of divine favor), let me restate his point as follows: God, in Christ, has given us ample reason to love him, so our failure to respond to God in love is just that—our failure.

To say that love in a fallen world is demonstrated through suffering raises the question of what love would look like in a nonfallen world. In a world untouched by sin, love is expressed through the gift of sacrifice. To see this, consider that the very existence of the world depends on such a gift. A common challenge to the Christian doctrine of creation is to ask whether, in creating the world, God augmented himself since it would appear that God plus the world is greater than God alone. This is supposed to raise an insuperable difficulty for Christian orthodoxy, which regards God as perfect and thus as not improvable through the addition of anything external to God, such as the world.

But, in fact, God plus the world is less than God alone. To see this, consider that God could have created any world whatsoever. All were possibilities before him. Yet, in the very act of creating this world, he gave up creating others. Creation gives existence to one possibility by withholding existence from the other possibilities that exclude it. In creating the world, God jealously gives himself to it and expects the same loyalty from it, a fact to which all the covenants in the Old and New Testaments testify. Creation is inherently covenantal. Thus, in creating this world, God, far from expanding himself, contracted himself by limiting his possibilities. G. K. Chesterton put it this way:

Every act of will [and that includes divine creation] is an act of self-limitation. To desire action is to desire limitation. In that sense every act is an act of self-sacrifice. When you choose anything, you reject everything else. . . . Every act is an irrevocable selection and exclusion. Just as when you marry one woman you give up all the others, so when you take one course of action you give up all the other courses.[18]

The lesson here is that even apart from evil and sin, it is possible for intelligences (whether created or uncreated) to give irrevocably so that they deny and thereby sacrifice other options. Christian theology has always regarded God's creation of the world as an act of love. In the act of creation, God gives himself irrevocably to this world to the exclusion of all others.[19] Creation is a gift of sacrifice—the giving of what holds ultimate value by giving up everything of lesser value. As beings created in God's image, we are likewise able, and indeed called, to offer such gifts of sacrifice. Moreover, such acts of love would be ours to perform even if we had never sinned.

In a fallen world, however, sacrifice by itself is not enough to assure love. The problem is that fallen creatures like us know very well about delayed gratification of rewards, that is, we sacrifice an immediate good for a foreseeable greater benefit down the road. There is nothing wrong, in principle, with delayed gratification or sacrifice in this sense. But sacrifice ceases to be a gauge for love when it becomes an instrument of exchange, part of a system of reciprocity in which persons are duly compensated for costs incurred. This is why Jesus states, "Greater love hath no man than this, that a man lay down his life for his friends" (John 15:13). In laying down his life at the Cross, Jesus offered himself in a sacrifice of suffering that cannot be compensated (certainly not by us). Only the sacrifice of a suffering that cannot be compensated and does not ask to be compensated is a true gauge of love in a fallen world.

It is vital here to form a correct picture of Christ's redemption and our role in it. In allowing evil and then redeeming us from it, God is not an arsonist who starts a fire, lets things heat up for us, and then, at the last moment, steps in so that he can be the big hero. Nor is God a casual bystander, who sees a fire start spontaneously and then lets it get out of control so that he can be the big hero to rescue us.

[25]

We are the arsonists. We started the fire. God wants to rescue us not only from the fire we started but also, and more importantly, from our disposition to start fires, that is, from our life of arson. But to be rescued from a life of arson requires that we know how destructive arson is.[20] Fires always start out small. If God always instantly put out the fires we start, we would never appreciate the damage fires can do.

We started a fire in consenting to evil. God permits this fire to rage. He grants this permission not so that he can be a big hero when he rescues us but so that we can rightly understand the human condition and thus come to our senses. In rescuing us by suffering on the Cross, God does end up being a hero. But that is not the point of his suffering. The point is to fix a broken relationship between God and humanity.

In the Garden of Gethsemane, Jesus beseeched the Father to let this cup pass from him if it were possible. But there was no other way. Our sin demanded the ultimate cost. It is a cost our Lord willingly paid. He paid it at the Cross. He bears the marks of the Cross to this day.

TWO

EVIL'S ORIGIN

T HE Cross is God's answer to evil. But whence evil? Mainstream
Christian theology used to explain the origin of evil as follows: Evil
results from a will that has turned against God. Just why a will should turn
against God, however, is a profound mystery. Second Thessalonians 2:7,
for instance, refers to "the mystery of iniquity." Since everything is created by God, a will that turns against God is one of his creations. But a
good God presumably created a good will. How, then, could a good will
turn against God? I'm not sure that any final answer can be given to this
question. Invoking freedom of the will is little help here. Certainly, freedom of the will contains within it the logical possibility of a will turning
against God. But why should a good will created by a good God exercise
its freedom in that way (for instance, Christian theology teaches that there
are good angels whose wills never turned against God)?[1]

Perhaps the best we can do is offer a psychological explanation: Precisely because a created will belongs to a creature, that creature, if sufficiently reflective, can reflect on its creaturehood and realize that it is not
God. Creaturehood implies constraints to which the Creator is not subject.
This may seem unfair (certainly it is not egalitarian). The question then
naturally arises, Has God the Creator denied to the creature some freedom
that might benefit it? Adam and Eve thought the answer to this question
was yes (God, it seemed, had denied them the freedom to know good and

evil). As soon as the creature answers yes to this question, its will turns against God. Once that happens, the will becomes evil. Whereas previously evil was merely a possibility, now it has become a reality. In short, the problem of evil starts when creatures think God is evil for "cramping their style." The impulse of our modern secular culture to cast off restraint wherever possible finds its root here.

I've just described what is commonly referred to as the Fall. Mainstream Christian theology used to regard the Fall as a bad thing—the Fall fundamentally disordered humanity's relationship with God. No longer able to trust God, humanity turned inward and sought fulfillment in its creaturehood rather than in the source of its being, the Creator. Maximus the Confessor describes this disordering of our priorities as follows:

> If all things have been made by God and for his sake, then God is better than what has been made by him. The one who forsakes the better and is engrossed in inferior things shows that he prefers the things made by God to God himself. . . . If the soul is better than the body and God incomparably better than the world which he created, the one who prefers the body to the soul and the world to the God who created it is no different from idolaters.[2]

Sin, the condition of a fallen will that no longer finds fulfillment in God, leads to numerous individual sins—what may be called moral or personal evil. But besides personal evil, sin propagates through nature and brings about natural evil. So the disordered state of nature mirrors the disordered state of our souls.

Redemption from sin then means turning back a fallen will to God. Hence, in the Christian doctrine of salvation, the emphasis on repentance and faith. Repentance signifies a will that turns back to God and faith signifies a will that trusts God and no longer questions his wisdom and benevolence. This turning back to God cannot be coerced. Just as the will turned against God without coercion, so too must it turn back to God without coercion. But the picture of redemption is broader still. Everything that has been disordered as a result of human sin must also be restored. Thus nature, which now reflects humanity's fallen state, needs to be restored (see Rom 8:19–23). Christianity finds this redemption in the Cross and Resurrection of Jesus Christ.

This account of evil's origin, outworking, and ultimate overthrow through the redemption in Christ is entirely traditional. At the same time, it no longer sits well with our current mental environment. Mainstream theology these days doubts that there even was an actual, historical Fall of humanity. And, insofar as it is willing to entertain the Fall at all, mainstream theology tends not to regard it as a bad thing.[3]

Patricia Williams, for instance, in her book *Doing Without Adam and Eve*, even regards the Fall as a good thing.[4] According to her, the serpent in the Garden told Eve the truth—Eve did not die when she ate the fruit, and she gained the knowledge she was after (i.e., knowledge of good and evil that made her more like God). Far from regarding the Fall as the ruin of humanity, Williams regards it as a liberation from self-imposed and biological constraints. C. S. Lewis had a reply to theologians like Williams:

> They say that the story of the Fall in Genesis is not literal; and then go on to say (I have heard them myself) that it was really a fall upwards—which is like saying that because "My heart is broken" contains a metaphor, it therefore means "I feel very cheerful." This mode of interpretation I regard, frankly, as nonsense. For me the Christian doctrines which are "metaphorical"—or which have become metaphorical with the increase of abstract thought—mean something which is just as "supernatural" or shocking after we have removed the ancient imagery as it was before.[5]

Theologians who don't take quite so optimistic a view of the Fall as Williams still find much to commend in it. John Hick, for instance, regards the Fall as an occasion for "soul-making." Yes, the Fall has negative consequences, but it also makes us better people by forcing us to deal with and overcome evil.[6] And then there are theologians like John Polkinghorne who see a certain inevitability in the Fall because they regard sin and evil as a necessary cost of God's bestowing freedom on creation. Thus, in coming to terms with natural evil, Polkinghorne will recount the following anecdote:

> Austin Farrer once asked himself what was God's will in the Lisbon earthquake (that terrible disaster of 1755, when 50,000 people were killed in one day). Farrer's answer was this—and

it's a hard answer, but I think a true answer—that God's will was that the elements of the earth's crust should behave in accordance with their nature. God has given them freedom to be, just as he has given us freedom to be.[7]

The example of choice for natural evil these days is the great Asian tsunami of 2004 that killed more than 200,000 people.

In any case, invoking the freedom of creation does little to answer the worries raised by such natural evils. We can imagine a world far more violent than ours in which many more people die annually of natural disasters. Alternatively, we can imagine a world far more halcyon than ours in which no one dies of natural disasters because the whole world is a serene tropical paradise. Ascribing natural evil to the freedom of creation does nothing to address the amount of natural evil in creation or whether the freedom of creation could have taken a different form so that there would be less of it (or perhaps none at all).

Referring natural evil to the freedom of creation rather than to the Fall has become a consistent pattern in contemporary theology, which seeks to redress the Fall by rationalizing why the Fall isn't, as it seemed to previous generations of theologians, a horrible tragedy. Such rationalizations are absent from the *O felix culpa* (*O fortunate fault*) tradition of classical Christian theology. This tradition redresses the Fall by pointing to the great redemption in Christ that the Fall elicits.[8] In that tradition, just because a good outweighs an evil does nothing to make the evil less evil. Yes, in the end we will be better off because Jesus saved us from evil rather than because we happened to be descendants of an Adam and an Eve who escaped evil by never sinning. But their sin and its consequences must, even in the *O felix culpa* tradition, be viewed as a tragedy.

Contemporary strategies to ease our concerns over the Fall create worse difficulties than they resolve. Take John Polkinghorne's example of the Lisbon earthquake. Was this disaster really nothing more than a consequence of the freedom of the earth's crust? How does such an answer comfort the victims and survivors? As suggested earlier, why didn't God simply place us on a less dangerous planet where earthquakes don't ravage human life? Or was this not an option for the Creator, and if not, why not? What are we to make of divine providence in a world with the freedom to crush us? Why, in most classical liturgies of the Christian churches, do we pray for favorable seasons and good crops if the freedom of creation means that the land is going to do what it will regardless? Or does God constrain the freedom of creation? But, if so, why doesn't God place tighter constraints on this freedom in relation to evil?

An irony gets lost in many of these discussions about the world's freedom: How can the freedom of creation, which results from a freely acting God who freely bestows freedom on creation, *force* us to become sinners and *force* the world to be a dangerous place full of natural evil? Shouldn't the freedom of creation rather give us freedom *not* to sin? And shouldn't it be possible for God to create a world whose freedom is not destructive and does not entail natural evil? Such theodicies of freedom require, at crucial points, the sacrifice of freedom.

The earth as a place for soul-making also leaves much to be desired. The metaphor here is that of a school that attempts to train us to become great souls. But rigors of a curriculum are one thing; Lisbon earthquakes and Asian tsunamis, not to mention Auschwitz and the Killing Fields, are another. Do we really need a curriculum that grinds so many of its pupils to powder? If the earth is indeed a place for soul-making, how many great souls does it produce? Is it not a tiny, tiny minority? How many flunk out of Hick's school of soul-making? How many do not merely flunk out but end up in the gutter, addicted to sensuality, money, fame, or power? How many cannot be said to have enrolled in any school whatsoever, whose days are consumed simply in the struggle to survive (think of barefoot children scouring garbage dumps to eke out an existence)?

Finally, consider the knowledge gained by eating the fruit in the garden—was it worth it? Contrary to Aristotle, knowledge is not always a good thing, and people do not always desire to know.[9] We can think of many things we'd rather not know—ask any Holocaust survivor. As for the serpent's promise that Adam and Eve would not die, it's true that their bodies continued to live after eating the fruit. But their relationship with God, the source of life, was broken. Whereas previously they communed with God, they now hid in fear of God, conscious of their nakedness (Gen 3:10). And eventually their bodies did die. If the Fall was such a great blessing, why did God employ angels and a flaming sword to keep humanity from trying to get back into the Garden—to their pre-Fall state (Gen 3:24)?

THREE

Tracing the World's
Evil to Human Sin

CONTEMPORARY strategies for redressing the Fall consistently run aground because they attribute at least some of the evil that humanity suffers to factors other than human guilt. In such approaches, God lets humanity suffer evils of which it is entirely innocent—evils for which it is not responsible and which it therefore does not deserve. For a good God to permit such evils thus presupposes a limitation on God's power and knowledge. For presumably, if God's power and knowledge were up to the task, he would be both able and morally obligated, as a matter of justice, to prevent evils of which we are innocent from afflicting us. This is why process and openness theologies have become increasingly attractive. They give us a God who means well but is limited in stemming the tide of evil.[1]

Rabbi Harold Kushner's *When Bad Things Happen to Good People* provides a well-known example of this theology. The following passage from that book encapsulates the contemporary push to defend God's goodness at the expense of his power:

> I believe in God. But I do not believe in the same things about
> Him that I did years ago, when I was growing up or when I was
> a theological student. I recognize His limitations. He is limited in
> what He can do by laws of nature and by the evolution of human

nature and human moral freedom. I no longer hold God responsible for illnesses, accidents, and natural disasters, because I realize that I gain little and I lose so much when I blame God for those things. I can worship a God who hates suffering but cannot eliminate it more easily than I can worship a God who chooses to make children suffer and die, for whatever exalted reason. . . . The painful things that happen to us are not punishments for our misbehavior, nor are they in any way part of some grand design on God's part. Because the tragedy is not God's will, we need not feel hurt or betrayed by God when tragedy strikes. We can turn to Him for help in overcoming it precisely because we can tell ourselves that God is as outraged by it as we are.[2]

Kushner, in offering these reflections, no doubt means well—just as his God means well. But he fails to address the obvious question: Did God, as Creator, set up the conditions by which the laws of nature, evolution, and human freedom lead to painful things? If not, what sort of Creator is he? And if so, how is God any less complicit in our pain (see chapter 21)?

Kushner's semipowerful God is now a popular figure among evangelicals. For example, in an interview with Gary Stern, Tony Campolo remarked,

The only place where I would differ with Harold Kushner is that I believe that God has *chosen* to not be all-powerful. The reason God has chosen to not be all-powerful is simple: if God were in control of everything, there would be no such thing as human freedom. Without human freedom, we wouldn't be human in the first place. We would have no capacity to love, either God or other people. Love requires freedom. In the economy of God, love is more important than power. The loving God, in order to give us the capacity to love, has limited power. It was a choice. God made it. . . . I would contend that when the earthquake in Pakistan took place and this incredible suffering followed, God was the first one who cried.[3]

So, according to Campolo, God was at one point all-powerful but then gave up his power so that humans could experience free will. But now, like King Lear, God, having ceded his power, witnesses the wreckage of his kingdom and can't do anything about it. Campolo's self-limiting God raises several questions:

1. Isn't God culpable for voluntarily limiting himself and thereby allowing evil to run amuck? To say that free will was worth the cost seems hardly fair since humans are the ones picking up the tab.
2. Why should human free will require natural evil? It's easy enough to imagine a far safer world in which we retain our free will.
3. What are we to make of the biblical teaching that God performs miracles?[4] If God can intervene in the world miraculously, then why doesn't he use that power more frequently and effectively to reduce our suffering (rather than just crying about Pakistani earthquakes)? And if he can't perform miracles, what does that do to biblical exegesis?

With four million copies of Kushner's book in print,[5] with evangelicals like Campolo embracing Kushner, and with Kushner's doctrine of God increasingly taught at our seminaries and divinity schools (e.g., as process and open theism), a "diminished God" is now part and parcel of our mental environment. Such a God wrings his hands over the world's evil and, like an ineffectual politician, tries haltingly to make the world a better place. To our hardier theological forebears, this God would have seemed pathetic (to say nothing of heretical). But each age constructs gods in its own image, and in this touchy-feely age, a diminished God who shares our vulnerabilities and weaknesses is all the rage. In this theology, human sin is not responsible for the world's evil because God doesn't have the power to link the two. Thus, to identify human sin as responsible for the world's evil is now widely regarded as misguided and even gauche.

But that wasn't always the case. A tight link between human sin and the world's evil used to seem quite reasonable. What changed? To answer this question, we need to understand why throughout much of the history of Christian thought, a tight link between the world's evil and human sin seemed eminently plausible. The short answer is that, until the last two or three centuries, the first chapters of Genesis seemed to make perfect sense as both theology and history. Genesis gave a historical justification for the Fall. Specifically, Genesis was thought to describe how, in space and time, the human will turned against God and became evil.[6]

In this traditional reading of Genesis, God creates a good world in a short period of time (six 24-hour days). This original world is orderly and innocuous—it is paradise. Having introduced humans into this world, God explicitly warns them about turning against him by attempting to transcend their creaturehood. This warning is symbolized in the prohibition against eating the forbidden fruit. Nonetheless, the first humans, Adam and Eve, disregard the warning, eat the fruit, and so must live with the consequences of their actions. Those consequences include a disruption of human relations (personal evil) as well as a disruption of nature (natural evil—notably animal death and suffering). God's first promise to humanity is that he will undo the effects of the Fall (Gen 3:15). This promise of redemption is fulfilled in Jesus Christ, who through his Cross and Second Coming restores humanity to a right relationship with God and releases nature from the corruption caused by human sin (Rom 8:19–22). Until recent times, understanding Creation, Fall, and Redemption this way seemed perfectly reasonable and was mainstream Christian theology, both Catholic and Protestant.

Today this traditional reading of Genesis seems less reasonable. Especially problematic in the current mental environment is attributing natural evil to the Fall. Consider the following remarks by well-known Christian thinkers who explicitly deny that natural evil results from humanity's Fall:

C. S. Lewis: "The origin of animal suffering could be traced, by earlier generations, to the Fall of man—the whole world was infected by the uncreating rebellion of Adam. This is now impossible, for we have good reason to believe that animals existed long before men. Carnivorousness, with all that it entails, is older than humanity."[7]

John Polkinghorne: "Of course, physical death did not originate with our hominid ancestors, nor did the emergence of humankind bring about change in the physical constitution of the cosmos."[8]

Ian Barbour: "At some points, the theologian may need to reformulate traditional ideas. For example, theologians must ask how they can express the idea of sin and the fall without assuming death came into the world with Adam and Eve."[9]

Patrick Miller: "The effects of sin are depicted [in Isa 24–27] as both divine activity and an undoing from within, that is, as both retribution and an organic outworking of the deeds of the earth in which acts have consequences arising from them. This raises the difficult question of how the transgressions of human beings and the 'shaking' of the earth, that is, human acts and cosmic effects, can be related to each other in an intelligible fashion. It is hardly plausible to argue that the death of the solar system in the burning out of the sun or the contingent possibilities of [the] world ending are to be seen as causally related to human acts on earth."[10]

Denis Alexander: "In the evangelical circles in which I was raised it was common to believe that there was no pain, disease or suffering of any kind before the Fall, but that all these came into being following Adam and Eve's disobedience. . . . As I grew in the Christian faith, the position I had unthinkingly adopted seemed increasingly untenable. I started studying biology and learning incontrovertible evidence . . . that death has been present on the earth since the beginning of life."[11]

Jürgen Moltmann: "If . . . death came into the world only through sin, then we have to restrict this to the death of human beings, for the death of animals, the dying of trees, and the extinction of the dinosaurs can hardly be traced back to human sin. That would be a negative self-deification of human beings by way of an immense and presumptuous arrogation of guilt. Not every death in the world can be traced back to human sin."[12]

The claim that human sin has cosmic and transhistorical consequences has been a central theme of Christian orthodoxy. Protestations to the contrary by these Christian thinkers merely underscore its centrality—indeed, why are they making it an issue? Has our knowledge of the world, especially in light of modern science, so changed that this theme of Christian orthodoxy is no longer tenable? I will argue that cosmic and transhistorical consequences to human sin remain eminently reasonable. This is not because, as young-earth creationists contend, the science of astrophysics and geology have the age of the earth and universe wrong. In fact, I will argue that viewing natural evil as a consequence of the Fall is entirely compatible with mainstream understandings of cosmic and natural history.

Of the six thinkers cited here, five explicitly disconnect natural from personal evil. Only C. S. Lewis traces natural to personal evil, though for him the person in question is not Adam but Satan. According to Lewis, Satan, whose fall precedes that of humanity, is the source of natural evil.[13] Seeing no way to connect natural evil that predates the first humans to the Fall of humanity, Lewis nonetheless feels the force of connecting natural evil to the fall of some being capable of sin (the alternative, unacceptable to Lewis, is that God allows natural evil independent of personal or moral evil). Because Satan sinned before Adam and Eve, Lewis settles on the fall of Satan.

Mindful that attributing natural evil to the fall of Satan is unlikely to score points in the current mental environment, Lewis remarks,

> The doctrine of Satan's existence and fall is not among the things we know to be untrue: it contradicts not the facts discovered by scientists but the mere, vague "climate of opinion" [cf. mental environment] that we happen to be living in. Now I take a very low view of "climates of opinion." In his own subject every man knows that all discoveries are made and all errors corrected by those who ignore the "climate of opinion."[14]

In thus disparaging "climates of opinion," Lewis attempts to shield his own proposed resolution of the problem of natural evil from criticism. But tracing natural evil to the fall of Satan raises several exegetical and theological difficulties, including the following:

1. Satan and humanity reside in different orders of creation. How, then, does Satan, an angelic being not embodied in physical stuff, interact with the physical world and introduce natural evil into it?
2. Even if such supernatural intervention of an angelic being in the physical world is not in principle problematic, why should we think that God permitted such a fallen spiritual being to wreak havoc in the physical world prior to Adam and Eve? In particular, why should animals and humans be subject to the consequences of Satan's sin?

3. What sense does it make for God to call the creation "good" and "very good" if throughout the process of creation Satan has been infecting it?
4. What is the point in Genesis 1 of God's formally bestowing on humanity rulership of the earth if throughout its existence Satan has been undermining it with natural evil?

None of these difficulties decisively refutes Lewis's proposal that Satan—apart from humanity's fall—is responsible for natural evil. But until they are dealt with adequately, his proposal will languish, as it has now for decades. The first difficulty is actually no difficulty at all for classical theology, which takes seriously the Bible's teaching that spiritual agencies (God, angels, demons) can materialize and interact tangibly with the physical world.[15] This difficulty does, however, sit uneasily in the present "climate of opinion," which regards spirit–matter interactions as deeply problematic. Then again, as Lewis makes clear, climates of opinion are best viewed with skepticism. And he is right: reformations and revolutions in thought are only possible by breaking with climates of opinion.

The second difficulty is more serious. In classical theology, God owes Satan nothing, and just getting rid of him seems perfectly reasonable where only animal nature is concerned. The reason God does not simply get rid of Satan where human nature is concerned is that Satan and humanity are complicit in rebelling against God. As for the third difficulty, a thing might be good or very good even if corrupted, the way a painting could be a masterwork even though it requires cleaning. But does sin merely sully a masterwork so that underneath it remains intact, or does sin fundamentally distort the masterwork so that it can no longer properly be regarded as good? With the fourth difficulty, perhaps God did not intend humanity's rulership of the earth to be absolute but rather meant it to include ongoing resistance to Satan from the start. I do not hold that position, but it might be maintained.

What has become of Lewis's proposal to make Satan responsible for natural evil? Although his proposal has hardly won the day, it has more recently received a boost from open theism. Gregory Boyd, a proponent of open theism, has in fact written an entire book on the evils that may, in his view, properly be ascribed to Satan: *Satan and the Problem of Evil: Constructing a Trinitarian Warfare Theodicy*.[16] In that book, Boyd shifts to Satan the responsibility for natural evil.[17] Yet, in making that shift, Boyd embraces a dualism that Lewis would have rejected. Because open theism contracts the power and knowledge of God, God does not have Satan on a leash as he does in classical theism. Thus, for Boyd, Satan becomes an independent center of evil activity. This is not quite a Manichean dualism, in which good and evil are ontological equals (Satan for Boyd is still a created being). But it's close. Moreover, it's not clear how Boyd's theodicy absolves God of evil since as Satan's Creator, he must have realized the possibilities of evil inherent in his creation.

In any case, unless Satan's activity in bringing about natural evil can itself be traced to human sin (which is consistent with Lewis's proposal though it was not his original intent), Lewis's resolution of the problem of natural evil leaves unanswered why humans should be subject to Satan's wickedness. To say, without further elaboration, that God gave Satan permission provides little help here. In that case, we must face the question of why God should give Satan this permission, a question that invites the retroactive theodicy that is the subject of this book.

Thus, even though I follow Lewis in tracing natural evil to personal evil, I don't assign primary responsibility for natural evil to the person of Satan. Rather, I take the entirely traditional view that natural evil traces to the personal evil of the first humans (which, pace Lewis, allows that human evil opened the door to Satan to ravage the physical world, a view I do take—see chapter 20). At first blush the traditional view appears to contradict widely accepted claims from astrophysics and geology concerning the age of the earth and universe. Indeed, how could natural evil trace to the Fall of humanity if natural evil predates humans? But, as will become evident in later chapters, the soundness of viewing natural evil as a consequence of the Fall is, in fact, independent of scientific considerations.

Leaving aside for the moment science, which many interpret as showing that natural evil can't be traced to humanity's Fall, why should cosmic and transhistorical consequences of human sin seem implausible? If humans are indeed the crown of Creation, then it should, on theological grounds, seem entirely reasonable for human sin to have repercussions throughout the physical world. Moltmann, in the quote given earlier, describes such a view as presumptuous and self-congratulatory. But Moltmann is in danger of proposing a false humility that may well blind us to the truth about ourselves. If we alone among physically embodied creatures are made in the image of God, then our actions may well have cosmic and transhistorical consequences.

The Christian theological tradition is clear about humanity's unique status: God was incarnated, just once, as a human being in the person of Jesus Christ for our redemption and for that of the whole world. Consistent with this exclusive view of humanity, the Search for Extraterrestrial Intelligence (SETI) has not discovered a shred of evidence to suggest that embodied rational moral agents like us exist elsewhere in the universe.[18] Moreover, nonhuman animals have nothing like the conceptual and moral capacities of humans. Those who argue that there is merely a difference in degree rather than a difference in kind between chimpanzees, say, and us are fooling themselves.[19] As Bruce Thornton notes,

> What makes us recognizably human, then, is *not* what is natural about us but what is *un*natural: reason and its projections in language, culture, ritual, and technology; self-awareness, conscious memory, imagination, and the higher emotions; and, most important, values, ethics, morals, and the freedom from nature's determinism that allows us to choose, whether for good or ill. Nothing else in nature possesses *any* of these attributes, despite the wishful thinking of those who believe they are teaching chimps to "talk," or who consider a monkey digging up termites with a stick to be "using tools," or who label baboon rump-submission a "social practice," or who subjectively interpret the behavior of animals to indicate the presence of "self-awareness" or higher human emotions such as love, grief, regret, guilt, shame, or loyalty. For every dog that howls over the body of its dead master there is another that, if necessary, will happily eat his corpse.[20]

Such a high view of humanity (Peter Singer disparages it as "speciesism") has, however, been pounded out of us in the name of modern science. Advances in science are supposed to have left us no choice but to embrace the Copernican Principle (also known as the Super-Copernican Principle or the Principle of Mediocrity). According to this principle, there is nothing special about humans in the grand scheme of things. Yes, we are currently having our moment on the stage of history. But there's nothing cosmically significant about that, and soon enough our little drama will be done and forgotten.

The Copernican Principle expresses a sentiment deeply held in the current mental environment. Carl Sagan expressed it as follows:

Because of the reflection of sunlight . . . the Earth seems to be sitting in a beam of light, as if there were some special significance to this small world. But it's just an accident of geometry and optics. . . . Our posturings, our imagined self-importance, the delusion that we have some privileged position in the Universe, are challenged by this point of pale light. Our planet is a lonely speck in the great enveloping cosmic dark. In our obscurity, in all this vastness, there is no hint that help will come from elsewhere to save us from ourselves.[21]

Sagan here invokes the size and duration of the universe—as though against so vast a backdrop, we cannot but fade into insignificance. Nonetheless, such crassly materialist considerations are simply irrelevant to gauging humanity's true status in the great scheme of things. This is not to say that we should think of ourselves more highly than we ought. The words *human* and *humility,* after all, derive from the same source, indicating our solidarity with the ground (humus) from which our physical constitution derives. But it also means not thinking less of ourselves than we ought.

Sagan's attempt to make religious believers doubt the uniqueness and preeminence of humans among physically embodied beings does not withstand closer scrutiny. Indeed, effective responses to the Copernican Principle are easy to find. Take, for instance, the following observation by Pascal: "By space the universe encompasses and swallows me up like an atom; [but] by thought I comprehend the world."[22] Or consider Julian of Norwich, who had a vision of a small hazelnut that she held in her hand. "What is this?" she asked. She heard God answer, "It is all that is made."[23] Thus, for Julian of Norwich, the fullness of creation was captured in even the smallest things. My favorite theological response to the Copernican Principle is G. K. Chesterton's. Responding to Herbert Spencer, he wrote,

[Spencer] popularized this contemptible notion that the size of the solar system ought to overawe the spiritual dogma of man. Why should a man surrender his dignity to the solar system any more than to a whale? If mere size proves that man is not the image of God, then a whale may be the image of God. . . . It is quite futile to argue that man is small compared to the cosmos; for man was always small compared to the nearest tree.[24]

Nor do theological reflections alone lead us to reject the Copernican Principle. This principle is refutable on scientific grounds. Despite strident rhetoric from the popular science industry (Asimov, Sagan, Dawkins, etc.), arguments against the importance of humans in the cosmos that turn on either the size of the universe or the unimportance of Earth are not in fact supported by current science. A vast gap exists between actual science, whose claims are supported by evidence, and materialistically driven popularizations of science, which tend to fly in the face of evidence. The actual scientific evidence, as Guillermo Gonzalez and Jay Wesley Richards show in *The Privileged Planet*, suggests that our place in the cosmos is indeed special in that it was designed to foster not just intelligent life but also scientific discovery. According to them, among all the places in the universe from which to pursue scientific discovery, the planet we call home—Earth—is as good as it gets.[25]

FOUR

THE GRAVITY OF SIN[1]

I F we are serious about tracing the world's evil to human sin, we now face an uncomfortable question: Why would a benevolent God allow natural evil to afflict an otherwise innocent nature in response to human moral evil? To answer this question, we need to reexamine the origin of evil. Earlier I argued that evil results from a will that has turned against God. Clearly the unity of the Godhead is such that God's will does not, and indeed cannot, turn against God. Evil, therefore, is the result of a *creaturely* will turning against God. The essence of evil is rebellion of the creature. This rebellion constitutes sin (singular) and finds expression in numerous particular sins (plural). As a consequence, sin separates us from God. This rift between God and humanity, however, cannot be left to stand. To let it stand would thwart God's purpose for humanity, which is to be united to humanity in love. Once sin has entered the picture, God's overriding task is to find a way to heal the rift.

At this point one might ask why it should be God's task to heal the rift between humanity. Since we're the guilty party, why shouldn't that burden fall on us? Better yet, why doesn't God just "get over it" and forgive us? As Heinrich Heine is reported to have said on his deathbed, "*Le bon Dieu me pardonnera; c'est son metier*" ("The good God will forgive me; that's his job").[2] God is in the forgiving business, so why doesn't he just have at it? There are two problems with Heine's approach to divine forgiveness:

[43]

1. It presupposes that humans have the power to heal the rift with God by a straightforward act of the will, voluntarily desisting from their rebellion against God. That's Pelagianism. The clear teaching of Scripture is that humanity does not possess this power (see Romans 7 and 8).[3]

2. Forgiveness, in the uncomplicated sense of "I won't hold what you did against you," doesn't address the root cause of what led to the rift that calls for forgiveness. Without addressing this root cause, forgiveness becomes irresponsible, condoning what should not be condoned.[4]

The term for God's healing the rift between humanity and himself is *atonement*.[5] Within Christian theology, atonement comes through the redemptive work of Christ on the Cross (see chapter 1). *Redemption* is a business term and can be usefully illustrated by business practices. It denotes an exchange that restores to one party something previously belonging to it but now in the hands of another. For instance, the period after a real estate foreclosure sale during which the original owner has the right to reclaim the foreclosed land is called the "redemption period." Pawn shops, in which people leave items and can reclaim them later, also illustrate this concept. In Christian theology God is the Redeemer. Humanity used to belong to God. But through sin, humanity has become captive to evil. The redemptive work of God in Christ on the Cross restores humanity back to God.[6]

This picture of Christ's redeeming work is accurate as far as it goes, but it omits one crucial element: humanity, in becoming captive to evil, gave its consent. Humans are complicit in the evil from which God is striving to deliver us. For redemption effectively to deliver humanity from evil therefore requires us to be clear as to precisely what we have consented to in rebelling against God and embracing evil. To achieve this clarity, humanity must experience the full brunt of the evil that we have set in motion, and this requires that the creation itself fully manifest the consequences of humanity's rebellion against God. This does not mean that the creation has to become as corrupt as it could possibly be. But it does mean that the creation must not conceal or soft-sell the gravity of sin. It also helps us understand why God, despite having the power to intervene and stop specific evils, may refrain from doing so.

In answer, then, to why a benevolent God would allow natural evil to afflict an otherwise innocent nature in response to human moral evil, we can say that it is to manifest the full consequences of human sin so that when Christ redeems us, we may clearly understand what we have been redeemed from. Without this clarity about the evil we have set in motion, we will always be in danger of reverting back to it because we do not see its gravity. Instead, we will treat it lightly, rationalize it, shift the blame for it—in short, we will do anything but face the tragedy of willfully separating ourselves from the source of our life, who is God. Additionally, we will fail to recognize the enormity of Christ's suffering on the Cross to redeem us. As a result, we will not be moved to repent of our sin and return to God in trust and humility.

In saying that God uses natural evil to get us to understand the gravity of sin, I might seem to be merely amending Hick's view of the world as a school for soul-making, a view I previously dismissed as inadequate. Let me suggest that the difference in our views goes far deeper. The point of natural evil in the theodicy I am proposing is not merely to assist us in acquiring an intellectual or practical understanding of the sort that schools are typically designed to give their students. The point, rather, is to get our attention, to impress on us the gravity of sin, and, most significantly, to bring us to our senses and thereby to restore our sanity.

Where Hicks offers a school, I offer an insane asylum. Students at a school need to be trained and cultivated. Inmates of an insane asylum need to be cured and delivered. (Indeed, why did Jesus devote so much of his ministry to healing the sick and casting out demons?) Sin has rendered us insane. Granted, many don't see it that way and take offense at the very suggestion. But if God is all that Christian theology teaches that he is, then it is nothing short of insanity for us to be constantly constructing idols that divert us from finding ultimate satisfaction in the God who alone is our light and salvation (Ps 27:1), who alone loves us so totally that he makes his life ours (Gal 2:20; Col 3:1–4).

The gravity of sin consists in offending a holy God. Our natural inclination is to think that God is too generous to grudge any offense that we commit against him. The problem isn't that God can't take it but that we can't take it—in offending God, we ruin the image of God in ourselves and so lose our true self. Because God is all that Christian theology teaches that he is, offending this God is the worst thing imaginable and trumps all the offenses that we commit against one another. But we refuse to see this. Thinking that God is obliged to excuse our sin, we offend God further by accusing him of injustice because those who suffer the most in this life are often not those most evidently responsible for evil. Thus, when we rank the sins that humans commit against one another, we find that punishments tend not to match up with our rankings. But God is not unjust. All of us are sinners (Rom 3:23), and our sin is principally against God (Ps 51:4).

We need to take seriously Jesus' parable of the unforgiving servant in Matt 18:23–35: the debt we owe to God on account of our sin against him (i.e., the "ten thousand talents" owed by the servant) completely overshadows any debt owed to us by others (i.e., the "hundred pence" owed to the servant). The lesson of this parable is that we must, without conditions or qualifications, forgive others. Failure to forgive means that God will not forgive us (see also Matt 6:14–15 and Mark 11:25–26). Why won't God forgive us if we refuse to forgive others? Unforgiveness says, "I have the right to hold your sins against you." But in sinning against God, we forfeited any such right. God is just and will, come Judgment Day, right the inequities of this life. The promise of redemption is that Christ has taken on himself the judgment merited by our sins (see Isaiah 53 and 2 Cor 5:21).

The view of God's redemption in Christ sketched in this chapter is basic Christian theology. I regard it as not only true but also mandatory for sound Christian faith. Nonetheless, it presupposes that all evil in the world ultimately traces back to human sin. For this understanding of evil to be plausible within our current mental environment therefore requires an explanation of how natural evil could precede the first human sin and yet proceed from it. I'll address this question in due course. But first we need to see why the traditional view that all evil, both moral and natural, traces to human sin used to seem eminently plausible. The short answer is that Genesis used to be read as plain history, and therefore no pressing reason existed to doubt the traditional view. We turn now to the long answer.

PART II

YOUNG- AND OLD-EARTH CREATIONISM

FIVE

THE ATTRACTION OF A YOUNG EARTH

I F human sin no longer seems responsible for natural evil, that's because science has made it difficult to see how human sin could be responsible for natural evil. Standard astrophysical and geological dating (13 billion years for the age of the universe, 4.5 billion years for the age of the earth) gives a world that long predates the arrival of humans. How then can humans, whose sin precipitates the Fall, be responsible for the history of violence and cruelty that predates them (a history exhibited in the fossil record)? A world in which natural evils such as death, predation, parasitism, disease, drought, floods, famines, earthquakes, and hurricanes precede humans, and thus appear disconnected from the Fall, seems hard to square with a creation that, from the start, is created good.

Young-earth creationists deserve credit for highlighting the difficulty of reconciling an old earth with the Fall. In particular, they see the theological necessity of linking natural evil to human sin. That's why, when asked what's riding on a young Earth, proponents of this position cite Rom 5:12, which speaks of death as a consequence of human sin.[1] Sure, one can try to make an exegetical argument that passages like Rom 5:12 speak strictly about human death. But young-earth creationists have the stronger case here, both exegetically and theologically, in interpreting such passages as speaking about death and corruption generally and not just about human death. Without a young earth (i.e., an earth created in six 24-hour days and spanning a history of only a few thousand years), how can natural evil be traced back to human sin?

Young-earth creationism presents a straightforward chronology that aligns the order of creation with a traditional conception of the Fall: God creates a perfect world, God places humans in that world, humans sin, and the world goes haywire. In this chronology, theology and history march in sync so that the first human sin predates and is causally responsible for natural as well as moral evil. But what if the universe is 13 billion years old? What if the earth formed 4.5 billion years ago? What if unicellular life got started after the planet cooled 3.9 billion ago? What if multicellular life dates from 600 million years ago?[2] In that case, the bulk of natural history predates humans by billions of years. In that case, for hundreds of million of years, multicelled animals have been emerging, competing, fighting, killing, parasitizing, torturing, suffering, and going extinct. Given such a past, young-earth creationism's harmony of theology and history appears insupportable. Natural history as described by modern science therefore appears irreconcilable with the order of creation as described in Genesis.

Precisely such considerations led Russell Moore, dean of the Southern Baptist Theological Seminary, to convert from an old-earth to a young-earth view. As he put it,

> For a long time, I believed that Scripture was silent on the question of the age of the universe. After all, "day" in Scripture can and often does refer to a long period of time (the "day" of the Lord, for example). In recent months, however, as I have been teaching through Genesis and working on a lengthy article on general revelation, I have slowly changed my mind. The main issue for me is not the exegetical arguments for the use of the word "day." . . . What convinced me that the universe is much younger than we've been told was an episode of television's "Animal Planet." Specifically, the problem for Christian theology is the picture of a python swallowing a pig.[3]

Moore concluded that Romans 8, properly interpreted, teaches that all evil in "the entire created order" arises from human sin and thus demands a young earth.

Moore's move from old-earth to young-earth creationism epitomizes the attraction of a young earth. How else can a robust view of the goodness of creation be preserved unless all evil in it can somehow be traced to humanity's Fall? And how else can all evil be traced to humanity's Fall unless the Fall temporally precedes the entrance of evil into the world? And how else can the Fall temporally precede the entrance of evil into the world unless humans inhabit creation from the start and not at the end of a bloody natural history that exhibits death and destruction? A theologically sound view of the Fall seems to demand that the corrupting effects of sin follow time's arrow. Thus, if humans, through their sin, are responsible for all corruption in the world, the world's corruption must postdate human sin. Causes, after all, precede their effects. Or do they?

The underlying assumption here is this: Human sin must precede all appearance of evil in the world; otherwise it cannot be responsible for it. That may seem axiomatic, but it can legitimately be questioned. Why, in the economy of a world whose Creator is omnipotent, omniscient, and transtemporal, should causes always precede effects? Clearly, such a Creator could act to anticipate events that have yet to happen. Moreover, those events could be the occasion (or "cause") of God's prior anticipatory action. By tacitly rejecting such backward causation, young-earth creationists insist that the corrupting effects of the Fall be understood *proactively* (in other words, the consequences of the Fall only act forward into the future). By contrast, I will argue that we should understand the corrupting effects of the Fall also *retroactively* (in other words, the consequences of the Fall can also act backward into the past). Accordingly, the Fall could take place *after* the natural evils for which it is responsible.

Such "retroactivity" has theological precedent. Take the saving effects of the Cross, which are held to act not only forward in time but also backward. Christians have always attributed the salvation of Old Testament saints to Christ's sacrifice on the Cross at the hands of the Romans even though Old Testament times predate Roman times by hundreds of years. In this way, an omnipotent God unbound by time makes a future event (Christ's sacrifice) the cause of an earlier event (the salvation of Old Testament saints).[4] Likewise, an omnipotent God unbound by time can make natural evil predate the Fall and yet make the Fall the reason for natural evil.

Such "backward causation" may seem counterintuitive, though science-fiction readers will recognize in it familiar paradoxes connected with time travel. The point to note is that what is impossible for science and paradoxical for science fiction can be standard operating procedure for the Christian God. Throughout Scripture God is portrayed as unbound by time. For instance, in Isa 46:9–10, one reads, "I am God, and there is none like me, declaring the end from the beginning, and from ancient times the things that are not yet done, saying, My counsel shall stand, and I will do all my pleasure." Scripture even explicitly states that God acts in anticipation of future events. Thus, in Isa 65:24, God says, "It shall come to pass, that before they call, I will answer; and while they are yet speaking, I will hear."

Many an answered prayer requires that God have prepared the answer before the prayer was actually offered. Take an answer to prayer recounted by physician Helen Roseveare, who served as a medical missionary in Zaire. A mother died in childbirth, leaving a two-year-old daughter and a premature baby, who required a water bottle to stay warm and alive. As Roseveare prayed with children from the local orphanage for this need, a ten-year-old girl named Ruth asked God to "send us a water bottle. It'll be no good tomorrow, God, the baby'll be dead; so please send it this afternoon. . . . And while You are about it, would You please send a dolly for the little girl so she'll know You really love her?" That afternoon a parcel arrived containing the water bottle and the doll. And when was it sent? Remarkably, "that parcel had been on the way for five whole months, packed up by my former Sunday School class." It was sent "five months earlier in answer to the believing prayer of a ten-year-old to bring it 'That afternoon!'"[5]

God can act retroactively, anticipating what from our vantage are present and future events. Both Scripture and Christian experience support this view of divine action. For the moment, however, let us set aside any retroactive effects of the Fall and take young-earth creationism on its own terms. Young-earth creationism invokes no temporal paradoxes. God creates a perfect world, humans fall, and the world becomes corrupt. Within young-earth creationism, this order of events is taken as an ordinary temporal progression. For those who regard the Scriptures as authoritative and accurate (as I do), a young-earth interpretation of Genesis seems natural and fitting.

Indeed, the history of biblical interpretation until the rise of modern science in the seventeenth century overwhelmingly supports a young-earth view. Young-earth creationism was the dominant position of Christians from the Church Fathers through the Reformers. The second-century Christian apologist Theophilus of Antioch examined the genealogies in the Greek translation of the Old Testament (the Septuagint) and calculated 5,698 years from creation to the death of the Emperor Aurelius Verus, who died in AD 169. That put the creation of the world at 5529 BC. The third-century Christian historian Julius Africanus made a similar calculation and put the creation of the world at 5531 BC.[6] Note that these numbers, derived from the Septuagint, add about 1,500 years to the age of the earth as compared to the standard Hebrew edition of the Old Testament (the Masoretic text) employed by the Reformers and translators of contemporary Bibles.

Even Origen and Augustine, who allowed some flexibility in interpreting the days of Genesis 1, accepted that the earth was only a few thousand years old. Countering the view of Celsus, who held to an eternal universe, Origen wrote in the third century: "After these statements, Celsus, from a secret desire to cast discredit upon the Mosaic account of the creation, which teaches that the world is not yet ten thousand years old, but very much under that, while concealing his wish, intimates his agreement with those who hold that the world is uncreated."[7] Origen here clearly agreed that the earth is "not yet ten thousand years old." Likewise Augustine, in the fifth century, wrote, "They are deceived, too, by those highly mendacious documents which profess to give the history of many thousand years, though, reckoning by the sacred writings, we find that not 6,000 years have yet passed."[8]

Fast-forwarding to the middle ages, we find the preeminent scholastic theologian, Thomas Aquinas, interpreting Genesis so literally as to make any contemporary young-earth creationist proud. He explicitly rejected that God used intermediate or secondary causes to create humanity: "The first formation of the human body could not be by the instrumentality of any created power, but was immediately from God."[9] Thus Aquinas would have rejected any evolutionary account of human origins. Indeed, he would have dismissed the "Thomistic evolutionism" promoted by contemporary neo-Thomists as an oxymoron.[10]

Aquinas also held that the days of creation were literal 24-hour days: "The words 'one day' are used when day is first instituted, to denote that one day is made up of twenty-four hours. Hence, by mentioning 'one,' the measure of a natural day is fixed."[11] Holding that "the angels were created at the same time as corporeal creatures," Aquinas found himself at odds with other theologians, notably Jerome, who held that "the angels were created before the corporeal world."[12] Nevertheless, even though he differed with Jerome about when God created angels, Aquinas quoted with approval the following statement by Jerome: "Six-thousand years of our time have not elapsed [since the creation of the corporeal world]."[13] Aquinas was therefore a six-day, six-thousand-year young-earth creationist!

In the sixteenth century we find key Reformers such as Martin Luther and John Calvin also holding to a young earth. Thus, according to Luther, "We know from Moses that the world was not in existence before 6,000 years ago."[14] He also held to a literal interpretation of the Genesis days:

> [Moses] calls "a spade a spade," i.e., he employs the terms "day" and "evening" without allegory, just as we customarily do. We assert that Moses spoke in the literal sense, not allegorically or figuratively, i.e., that the world, with all its creatures, was created within six days, as the words read.[15]

Calvin's views on the age of the earth and on the days of creation coincided with Luther's. Indeed, Calvin was a hard-liner about such questions. In addressing the age of the earth, he criticized "obstinate persons" who "will not refrain from guffaws when they are informed that but little more than five thousand years have passed since the creation of the universe, for they ask why God's power was idle and asleep for so long [i.e., prior to creation]."[16] Moreover, even though he conceded that God could have created the world in a moment or over any length of time, Calvin insisted that the creation occurred in six ordinary days: "Six days were employed in the formation of the world; not that God, to whom one moment is as a thousand years, had need of this succession of time, but that he might engage us in the contemplation of his works."[17]

Given such a long and venerable history of outstanding Christian thinkers who embraced a young earth, why should any Christian opt for an old earth? Doesn't faithfulness to Scripture and Christian orthodoxy demand a young earth? In his three-volume layperson's guide to the West-minster Confession, Christian apologist R. C. Sproul, despite a long career as an author and teacher, describes his own eleventh-hour conversion from old-earth to young-earth creationism: "I have now changed my mind. I now hold to a literal six-day creation. . . . Genesis says that God created the universe and everything in it in six twenty-four-hour periods. Accord-ing to the Reformation hermeneutic, the first option is to follow the plain sense of the text. One must do a great deal of hermeneutical gymnastics to escape the plain meaning of Genesis 1–2."[18]

Even so, many of Sproul's evangelical colleagues are reluctant to follow him in his conversion. Why? One thing and one thing alone: *science*.[19] As Sproul puts it, "In our time a considerable number of theories have arisen denying that the creation, as we know it, took place in six twenty-four-hour days. Common to these theories is the acceptance of the dominant scientific view that the earth and life on it are very old."[20] For science to trump the most natural reading of Genesis and the overwhelm-ing consensus of theologians up through the Reformation, either science has discovered momentous new truths or science has gone massively awry. In either case, science has raised a crucial challenge to young-earth cre-ationism. Let us now turn to that challenge.

SIX

NATURE'S CONSTANCY

THE young-earth solution to reconciling the order of creation with natural history makes good exegetical and theological sense. Indeed, the overwhelming consensus of theologians up through the Reformation held to this view. I myself would adopt it in a heartbeat except that nature seems to present such strong evidence against it. I'm hardly alone in my reluctance to accept young-earth creationism. In our current mental environment, informed as it is by modern astrophysics and geology, the scientific community as a whole regards young-earth creationism as untenable.

In response, some young-earth creationists grant that theirs is the weaker argument scientifically, conceding that the preponderance of scientific evidence goes against their position. Nevertheless, they feel compelled to maintain the young-earth position because they see Scripture as requiring it. They hope that science will eventually vindicate their position. John Mark Reynolds and Paul Nelson exemplify this approach:

> Presently, we can admit that as recent [i.e., young-earth] creationists we are defending a very natural biblical account, at the cost of abandoning a very plausible scientific picture of an "old" cosmos. But over the long term, this is not a tenable position. In our opinion, old earth creationism combines a less natural textual reading with a much more plausible scientific vision. They have many fewer "problems of science." At the moment, this would

> seem the more rational position to adopt. Recent creationism
> must develop better scientific accounts if it is to remain viable
> against old earth creationism. On the other hand, the reading of
> Scripture (e.g., a real Flood, meaningful genealogies, an actual
> dividing of languages) is so natural that it seems worth saving.
> Since we believe recent creation cosmologies are improving, we
> are encouraged to continue the effort.[1]

Thus, for Nelson and Reynolds, young-earth creationism's theological attractiveness outweighs its scientific difficulties.

Although some young-earth creationists grant that theirs is the weaker position scientifically, many refuse to make such a concession. Instead, they fault the mainstream scientific understanding of the age of the earth and universe, arguing that a young-earth position actually makes for better science.[2] To make their case, young-earth creationists start by pointing to scientific findings that they regard as anomalous if the Earth is old. For instance, they may point to polystrate fossils (fossils that span several geologic strata) as inconsistent with the slow rates of fossilization typical of an old earth. Or they may point to certain currently observed sedimentation rates that are so fast that, if extrapolated beyond a few thousand years, would have deposited far more sediment than is currently observed.[3] Of course, critics of young-earth creationism respond to such anomalies point for point.[4]

Anomalies that merely poke holes in an old earth, however, do not go far enough to support a young earth. Young-earth creationists do not merely want to show why the other side is wrong; they also want to show why their side is right. To show the superiority of their view, young-earth creationists thus need radically to revise our understanding of geology and astrophysics. Consider, for instance, the Institute for Creation Research's RATE project (RATE = Radioisotopes and the Age of the Earth), which attempts to demonstrate that our present scientific understanding of radiometric dating needs to be radically revised (in favor of a young earth). The RATE project is the crown jewel of young-earth creationist attempts to square natural history with a face-value interpretation of Genesis. And yet even this project faces serious objections. For instance, Donald DeYoung, in a book arguing for the young-earth view, outlines several "challenges" (his word) that confront the RATE project.

One such challenge is to explain how the rate of nuclear decay could have been much faster in the past than now. Such accelerated decay is required for the RATE project to establish a young earth. Yet, according to De Young,

> *The acceleration of nuclear decay gives rise to some basic un-answered questions.* Why did it occur and what was the mechanism? Exactly when did the decay rates increase? Each of these questions has both scientific and theological components. There is also a serious concern for the protection of plant, animal, and human life from increased nuclear radiation during the Genesis flood event. Further insight is needed on these issues.[5]

Accelerated nuclear decay would explain why rocks, given present decay rates, appear millions or billions of years old when, on a young-earth view, they can be only thousands of years old. But invoking accelerated nuclear decay fills one hole by digging several others. What accounts for the change of the decay rate? If it was much faster in the past, how were its destructive effects avoided (the increased decay rates required for a young earth imply lethal levels of radiation)? Is there any solid evidence for nuclear decay's acceleration that does not depend on the need to establish a young earth?

De Young's need to tinker with nuclear decay rates reflects a larger difficulty confronting young-earth creationists: to preserve a young-earth interpretation of Genesis, they must question the *constancy of nature*. Scientific investigation suggests that the physical universe has a determinate character—that nature tends to operate in certain ways and not in others. Thus, various physical processes appear to operate at certain fixed rates. For instance, measure the speed of light yesterday or today, and our best scientific instruments can tell no difference. Up to this point young-earth creationists will typically agree. Yet a persistent line of criticism among young-earth creationists against an old earth is to posit that these rates were substantially different in times past (usually faster) so that what appears to be a long time (millions or billions of years) is in fact a short time (only thousands of years).

In ascribing constancy to nature, I am not smuggling in the materialist assumption that nature is a closed system impervious to divine action.

Indeed, I find repugnant the idea that the world is a closed system of matter and energy operating by unbroken physical laws. As a classically orthodox Christian, I follow the traditional line that the world is radically dependent on God. Georges Florovsky referred to this radical dependence as "the absolute creatureliness and non-self-sufficiency of the world."[6] In particular, I believe that God performs miracles and thus can and does make exceptions to the regularities of nature, or what are typically called natural laws.

Interestingly, such exceptions to natural laws need not violate natural laws. Just as human laws do not cover every eventuality that arises in society, so the laws of nature need not cover every eventuality that may arise in physical reality. Simply put, the laws of nature may be incomplete. Thus, even though natural laws account for much that happens in nature, natural laws need not provide a complete account of what nature does or is capable of doing. Natural laws give God plenty of room to maneuver—or perhaps we should say that God designed natural laws to accommodate divine action. To act in the world, God does not need to violate natural laws; it's enough for him simply to work with and around them. On this view, natural laws are like stage props that provide a framework within which an actor must act but that also gives the actor plenty of freedom. Or, to change the analogy, the laws of nature are like a poetic meter: the meter constrains the poet; and yet the poet, working within the constraint, retains a great deal of freedom.

To say that nature is constant, therefore, differs from saying that it is causally closed. Causal closure means that no divine finger can get into nature. Constancy means that when the divine finger gets into nature, having assimilated the divine activity, nature resumes behaving as it always has. The constancy of nature reflects the covenant faithfulness of God—that just as God has a consistent character that we can count on, so God has given the world a consistent character that we can count on.[7] Divine activity may help nature accomplish things that, left to her own devices, nature never could; but divine activity does not change the nature of nature.

To illustrate the difference between causal closure and constancy, imagine two types of computerized chess programs. With one type of program, once it begins running, it cannot be interrupted; with the other type, its operation can be modified while it is running. Now imagine that Gary

Kasparov, widely regarded as the best chess player of all time, walks by as a game is being played. With the first type of program, he can see a brilliant move but can't make it because he can't input it during the operation of the program. With the second type he can pause the program and make the move, after which the program resumes its normal play. The second program is designed to allow pausing and intervention; no violation of the program occurs when Kasparov overrides it. The first program, on the other hand, is impervious to external influence. It illustrates causal closure by barring Kasparov from inputting any move. The second program illustrates constancy: once Kasparov inputs his brilliant move, the program assimilates it and goes back to operating as it always has.

Young-earth creationists give up both causal closure and constancy, embracing instead an inconstant nature. To illustrate inconstancy, we might imagine a chess program that radically changes its behavior at different times in the game: at the beginning it plays full strength, in the middle it limits itself to evaluating only a few dozen chess positions, and toward the end it gives up material and tries to lose. With such a program, Kasparov might still be able to input a brilliant move, but there would be no guarantees that the program would take best advantage of it. Similarly, an inconstant nature would still be open to divine activity, but its characteristic behavior could change so radically at different times that it might be unclear whether a given event is a miracle. For instance, one day, when cyanide acts as a poison, surviving its ingestion is a miracle. The next day, when cyanide acts as a supernutrient, surviving its ingestion becomes fully natural and even healthy.

In illustrating how divine action and nature's constancy relate, the analogy of Kasparov overriding a computer chess program is imperfect. The analogy rightly highlights nature's (cf. the computer program's) determinate character—that it has certain capacities and lacks others. But it also suggests that divine action (cf. Kasparov's moves) is episodic—that nature typically does whatever is in its character to do, only to be interrupted periodically by divine acts that suspend its character. Edward Oakes calls this "Deism put under a stroboscope."[8] Divine action within a constant nature, however, need not work this way. Instead of divine action and nature's constancy switching a baton back and forth, so that only one or the other operate at a given time (as in the chess example), both can operate continuously and in tandem. Consider, for example, Joseph's brothers selling him into slavery. According to Joseph, his brothers, acting according to their natural disposition, meant it for evil; yet God, acting also in this situation through his brothers, meant it for good (see Gen 50:20). In this case, divine and human action were continuous and simultaneous. Likewise, God and nature may act continuously and simultaneously.

In claiming that nature is constant, are we asserting an inviolable principle of reason? Are we proposing a hermeneutic principle necessary for interpreting Scripture aright? Are we presenting a regulative principle for scientific and historiographical inquiry? No. Nature's constancy is a *presumption*. In other words, we treat it as true and let it guide inquiry until we have good reason to think otherwise. To reconstruct the past (whether as scientists or as historians), we have little choice but to invoke the constancy of nature: We know how nature operates in the present. We infer how nature operated in the past by projecting its present operation onto the past (it is our best and only shot at understanding the past). Yet to legitimately project the present onto the past, nature must to some degree be constant, its past operation paralleling its present.

To say that nature's constancy is a presumption means that the burden of proof is on those who would contend that it is inconstant. Thus, given independent evidence that nature has acted inconstantly, questioning nature's constancy could be entirely appropriate. For instance, evidence of the earth's cooling may suggest that volcanoes have been more active in the past than they are now. If this is correct, however, it is the level of volcanic activity in different times and circumstances that is inconstant, not the laws that govern volcanism.

When young-earth creationists question the constancy of nature, however, typically it is not because they have independent evidence to question it but because their belief in a young earth requires that nature behave inconstantly. Thus they argue, as we discussed earlier, for the acceleration of nuclear decay in times past. Or consider their response to ice sheets in Antarctica and Greenland, which appear to accumulate at a steady rate by forming annual layers (much as trees form annual rings). If one drills ice cores (sometimes one or two miles deep), present rates of accumulation suggest that the cores record more than one hundred thousand years of natural history (which, of course, exceeds the age of a young earth).[9]

Young-earth creationists therefore counter that as one goes down the core, compression of the ice destroys our ability to distinguish annual layers. Dismissing what they call a "uniformitarian model" of ice sheet formation, they substitute their own "post-flood rapid ice age model."[10]

As another example of this mode of reasoning, consider the creationist proposal of *catastrophic plate tectonics*, in which "new ocean floor was being created during the Flood at miles per hour with reversals occurring every couple of weeks."[11] Rather than provide independent evidence that something like this actually occurred, young-earth creationists attempt to explain how such an acceleration of ordinary plate tectonic movement, in which the earth's crust moves at miles per hour rather than at the present rate of centimeters per year, can avoid the destructive effects of heat that would be generated by such acceleration. Thus John Baumgardner points to ultralow friction for certain silicate minerals.[12] To be sure, Baumgardner is a competent geophysicist. But showing that there are theoretical models in which catastrophic plate tectonics can avoid horrendous destruction of the earth is hardly the same as showing that catastrophic plate tectonics is a real phenomenon. The inference that it is a real phenomenon comes less from the evidence of science than from the presupposition of a young earth.

"Uniformitarianism" is always a dirty word for young-earth creationists in such discussions, signifying an unwillingness by the scientific community to question the constancy of nature and thus to make room for a young earth. When young-earth creationists challenge uniformitarianism, they seem less interested in understanding nature on its own terms than in devising loopholes to support an otherwise untenable position. The layering of ice cores, for instance, admits a straightforward interpretation suggesting tens of thousands of annual layers. Young-earth creationists argue that this interpretation is incorrect not by presenting a compelling vision of what actually happened but by raising doubts about the interpretation. Maybe they are right—I'm not an expert in the relevant fields. But as an expert in logic and critical reasoning, I find this mode of argumentation troubling. Anyone without a stake in the age of the earth, it seems to me, is unlikely to find such arguments persuasive. A good reality check in such discussions is to ask yourself what age you would estimate if you didn't feel the need to square the age of the earth with a young-earth interpretation of Genesis 1–11.[13]

Although young-earth creationism suggests that the constancy of nature is easily questioned, in fact the defense of the Christian faith would suffer a hard blow if it were questioned willy-nilly. Indeed, the presumption of nature's constancy is absolutely critical to historical apologetics, which attempts to establish the occurrence and significance of certain key biblical events. Take the Resurrection of Christ. If at different times in human history people who experienced violent deaths spontaneously revived and returned to business as usual, the unique significance of Christ's Resurrection would be lost. Precisely because nature is constant regarding death (dead people stay dead apart from divine intervention), Christ's Resurrection assumes its significance for salvation, showing that God in Christ has decisively conquered death. Apart from nature's constancy, that conclusion could not be drawn.

To see the importance of nature's constancy to historical apologetics, however, one need not look only to such dramatic events as the Resurrection. Historiographical, archeological, and anthropological methods that presuppose the constancy of nature have been enormously helpful in confirming events, places, and persons recorded in Scripture. Using such methods, F. F. Bruce argues for the authenticity of Acts as a first-century document. Thus he infers that "the historical, geographical and political atmosphere of Luke-Acts as a whole, and of Acts in particular, is unmistakably that of the first century and not of the second."[14] Or consider that biblical critics of the nineteenth century doubted whether references in Scripture to the Hittites were factual (see the references to the "sons of Heth" in Genesis). Subsequent archeological research revealed a Hittite civilization flourishing in the second millennium BC.[15]

Young-earth creationists accept these research methods when they confirm events going back to Abraham as described in Genesis 12. Yet, when these same methods get pushed back before Genesis 12, they balk. The reason is that these methods give evidence of human activity that should not have survived a universal flood (which young-earth creationists place around 2500 BC, or 4,500 years ago). Accordingly, archeologists claim to find evidence of human writing at Uruk going back 5,000 years, well before Noah's flood on a face-value reading of Genesis 6–8.[16] Moreover, they claim to find evidence of artifacts, such as dolls, going back 7,000 years, well before the creation of Adam on a face-value reading of Genesis

1 and 2 (young-earth creationists place the creation of Adam around 4000 BC, or 6,000 years ago).[17]

To invoke the constancy of nature when it suits the apologetic case one is making and then to renounce it when it proves inconvenient damages Christian apologetics. Notwithstanding, young-earth creationism has adopted this double standard. Thus we see Henry Morris, the preeminent young-earth creationist of the twentieth century, tacitly appeal to the constancy of nature when he offers a historical defense of events recorded in the Bible (see his *Many Infallible Proofs*); yet he dispenses with it when he argues for a young earth (see his *Scientific Creationism*).[18] In the absence of strong countervailing evidence that nature has changed its ordinary course of operation in the last few thousand years, to question the constancy of nature smacks of special pleading: where science appears to challenge a particular interpretation of Genesis, question nature's constancy; where that interpretation appears safe, leave nature alone.

SEVEN

THE APPEARANCE OF AGE

I N challenging the constancy of nature, young-earth creationists tacitly
admit that the world, even if it is not actually old, appears to be old. Indeed, the appearance of age is a dominant theme in young-earth creationist
writings. Their attempt to explain it away is a prime reason the scientific
mainstream rejects young-earth creationism. Philip Gosse's *Omphalos*
epitomizes the problem.[1] Gosse wrote *Omphalos* in 1857 to address arguments current at the time that the earth was much older than Genesis
would indicate. Gosse argued that creation ex nihilo requires God to create
a world that gives the appearance of age even at the instant of creation.

Omphalos means "navel." Adam, because he was created directly by
God, would not have had a human mother and thus would not have had an
umbilical cord requiring a navel. Thus Adam's navel (Gosse assumed he
had one) would be part of God's initial creation and would therefore suggest a prehistory that never occurred. When Gosse's book appeared, hardly
anyone was satisfied by this reasoning. Scientists holding to an older earth
saw it as flying in the face of the scientific evidence. And theologians holding to a God of truth saw it as turning nature into a divine hoax. A world
that—at the moment of its creation—appears older than it is suggests a
bogus history and therefore a deception unworthy of God.

But that raises a question: How could God create a world that gives
no evidence of a bogus history, a world that appears as old as it actually

is? For old-earth creationists the answer is simple: the Big Bang. The Big Bang, conceived as the moment of creation, is initially an infinitely dense concentration of energy, which mathematicians describe as a "singularity." Now, you can do various things mathematically with singularities, but one thing you can't do is extrapolate equations of motion backward from them. In other words, there is no way to run history backward from a singularity like the Big Bang. Accordingly, there is no history prior to the Big Bang for science to infer. History, insofar as science can make sense of it, can begin with a Big Bang but cannot precede it. The Big Bang therefore disproves Gosse's view that creation ex nihilo necessarily requires a fictitious history.

Despite its selling points, the Big Bang has not fared well among young-earth creationists. The problem is that the Big Bang suggests a creation not thousands but billions of years old. Light travels at a fixed speed of 186,000 miles per second. Moreover, as a light source moves away from an observer, the light's wavelength increases. Thus, when we look at the light from stars in distant galaxies and see the light's wavelength increase, we infer that those galaxies are moving away from us. If we now extrapolate back into the past, we find that these stars and galaxies were once closer to us. As we keep extrapolating, we find that our equations of motion can take us only so far—until the stuff of the universe comes to a dead stop at a singularity. Given the fixed speed of light, the fact that nothing travels faster than light, and the billions of light-years separation between us and other stars, it follows that the universe is billions of years old.

To get around this conclusion, young-earth creationists have adopted three main approaches: (1) embrace a fictitious history of the universe in the spirit of Gosse's *Omphalos*; (2) view the speed of light as having decayed over time; (3) interpret Einstein's theory of general relativity so that during an "ordinary day as measured on earth, billions of years worth of physical processes take place in the distant cosmos."[2] The late Henry Morris was a proponent of the first approach, Barry Setterfield of the second, and Russell Humphreys of the third. Each of these approaches is, in my view, deeply problematic.

Take Henry Morris's modern rendition of *Omphalos*. As he saw it, God specially created not merely the sources of light in the heavens (i.e., the stars) but also the very shafts of light that would issue from them:

The creation was "mature" from its birth. It did not have to grow or develop from simple beginnings. God formed it full-grown in every respect, including even Adam and Eve as mature individuals when they were first formed. The whole universe had an "appearance of age" right from the start. It could not have been otherwise for true creation to have taken place. "Thus the heavens and the earth were finished, and all the host of them" (Gen 2:1).

This fact means that the light from the sun, moon and stars was shining upon the earth as soon as they were created, since their very purpose was ". . . [*sic*] to give light on the earth" (Gen 1:17). As a matter of fact, it is possible that these light-waves traversing space from the heavenly bodies to the earth were energized even *before* the heavenly bodies themselves in order to provide the light for the first three days.

[Here Morris adds in a footnote: "The light for the first three days obviously did not come from the sun, moon and stars, since God did not make them and place them in the heavens until the fourth day (Genesis 1:16–19). Nevertheless, the light source for the first three days had the same function ('to divide the light from the darkness') as did the heavenly bodies from the fourth day onward (Genesis 1:4,18). This 'division' now results from the sun and moon and the earth's axial rotation. For practical purposes, therefore, the primeval light must essentially have come from the same directions as it would later when the permanent light-sources were set in place."]

It was certainly no more difficult for God to form the light-waves than the "light-bearers" which would be established to serve as future generators of those waves.[3]

In its favor, this approach does not entail a flat contradiction. God in his omnipotence could presumably have done things that way. But absence of contradiction is about all that can be said in its favor. The shafts of light that God created independently of the stars (and that seemingly arise from them) project onto the earth a history of the cosmos that never in fact happened. For instance, if human astronomers see what appears to be a supernova exploding in a galaxy millions of light-years away, Morris's approach means that no supernova ever exploded. Rather, God specifically created a beam of light six thousand years ago that has only now reached earth and that gives the appearance of a supernova exploding. In Morris's approach, astronomy is not about how actual stars looked in the distant past but about how fake stars might look in a 3-D animation made by God. It is difficult, in my view, to reconcile such a God with a God of truth.

Barry Setterfield's idea of c-decay attempts to get around the problem of light created "in flight" and the bogus history of the cosmos that entails. Setterfield, in the 1980s, argued that light originally traveled much faster than it does now.[4] Thus stars that seem billions of light-years from earth, given light's present speed, would be only a few thousand light-years from earth once we factor in how much the speed of light has decayed. The idea that light might be "getting tired" or "running out of steam" has a certain plausibility if one is committed to a young earth. But difficulties arise as soon as one asks for independent evidence of c-decay. Setterfield, for instance, examined measurements of the speed of light over the last 300 years and found that its speed had diminished. But the changes in speed over the time that Setterfield recorded (most of them within one percent of today's best estimate for the speed of light) suggest not an actual change in light speed but a margin of error consistent with a constant speed of light (especially when one considers that the methods for measuring the speed of light 300 years ago were primitive and have improved considerably since).

But deeper problems confront Setterfield's proposal. The fundamental constants of nature seem finely tuned to one another so that even small changes in their values would fundamentally disrupt the universe (for example, by preventing the formation of stars, planets, or life).[5] Perhaps the most famous scientific formula of all time is Einstein's $E = mc^2$. The "c" here is the speed of light in a vacuum. This formula shows that energy is proportional to the speed of light. Thus, given a vastly increased speed of light in times past, chemical and physical reactions would have been much more energetic. It follows that increasing the speed of light would upset the fine-tuning of the universe.

For instance, the production of carbon depends on a specific nuclear resonance.[6] Accordingly, only a narrow range of energies would allow for the formation of carbon. Yet this resonance would be crippled if c were drastically altered. In consequence, carbon production would vastly diminish, and life as we know it would be impossible. Thus, in addition to c, many other constants would need to change as well to preserve the stability and life-permitting structure of the cosmos (for example, Setterfield concedes that Planck's constant h would also need to change). So suddenly we're no longer talking just about c-decay but about changing all of physics simply to circumvent an old universe suggested by a constant speed of light.

While Henry Morris's *"omphalos"* approach to starlight may have been acceptable to young-earth creationists in the 1970s and while Barry Setterfield's c-decay approach may have seemed promising in the 1980s, since the 1990s Russell Humphreys's use of Einsteinian relativity to resolve the problem of distant starlight has been the young-earth cosmology to beat. Here is one reaction from his young-earth creationist colleagues:

> The c-decay theory stimulated much thinking about the issues. Creationist physicist Dr. Russell Humphreys says that he spent a year on and off trying to get the declining c theory to work, but without success. However, in the process, he was inspired to develop a new creationist cosmology which appears to solve the problem of the apparent conflict with the Bible's clear, authoritative teaching of a recent creation. . . . This sort of development, in which one creationist theory, c-decay, is overtaken by another, is a healthy aspect of science. The basic biblical framework is non-negotiable, as opposed to the changing views and models of fallible people seeking to understand the data within that framework.[7]

Since Einsteinian relativity is our best theory of the large-scale structure and dynamics of the universe, Humphreys rightly went with it. According to Einsteinian relativity, clocks maintain different times depending on the gravitational field in which they find themselves. Humphreys made this insight the basis of his new cosmology:

> What this new cosmology shows is that gravitational time distortion in the early universe would have meant that while a few days were passing on earth, billions of years would have been avail-

able for light to travel to earth. It still means that God made the heavens and earth (i.e., the whole universe) in six ordinary days, only a few thousand years ago. But with the reality revealed by GR [General Relativity], we now know that we have to ask—six days as measured by *which clock*? In which frame of reference? The mathematics of this new theory shows that while God makes the universe in six days *in the earth's reference frame* ("Earth Standard Time," if you like), the light has ample time *in the extra-terrestrial reference frame* to travel the required distances.[8]

To reconcile how distant stars that appear to be billions of years old can be compatible with a young earth, Humphreys therefore set up a relativistic model in which the rate at which time passes changes dramatically in different parts of the universe. Thus, what looks like 6,000 years on earth may correspond to billions of years elsewhere in the universe.

But there is a problem with this proposal. Humphreys, despite having over a decade to shore up his cosmology, has been unable to get his numbers to come out right. University of Sydney mathematician Edward Fackerell comments:

> One of the major scientific challenges to young-earth creationism, that is, the view that God created the universe less than 10,000 years ago, has been the difficulty of reconciling this view with the tremendous size of the universe. If the universe is 13 billion light years across, in the sense that there are objects 13 billion light years from earth, then any straightforward scientific theory of the propagation of light leads to the conclusion that the universe is at least 13 billion years old. Nevertheless, many young-earth creationists are of the opinion that a reconciliation of six-day creationism with general relativistic cosmology has been carried out successfully by D. Russell Humphreys in his little book *Starlight and Time*. . . . His goal is to reconcile general relativistic cosmology with a short time-scale for the universe, essentially by claiming that cosmological models exist in which differential aging takes place between nonequivalent fundamental observers. Humphreys has used three different approaches to substantiate this claim of differential aging.[9]

Fackerell then proceeds to refute "the mathematical errors and the errors in general relativity in three crucial claims made by Humphreys."[10]

On its face Humphreys's idea holds promise. But the devil is in the details, and to date Humphreys has not been able to make his model work. Fackerell is not the only expert to critique the nitty-gritty of Humphreys's model. Physicists Samuel Conner and Don Page (Page is an evangelical Christian and a world-class relativist who has worked with Stephen Hawking) have also analyzed it and found it defective.[11] Even though I'm not an expert in relativity theory, as a mathematician who has read both sides of this discussion, I would say that Humphreys's model is, at least for now, dead in the water. I say this without a vested interest in this debate. Cosmologists and mathematicians are happy to consider counterintuitive models of space and time, and I personally would regard it as a neat result if relativity theory could somehow combine a young earth with an old distant universe.

But even if the numbers in Humphreys's model could be made to come out right, we would still be a long way from confirming that this model accurately reflects the true state and history of the universe. Einsteinian relativity allows for numerous geometric models of the universe. Humphreys, to support a young earth, requires one that is bounded, spherical, symmetric, pressureless, and dust filled. Maybe this is the sort of universe we inhabit. But where is the independent evidence that confirms this model over other relativistic models? And even with a mathematically coherent model that reconciles old distant stars with a young earth, the ad hoc special pleading that infects so many young-earth models would still be a problem here.

It only takes a few sips from an ocean to realize it's salty. The persistent failure of young-earth creationist attempts to account for the appearance of age in the universe should therefore give us pause. Young-earth creationists, it would seem, hold to a recent creation not because of but in spite of the scientific evidence. To be sure, one can question the constancy of nature if one has good independent grounds for doing so. But even here, one questions nature's constancy on a case by case basis, sizing up particular instances where nature seems to have changed its habits. On the other hand, questioning the constancy of nature as a whole does not seem possible. For in the very act of questioning one must hold constant the backdrop against which the question is posed. Questioning nature's constancy in general would deny this backdrop and thus be self-defeating.

EIGHT

Two Books

T O undermine the constancy of nature for theological gain preserves the integrity of neither science nor theology. God gave humanity two primary sources of revelation about himself: the world that he created and the Scripture that he inspired. These are also known as general and special revelation, or sometimes as the Book of Nature and the Book of Scripture. God can thus be viewed as the author of two books. The Book of Nature reveals what God did in creating, structuring, and guiding the natural world (it reveals what sometimes is called the Law of Creation). The Book of Scripture reveals what God did in redemption history to restore humanity and the world to a right relation with himself (it reveals what sometimes is called the Law of Redemption).[1] We study science to understand the first of these books, theology to understand the second.

As distinct witnesses to the work of God, these books can be read individually or together. When read individually, they have an integrity of their own that must not be undermined by using one to invalidate the other. Theology may lead us to question certain claims of science, but any refutation of those claims must ultimately depend on scientific evidence (as ascertained by carefully reading the Book of Nature). Likewise, science may lead us to question certain claims of theology, but any refutation of those claims must ultimately depend on exegetical evidence (as ascertained by carefully reading the Book of Scripture).

Theologians, for instance, bristle when scientists claim that quantum mechanics, by introducing an irreducible indeterminism into nature, makes divine foreknowledge impossible (at least they used to bristle before being seduced by process and open theism). So too, scientists bristle when theologians claim that their estimates of the age of the earth must be wrong because Genesis teaches the opposite. If we are to reject divine foreknowledge (which the Book of Scripture teaches), then we must have sound theological and exegetical reasons for doing so. Likewise, if we are to reject an old earth (which the Book of Nature teaches), then we must have solid scientific evidence for doing so. God is a God of truth. As the author of both books, he does not contradict himself. Accordingly, our task in understanding the relation between the Book of Scripture and the Book of Nature is to bring them into consonance so that they are mutually illuminating and yet preserve their individual integrity.

The tendency in science-theology discussions these days, however, is either to elevate one of these books at the expense of the other or to so separate them that they are completely independent. Stephen Jay Gould's "non-overlapping magisteria" (NOMA) exemplifies the latter approach. According to Gould, science and theology (or religion) operate as separate authorities (*"magisteria"*) over completely separate realms so that neither can substantively interfere with or influence the other. Gould allocates to science the realm of facts and experience whereas to religion he allocates the realm of ethics and ultimate meaning.[2]

Gould's compartmentalization of science and religion doesn't hold up under scrutiny. For instance, if it is a fact that we are evolved beings who spent much of our evolutionary history as hunter-gatherers, thereby becoming adept killers of other animals and fellow humans, then this fact will have profound implications for ethics, suggesting that certain tendencies to violence in us are natural, resulting from our evolutionary conditioning. In particular, it would be inappropriate to regard such tendencies as sinful, the result of conscious rebellion against our Creator. So too, if, as Christians, our ultimate meaning derives from Christ's sacrifice on the Cross and his Resurrection from the dead, then historical facts play a central role in Christianity. In that case, religion cannot be reduced simply to ethics and meaning. The realms of fact and value are thus intimately connected, and there is no way to divorce one from the other.[3]

Gould, as a defender of "scientific correctness," wanted to separate science from theology in order to stop pesky theologians (especially creationists) from interfering with science. For Gould, science was a fully materialistic enterprise that could never provide any evidence for an intelligence behind the world (design, for him, was scientifically undetectable). Yet, if Gould wanted to keep theologians out of his hair, theologians likewise have been motivated to keep scientists out of their hair. Karl Barth, for instance, held that nature can reveal nothing about God and that divine revelation must come directly from God unmediated by nature ("perpendicular from above" was Barth's catch phrase to describe how God reveals himself to humanity).[4]

Barth, writing in the first half of twentieth century, was reacting to the positivistic mental environment of his day, in which science was used as an ideological weapon to contract theology's reach. In thereby placing theology beyond the reach of science, Barth sought to preserve classic teachings of the Church that liberal theology had, in his view, betrayed. Barth's strategy for protecting theology from science, however, failed for the same reason as Gould's strategy for protecting science from theology. The problem is that even though science and theology are distinct, they interact.

Barth eschewed all forms of "natural theology" and thus denied that God could reveal himself via nature (thereby also denying any relevance of science to theology).[5] Yet theology requires metaphors and concepts that come from our understanding of nature and therefore from science. How can we understand that Jesus is the "Lamb of God" without knowing something about biology? How can we understand that God is light without knowing something about physics? How can we understand that faith can move mountains without knowing something about orology?

Placing science and theology in tight compartments ignores the reality of their interaction. But what about pitting them against each other so that one trumps the other? Consider Richard Dawkins's dismissal of theology in the name of science and, in particular, his invocation of Darwin to support atheism: "Although atheism might have been *logically* tenable before Darwin, Darwin made it possible to be an intellectually fulfilled atheist."[6] Since making this remark, Dawkins has increasingly used science as a club to beat theology, a practice that is now widespread among atheists.

In response, theists have adopted two main strategies. One strategy, advanced by Alister McGrath, argues that science cannot legitimately be used to mount a fundamental critique of theology. Science empirically investigates the material world; theology critically reflects on ultimate realities. Thus, for McGrath, the two complement each other and are not in a position to conflict.[7] The other strategy, advanced by the intelligent design community, argues that the very theory of evolution that Dawkins and his colleagues deploy against theology is itself problematic. Moreover, they argue that when the natural world is properly understood, it provides solid scientific evidence for an intelligence that structures and directs the world. While there is merit to the first strategy, and while the second does not invalidate the first, the second is far more radical, cutting the ground out from under those who, like Dawkins, want to use science to nullify theology. McGrath criticizes the enterprise of using science as a club to beat theology but does not question the science that is being used as a club. Design theorists, by contrast, criticize the very science that is supposed to nullify theology.

Among those who think that science and theology conflict, Dawkins's use of science to trump theology stands at one extreme. The opposite extreme is to use theology to trump science. In popular retellings of the Galileo episode, the Catholic Church is said to have done just that, forcing Galileo to retract heliocentrism because Church dogma demanded geocentrism. The actual Galileo episode, however, was far more complex. Certainly, Galileo didn't help himself by ridiculing Church authorities for their scientific obtuseness.[8] But in fact, the Church operated with a reasonably sophisticated philosophy of science. The Church recognized that if a scientific theory was to have any validity, it must match up with observational data. At the same time the Church also understood that any set of observational data is compatible with more than one scientific theory (what philosophers of science call "the underdetermination of theory by data"). The Church was therefore willing to allow Galileo to treat heliocentrism as a provisional (though not necessarily true) theory for representing planetary motion.[9]

If Dawkinsian atheists provide the best current example of science trumping theology, then young-earth creationists provide the best current example of theology trumping science. For hard-core atheists, all scientific evidence is uniformly against belief in God. So likewise, for hard-core creationists, no scientific evidence can undercut belief in a young earth. In each case, a particular understanding of science or theology is non-negotiable and trumps the other. As an example of hard-core atheism, we've already considered Richard Dawkins. As an example of hard-core creationism, consider Kurt Wise.

Wise and I began our undergraduate studies at the University of Chicago in 1977. He went on to Harvard to earn his Ph.D. in paleontology with Stephen Jay Gould. I returned to the University of Chicago to earn my Ph.D. in mathematics with Patrick Billingsley and Leo Kadanoff. In perhaps his best known statement (publicized widely by Richard Dawkins[10]), Wise admits,

> Although there are scientific reasons for accepting a young earth, I am a young-age creationist because that is my understanding of the Scripture. As I shared with my professors years ago when I was in college, if all the evidence in the universe turns against creationism, I would be the first to admit it, but I would still be a creationist because that is what the Word of God seems to indicate. Here I must stand.[11]

Wise claims that his interpretation of Genesis (as he puts it, "what the Word of God seems to indicate") trumps all scientific evidence favoring an old earth. But that raises a question: Why should Wise's particular interpretation of Scripture occupy such a privileged place? Although the truth of Scripture is inviolable, our interpretations of it are not. The history of biblical interpretation simply does not support that a well-established interpretation of Scripture should always trump alternative interpretations. In fact, the history of biblical interpretation includes cases where interpretations of Scripture once universally held were later abandoned— and for scientific reasons no less! For instance, at the time a young earth was unquestioned, the Church also taught that the earth was stationary. Psalm 93 states that the earth is established forever and cannot be moved. A face-value interpretation of Psalm 93 seems to require geocentrism. And yet young-earth creationists accept the Copernican Revolution. We read this psalm today as endorsing not geocentrism but the stability of God's works.

[75]

In reading Scripture, we begin with a face-value interpretation. But sound biblical hermeneutics need not end there. Indeed, sound biblical hermeneutics needs to know when to leave off face-value interpretation. Consider Matt 18:8–9:

> If thy hand or thy foot offend thee, cut them off, and cast them
> from thee: it is better for thee to enter into life halt or maimed,
> rather than having two hands or two feet to be cast into ever-
> lasting fire. And if thine eye offend thee, pluck it out, and cast
> it from thee: it is better for thee to enter into life with one eye,
> rather than having two eyes to be cast into hell fire.

Anyone who interprets this passage at face value is likely to land in a straitjacket.

As Christians we are obligated, as the apostle Paul put it, to "rightly divide" (i.e., interpret) the Scriptures (2 Tim 2:15). But what guides our interpretation of the Scriptures? Clearly, our knowledge of the world plays some role. Our knowledge of physics from the seventeenth century on-wards has rendered geocentrism untenable. Nineteenth-century Princeton theologian Charles Hodge faced the challenge of balancing the science of his day with the interpretation of Scripture. Early in his systematic theol-ogy, he noted that even though Scripture is true, our interpretations of it can be in error; as a consequence, it can be a trial for the Church when long-held interpretations are thrown into question. As he put it,

> Christians have commonly believed that the earth has existed
> only a few thousands of years. If geologists finally prove that
> it has existed for myriads of ages, it will be found that the first
> chapter of Genesis is in full accord with the facts, and that the
> last results of science are embodied on the first page of the Bible.
> *It may cost the church a severe struggle to give up one interpre-*
> *tation and adopt another*, as it did in the seventeenth century
> [when the Copernican system displaced the Ptolemaic system of
> the universe], but no real evil need be apprehended. The Bible
> has stood, and still stands in the presence of the whole scientific
> world with its claims unshaken.[12]

Despite the Galileo episode, the Church in the end willingly relin-quished geocentrism. Contrary to the widespread misconception that the

Copernican revolution demoted us from a privileged place in the universe, the center of the universe was, in the Ptolemaic-Aristotelian cosmology that held sway prior to Copernicus, the place of least privilege. It was a place of corruption and mortality. For incorruption and immortality, one had to go beyond the earth to the heavenly bodies, which moved around the earth in unending circular orbits and were therefore regarded as the realm of eternity. At the outer reaches of heaven was the Empyrean, conceived by the ancients as a realm of pure fire or light and within medieval Christian theology as the abode of God and the angels.[13]

Except for preserving the face-value interpretation of certain Old Testament passages (like Psalm 93), nothing of theological importance is riding on geocentrism. The same cannot be said for a young earth. A young earth seems to be required to maintain a traditional understanding of the Fall. And yet a young earth clashes sharply with mainstream science. Christians, it seems, must therefore choose their poison. They can go with a young earth, thereby maintaining theological orthodoxy but committing scientific heresy; or they can go with an old earth, thereby committing theological heresy but maintaining scientific orthodoxy.

Are the Book of Scripture and the Book of Nature therefore irreconcilable? No. As we will see, a traditional understanding of the Fall is tenable regardless of one's view of the age of the earth. In particular, one does not have to be a young-earth creationist to adopt a traditional understanding of the Fall. But that conclusion requires further argument.

NINE

THE PROBLEM WITH OLD-EARTH CREATIONISM

O UR dilemma is to preserve both theological orthodoxy about the Fall and scientific orthodoxy about the age of the earth. Atheists, agnostics, and skeptics are only too happy to give up theological orthodoxy. On the other hand, by requiring a 6,000-year-old earth, young-earth creationists seem too ready to give up scientific orthodoxy. What about old-earth creationists? Have they done better at grasping both horns of this dilemma? Have they, in other words, successfully reconciled scientific and theological orthodoxy? The actual attempts at reconciliation that I've seen from old-earth creationists have struck me as inadequate if by theological orthodoxy one means a traditional understanding of the Fall that traces all natural and personal evil in the world to human sin.

Take Hugh Ross. Ross does not believe the Garden of Eden was free of death, decay, pain, and suffering. For him there never was a perfect paradise. To justify this claim scripturally, Ross cites Gen 3:16, in which God informs Eve after she has sinned that he will greatly multiply her pain in childbirth. Since zero multiplied by anything remains zero, Ross infers that God did not initiate Eve's pain but rather increased her existing pain in childbearing.[1] More generally, Ross suggests that God uses randomness, waste, and inefficiencies to bring about the "very good" world into which he placed Adam.[2] The difficulty with this suggestion, which is made throughout the old-earth creationist literature, is that natural evil becomes simply a tool for furthering God's ends rather than a consequence of human sin. Old-earth creationism thus opens God to the charge of inflicting pain simply to advance a divine agenda.

Mark Whorton follows this same pattern. In his book on the age of the earth, he attempts to justify the creation of a less than perfect world into which God then places humans who have yet to sin (again, the lack of perfection of the world is not attributed to human sin). To argue his point, Whorton contrasts what he calls a Perfect Paradise Paradigm with a Perfect Purpose Paradigm:

> The two creation paradigms offer diametrically different perspectives on the problem of suffering. The Perfect Paradise Paradigm views suffering in light of the past. All suffering is traceable back to the original sin of Adam in the garden. It was never God's intent for His creation to suffer or be blemished in any way because He created it to be "very good." In stark contrast, the Perfect Purpose Paradigm sees suffering in light of the future. God has a plan, and history is unfolding in a providentially directed process that will ultimately accomplish His eternal purpose. Until the end, the plan will not be complete and the purpose will not be fully accomplished. . . . Suffering in this life can only be reconciled from the eternal perspective of the Master's plan.[3]

Thus, according to Whorton's Perfect Purpose Paradigm, God creates a world of suffering not in response to human sin but to accomplish some future end (i.e., "the Master's plan"). But this, again, makes human suffering a means to an end. And even if this end is lofty, we are still being used. Used is used, and there is no way to make this palatable, much less compatible with human dignity. That's why Kant taught that we must treat fellow human beings not as means but as ends in themselves. And that's why, unless human suffering is permitted by God because we have, in some way, brought it on ourselves, Whorton's Perfect Purpose Paradigm becomes a cynical manipulation of means to justify otherwise high ends.

In making sense of the Fall in light of modern science, old-earth creationists often deny that natural evil is morally significant.[4] Their rationale is that personal evil (the harm we intentionally cause to ourselves and others) doesn't arise until humans first sin. So, by denying that natural evil is morally significant, old-earth creationists, like their young-earth counterparts, are able to attribute all morally significant evil to human sin after all. On this view, personal evil is morally significant, but natural evil doesn't become morally significant until humans experience it as alienation from God, which they do once they have sinned (i.e., after the Fall).

One way to justify that natural evils are not morally significant, inspired by Descartes but no longer popular, is to characterize animals as automatons (i.e., as complex machines consisting of bones, muscles, and organs that in principle could be replaced with cogs, cams, and pistons) and thus to deny their ability to suffer like humans. Accordingly, only souls made in the image of God can truly suffer and experience natural evil as morally significant. Needless to say, in our pet-friendly culture, this way of dealing with natural evil does not sit well with our mental environment. Nor should it. The affection that dogs (and some would argue cats) display for their masters has nothing machine-like about it.

Another way to justify that natural evils are not morally significant is to grit one's teeth and boldly assert that God takes full responsibility for natural evil, that he directly created it, that he even takes pleasure in it, and that, however counterintuitive it may seem, natural evil is entirely compatible with the goodness of God in creation. Thus, we are mistaken if we take death, predation, parasitism, disease, drought, floods, famines, earthquakes, and hurricanes as evidence against the creation being "very good." On this view, the challenge of theodicy is not, as Mark Whorton advises, to trust that God's good purposes will be accomplished somewhere down the road but rather to get over our squeamishness. David Snoke, in justifying that a good God could create dangerous animals and be directly responsible for bringing about natural evil, puts it this way:

> The young-earth creationist and the atheist Darwinist have in common their belief that God would never create killer things. The atheist removes God from the picture to account for the natural evils of this world, while the young-earth creationist removes the record of killer animals from the picture to preserve the goodness of God. Both of these views need to interact with a fully biblical picture of God, as he is revealed in Scripture and in nature—powerful, uncontrollable, and able to pour out extreme

violence, yet also just, merciful, and able to bless beyond all our expectations.[5]

But how is a God who creates killer things and pours out extreme violence to be regarded as benevolent except insofar as such acts respond to human sin and have redemptive significance? Snoke gives no indication that God allowed natural evil for the greater good of helping to redeem humanity. Instead, he portrays the violence and cruelty of nature as a form of divine self-amusement: "God does claim direct responsibility for the creation of natural evil, that is, things in nature which terrorize us. . . . God neither apologizes for making these things, nor weeps over them—he glories in them."[6]

Elsewhere, Snoke recalls one of his grandfather's favorite acronyms: "NITRIC"—"Nature In The Rough Is Cruel."[7] The way Snoke portrays it, NITRIC is a positive virtue of nature rather than defect to be eradicated. Whatever happened to the lovingkindness of God not just for humanity but also for creation as a whole (the Hebrew *hesed*)? Whatever happened to love as the defining attribute of God (the Greek *agape*)? How can the love that 1 Corinthians 13 ascribes to God be reconciled with the violence that Snoke ascribes to God?[8]

Snoke has fallen into the trap of converting a problem into its own solution (and thereby creating a much bigger problem). It does nothing to alleviate the problem of natural evil to say that natural evil is really OK because God invents it and is proud of inventing it—full stop. If anything, such a claim exacerbates the problem of natural evil because it removes any redemptive element from it. The only way for natural evil, and the suffering it entails, to be redemptive is if it helps to free the creation from a deeper, more insidious evil. Natural evil constitutes a disordering of nature. A benevolent God will allow natural evil only as a last resort to remedy a still worse evil, not as an end in itself over which to glory.

PART III

DIVINE CREATION
AND ACTION

TEN

THE TRINITARIAN MODE OF CREATION

C ONTEMPORARY science holds that the Earth and universe are not thousands but billions of years old, that humans have been around only a minuscule portion of that time, and that prior to their arrival natural evils abounded. To see how natural evil could precede the first human sin and yet be a consequence of it, we need to explore what it means for God to create and then act within creation.

As we study creation in Scripture, the first thing that strikes us is how God creates: God speaks, and things happen. Why should a speech act be God's mode of creation? On reflection, this mode of creation makes perfect sense. Any act of creation actualizes an intention by an intelligent agent. In our experience, intentions get actualized any number of ways. Sculptors actualize their intentions by chipping away at stone; musicians by writing notes on lined sheets of paper; engineers by drawing up blueprints; etc. But in general, all actualizations of intentions can be realized in language. For instance, a precise enough set of instructions in a natural language can tell the sculptor how to form the statue, the musician how to record the notes, and the engineer how to draw up the blueprints. In this way language becomes the *universal medium* for actualizing intentions.[1]

The language that proceeds from God's mouth in the act of creation is, according to John's Gospel, the divine *Logos*, the Word that in Christ was made flesh and through whom all things were created (see John 1).

As such, the divine *Logos* is not just language in the ordinary sense (i.e., utterances that convey information), but the very ground and possibility of language. The divine *Logos* is in fact the second person of the Trinity. The full Trinity, acting freely without internal or external compulsion, takes part in every act of divine creation. In the act of creation, God the Father (first person of the Trinity) speaks the divine *Logos* (second person of the Trinity) in the power of the Holy Spirit (third person of the Trinity). Words need power to accomplish their end. God's Word has that power: "So shall my word be that goeth forth out of my mouth: it shall not return unto me void, but it shall accomplish that which I please, and it shall prosper in the thing whereto I sent it" (Isa 55:11).

Given that we are made in God's image, the trinitarian structure of divine creation is reflected in human speech. Thus, when we form an intention, this reflects God the Father forming an intention to initiate an act of divine creation. Thus, when we articulate an intention with our words, this reflects God the Son acting as the divine *Logos* in articulating the divine intention. And finally, when we utter those words by running air over our vocal chords and through our mouths, this reflects God the Holy Spirit empowering the divine Logos and thereby actualizing the divine intention (it's not coincidental that *spirit* means "wind" or "breath").

In this trinitarian account of human speech, each element is deeply personal. Certainly we see this in the forming of an intention—in our experience, intention is always associated with personhood and consciousness. Ditto for language. The one instance where personhood may seem less obvious is the power that takes words, considered abstractly, and supplies them with energy to express and communicate. But even here personality is central. What distinguishes a voice synthesizer from a live human is not the mechanical empowerment of words as mere sound waves but the timbre, inflection, and cadences that make a voice come alive (a point driven home to us in this age of voice menus).

Thus, we find communications expert George Thompson noting that "from the receiver's point of view," the quality of one's voice carries four times the weight of "the content element." He elaborates: "Your very message, which you may see as the most important part of the process [of communication], is the least-considered factor [by the receiver of your communication]."[2] Throughout the New Testament the Holy Spirit is described as the One who makes alive. Indeed, Christ's own Resurrection is credited to the power of the Holy Spirit: "But if the Spirit of him that raised up Jesus from the dead dwell in you, he that raised up Christ from the dead shall also quicken [i.e., make alive] your mortal bodies by his Spirit that dwelleth in you" (Rom 8:11). Interestingly, even though the Greek word for "spirit" (*pneuma*) is in the neuter gender (that is, neither male nor female), whenever pronouns are used in the New Testament to refer to the Holy Spirit, the gender is masculine—further confirming that the third member of the Trinity is fully personal.

This trinitarian model of divine and human creativity has a deep parallel in the mathematical theory of information. In the 1940s, Claude Shannon, doing cryptographic research, examined the reliability of transmitting information across a communication channel. Given noise along a channel, how should information be transmitted from one end so that it is accurately received at the other? In his classic 1949 book on the topic, *The Mathematical Theory of Communication,* Shannon presented what he called a "schematic diagram of a general communication system."[3] Here is the diagram as it appeared in that book:

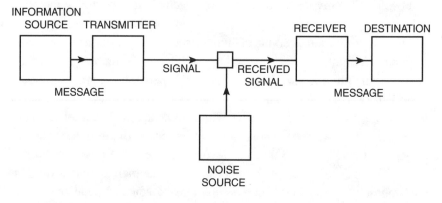

I draw your attention to the upper left portion of this diagram:

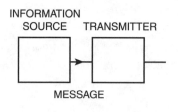

It is no accident that we find here a "trinity." The "information source" reflects God the Father, who is the source or fount of all being. The "message" reflects God the Son, the divine *Logos*. As the information source begets the message, so God the Father begets God the Son. Because this relation between Father and Son (source and message) is asymmetric (primacy in the communicative act residing with the Father), we find Jesus, who incarnates the divine *Logos*, appropriately acknowledge that "my Father is greater than I" (John 14:28).[4] Finally, the "transmitter" reflects God the Holy Spirit, who takes the message and empowers it. Accordingly, what the Father *purposes* and the Son *articulates*, the Holy Spirit *actualizes*.

The remaining portion of Shannon's communication diagram is also theologically significant. Just as the previous portion represents the Godhead, so the remaining portion represents the created order:

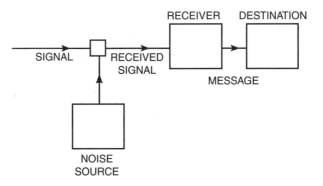

The "signal" reflects what in classic orthodox theology is called the "divine energy," namely, the manifestation of divine activity in creation. The "noise source" reflects the distorting effects of sin and the Fall, which attempt to frustrate the divine energy. Hence in the Lord's Prayer, "thy will be done on earth as it is in heaven": to the left of the noise source (in "heaven"), God's will is perfectly realized; to the right (on "earth"), God's will is only imperfectly realized. God speaks in heaven, and it is done; God speaks on earth, and his voice is routinely disobeyed. As all creation is restored through the redemption in Christ, creation will as fully reflect God's will as heaven does now.

Once the signal passes the noise source, it moves to the "receiver." The "receiver" is a matrix: it receives the signal as a divine seed in an act of conception (compare the imagery in the Parable of the Sower in which God sows the seed, which Jesus identifies as the Word of God and which yields a harvest—see Luke 8:11). The "message," now on the receiver rather than on the sender end, is no longer the divine Logos as in the previous diagram. Here it reflects the product of conception by receiver—it's what the receiver, as matrix, "gives birth to" in consequence of "impregnation" by the signal. And finally, the "destination" is the destiny of the message—what it accomplishes during its temporal existence.[5] To say that God's Word does not return void (Isa 55:11) is thus to say that the divine intention at the "source" is fully realized at the "destination." Thus, even though God's precepts may be disobeyed, God's purposes are always accomplished.

Noise cannot stop the realization of God's intentions. It might seem that noise along a communication channel means that the message received will necessarily be a corrupted version of the message sent. But that's not the case. To prevent corruption from entering the message received requires that both ends of the communication channel employ *effective error correction*. Without error correction, corruption will enter the message received; with it, error can effectively be eliminated.

We experience effective error correction all the time whenever we successfully send an e-mail to someone. All the communication channels that make up the Internet are subject to noise. But the various file transfer protocols operating over the Internet employ error correction that effectively prevents noise from corrupting files in transmission. Without effective error correction, the Internet could never have gotten off the ground. With it, it thrives. Communication theory includes an entire branch for dealing with error correction: the theory of error-correcting codes.[6] Presumably God, in revealing himself to us, both in nature and in Scripture, has employed effective means for controlling error.

None of the preceding analogies between information theory and the God-world relation is, I submit, strained. Quite the contrary, they match up precisely and capture the essence of Christian metaphysics. Shannon's communication diagram is refreshingly evocative. It makes the trinitarian relations within the Godhead appear less arbitrary and more reasonable. It explains why masculine language for the deity and feminine language for nature and the creation is normative (and non-negotiable!) within Christian theology.[7] It underscores why language is the trait that most clearly demonstrates that humans are made in God's image.[8]

The concept of information is central not only to theology but also to science. John Wheeler, one of the outstanding theoretical physicists of the twentieth century, describes his career as falling into three stages:

> In the first period, extending from the beginning of my career until the early 1950s, I was in the grip of the idea that Everything Is Particles. I was looking for ways to build all basic entities—neutrons, protons, mesons, and so on—out of the lightest, most fundamental particles, electrons, and photons. This same vision of a world of simple particles dominated my work with Feynman. We were able to formulate electrodynamics in terms of particles acting at a distance on one another without the need for intermediate electric or magnetic fields. . . .[9]
>
> I call my second period Everything Is Fields. From the time I fell in love with general relativity and gravitation in 1952 until late in my career, I pursued the vision of a world made of fields, one in which the apparent particles are really manifestations of electric and magnetic fields, gravitational fields, and space-time itself. . . .[10]
>
> Now I am in the grip of a new vision, that Everything Is Information. The more I have pondered the mystery of the quantum and our strange ability to comprehend this world in which we live, the more I see possible fundamental roles for logic and information as the bedrock of physical theory. I am eighty-six as of this writing, but I continue to search.[11]

In describing how his thinking about the physical world changed from Everything Is Particles to Everything Is Fields to Everything Is Information, Wheeler is in fact tracing a revolution in physics and in our understanding of the world generally. Other scientists are now likewise beginning to see information as the fundamental stuff underlying physical reality.[12] Information is the rock-bottom of reality, providing the final bridge between science and theology.

ELEVEN

INFORMATION TRANSCENDING MATTER

M ATTER operates by physical causality. In physical causality, one
state of affairs (the cause) brings about another state of affairs (the
effect). Thus, for instance, light from the sun striking a flag pole causes a
shadow on the ground. Physical causality can operate deterministically,
as when the cause brings about exactly one effect. Or it can operate nondeterministically, as when the cause brings about one of several possible
effects each of which is a live possibility. In nondeterministic causation,
which of these possibilities occurs is governed by probabilities. A chunk
of uranium falling to the ground in the Earth's gravitational field operates
deterministically. That same chunk of uranium undergoing radioactive decay operates nondeterministically.

Information, unlike matter, cannot be reduced to physical causality.
True, information can be instantiated in matter (the information on the
page that you are reading is instantiated in ink on paper). But how does
the information get into matter, and where did it come from originally?
Information in matter must first be transmitted to it. Now, the transmission
of information is frequently mediated by transfers of energy across a communication channel, and thus can be tracked causally. So when a police
officer holds up his hand for you to stop, information is transferred from
him to you by light reflecting from his hand to your retina. But information
transfer can occur without energy transfer.

The transmission of information is properly understood in terms of the correlation between patterns at two ends of a communication channel—and thus without reference to any intervening physical process. Absent such an intervening physical process, information relationships can still hold. As Fred Dretske explains,

> It may seem as though the transmission of information . . . is a process that depends on the causal inter-relatedness of source and receiver. The way one gets a message from *s* [source] to *r* [receiver] is by initiating a sequence of events at *s* that culminates in a corresponding sequence at *r*. In abstract terms, the message is borne from *s* to *r* by a causal process which determines what happens at *r* in terms of what happens at *s*. The flow of information may, and in most familiar instances obviously does, depend on underlying causal processes. Nevertheless, the information relationships between *s* and *r* must be distinguished from the system of causal relationships existing between these points.[1]

To illustrate Dretske's point, imagine that astronomers have discovered a pulsar three billion light-years from the Earth. The pulsar is a rotating neutron star that emits regular pulses of electromagnetic radiation in the radio frequency range. The astronomers who found the star are at first unimpressed by their discovery—it looks like just another star to catalogue. One of the astronomers, however, is a ham radio operator. Looking over the pattern of pulses, he finds that even though the pulses occur at exact time intervals, their frequencies alternate between two levels. More surprisingly still, by interpreting these alternating frequencies as dots and dashes, he finds that the pulsar is communicating English messages in Morse code.

Word quickly spreads throughout the scientific community, and from there to the world at large. Radio observatories around the globe start monitoring what becomes known as the "Incredible Talking Pulsar." The pulsar isn't merely transmitting disjointed English messages but rather is intelligently communicating with the inhabitants of earth. In fact, once the pulsar has gained international attention, it identifies itself. The pulsar informs us that it is the mouthpiece of Yahweh, the God of the Old and New Testaments, the Creator of the universe, the final Judge of humankind.

To confirm this extraordinary claim, the pulsar offers to answer any questions we might put to it. The pulsar specifies the following method for posing and answering questions. People on earth are to make an ark like the Ark of the Covenant originally constructed under Moses to hold the tablets of the Law (see Exodus 25). This ark is to be placed on Mount Zion in Israel. Every hour on the hour, a question written in English is to be placed inside the ark. Ten minutes later the pattern of pulses reaching Earth from the pulsar will answer that question, framed as an English message in Morse code. If, for some reason, no question is placed inside the ark, the pulsar recites famous passages from the plays of William Shakespeare.

The information transmitted through the pulsar proves to be nothing short of fantastic. Medical doctors learn how to cure AIDS, cancer, and a host of other diseases. Archaeologists learn where to dig for lost civilizations and how to make sense out of them. Physicists get their long sought-after theory for unifying the forces of nature. Meteorologists are forewarned of natural disasters and weather patterns years before they occur. Ecologists learn effective methods for decontaminating and preserving the earth. Mathematicians obtain proofs for long-standing open problems. The list of credits goes on, but let us stop here and consider what light this thought experiment sheds on the nonmateriality of information.

Strange as it may seem, this thought experiment violates no physical law. Such a conclusion may seem counterintuitive because a physicist's first reaction is likely to be that it violates Einstein's theory of special relativity, according to which messages cannot be relayed at superluminal speeds (i.e., speeds faster than light). Indeed, since the pulsar is three billion light-years from Earth, any signal we receive from the pulsar was sent billions of years ago. Yet the pulsar is "responding" to our questions within ten minutes of the written questions being placed inside the ark. The pulsar's answers therefore precede our questions by billions of years.

Physical causality thus has no way of accounting for the correlation between events on earth (i.e., questions placed inside the ark) and radio transmissions from the pulsar (i.e., answers arriving ten minutes later). Fred Dretske's dictum therefore bears repeating: "The information relationships between source and receiver must be distinguished from the system of causal relationships existing between these points."[2] Precisely because there is no causal sequence of energy transfers linking questions placed inside the ark with answers arriving from the pulsar ten minutes later, there is no principle of physics to be violated.

Information, like God, is nonmaterial and eternal. To be sure, information can be realized in objects that are material and temporal. Moreover, when those objects disintegrate, the information in them will be lost— from those objects, that is. But the same information can always be recovered (certainly by God) and then realized in other objects. Information is *multiply realizable*. To say the information is multiply realizable is to say that the same information can be represented (i.e., made present again) in numerous distinct ways.

A musical composition, for instance, can be realized as notes written in ink on paper, as an electronically scanned version of that document, as a live performance, or as an audio file on your computer (to name just a few possibilities). The material embodiment of information can always be destroyed. But information itself is indestructible. It follows that, because we are creatures of God, the information by which God created us is also indestructible and eternal.

Information's multiple realizability demonstrates its nonmateriality and eternity. Multiple realizability lies at the heart of all communication. The best case scenario for any communication is that the same information gets realized at both ends of the communication channel (often the correlation of patterns across the channel is imperfect). Thus, when Jesus in John 17:21 prays for believers to be united with God, he is praying for a communication between God and humanity in which the Word of God is perfectly realized, without distortion, in the human heart.

Christ's promise is that once our present embodiment disintegrates (at death), the information that constitutes our essence will be freed from distortion and receive a new embodiment that God will preserve through eternity. Christ's Resurrection guarantees this promise. But it guarantees much more. Not only will who and what we are be realized again in an embodied form, but the body that realizes our form will be glorified, removing limitations that were necessary while we were still in the thrall of sin. Once our bondage to sin is past, our bodies can be set free. Christ's resurrection body exhibited this freedom. It lacked nothing of his former body, being able to eat and enjoy the things of this world (Luke 24:41–43). And yet it was free to pass through walls, materialize in unexpected places, and ascend to heaven (Luke 24:36–37; Acts 1:9).

When we are resurrected, not only is the information by which God created us realized again, but it is also *transposed* into a new medium that enriches and enhances who we are, thereby glorifying us.[3] We are all familiar with the transposition of information. Consider Beethoven's *Fifth Symphony*. It is a marvelously rich orchestral work. And yet a three-year old can play the main theme from the first movement with one finger on a piano. Here the transposition is from a richer to a poorer medium. Indeed, much is lost in transposing a full orchestral work to a piano version. But transposition need not be in the direction of impoverishment. It can also be in the direction of enrichment.

Take, for instance, a computer chess program. When identical computer chess programs are played against each other, the version that has greater computational resources tends to win (because it can examine more possible positions and thereby perform a deeper analysis of what moves are likely to succeed). Thus, even though I may write a computer chess program for my laptop computer, if I then run the program on the $133-million IBM Roadrunner supercomputer that operates at 1.7 petaflops (i.e., over a thousand trillion floating point operations per second, which is several orders of magnitude greater than the computing power of current laptops), I'll have transposed my program from a poorer to a richer medium. Provided the program is well designed, it will play far stronger chess in the richer than in the poorer medium.

For the ultimate computational transposition, consider what has been called the "super supercomputer," attributed to statistician David Blackwell.[4] This computer performs its first computational step in half a second, it's next computational step a quarter of a second, it's next in an eighth of a second, and so on (in general, the nth computational step takes 1 in 2^n seconds; note that the infinite mathematical series $\frac{1}{2^1} + \frac{1}{2^2} + \frac{1}{2^3} + \cdots$ sums to 1). Such a computer would therefore perform any computation whatsoever in one second. Because it would have infinite computational speed and memory, it could resolve any mathematical problem whatsoever. To an intellect endowed with such computational power, all mathematical truths would be, in Ludwig Wittgenstein's sense, "surveyable" or "perspicuous."[5] Will God give our minds such computing power when we are resurrected? Why wouldn't he?

Many of the transpositions in this life take the form of damage. Consider the information in a book. Damage to the book can affect its readability. A page torn from a crucial passage will destroy the sense of the book. Alternatively, age may cause the pages to disintegrate and thus render them unreadable. Books constitute "static texts." Our brains constitute "dynamic texts." Brains "think" in the same way that books "inform." A book informs when a reader with suitable background knowledge reads it. Likewise the brain thinks when a mind suitably connected to that brain interacts with it. The mind is that which makes sense of the brain. If that brain grows old or is damaged (as in Alzheimer's disease), a destructive transposition occurs. A damaged brain attempting to think is like misplaced fingers typing at a keyboard.

Despite all the destructive transpositions we encounter in this life, God promises that in the resurrection we shall experience a transposition that is wholly positive and expansive. In the resurrection our embodied form will not merely be reconstituted. It will be transposed to a new reality in which all wounds are healed, all sorrows are comforted, all limitations are overcome, and all aspirations are fulfilled. In the final transposition, nothing of value will be lost:

> And I saw a new heaven and a new earth: for the first heaven and the first earth were passed away; and there was no more sea. And I John saw the holy city, new Jerusalem, coming down from God out of heaven, prepared as a bride adorned for her husband. And I heard a great voice out of heaven saying, Behold, the tabernacle of God is with men, and he will dwell with them, and they shall be his people, and God himself shall be with them, and be their God. And God shall wipe away all tears from their eyes; and there shall be no more death, neither sorrow, nor crying, neither shall there be any more pain: for the former things are passed away. And he that sat upon the throne said, Behold, I make all things new. (Rev 21:1–5)

TWELVE

LOGOS

S CRIPTURE, as even a cursory examination reveals, places a premium on the words we speak. The trinitarian mode of creation makes clear why this is so: as the prime instrument of creation, words also have the greatest potential for blessing as well as ruin. Thus we read "death and life are in the power of the tongue" (Prov 18:21) and "every idle word that men shall speak, they shall give account thereof in the day of judgment" (Matt 12:36).

Any act of speaking is at once exclusionary and irrevocable: to affirm one thing is to exclude or rule out others; moreover, like the Law of the Medes and Persians described in Dan 6:15, once a word goes out, it cannot be taken back—it echoes through eternity. Thus, when Jacob lied to his father Isaac by telling him that he was Esau, he ruled out telling him other things, notably the truth about his identity. Moreover, when Isaac blessed Jacob, thinking he was Esau, he could not retract the blessing even though Jacob had elicited it on the sly and Isaac had meant to give it to Esau. This exclusionary and irrevocable aspect of speech acts holds not just for humans but also for God. Thus, every divine spoken word rules out those possibilities not spoken. Moreover, once the word is spoken, God himself cannot recall it. God can only modify the original word's impact by adding further words.

This analogy between divine and human speaking extends further. Just as no human speaker ever exhausts his or her natural language (think of how much poetry could, but never will, be written), so God, in creating through the divine spoken word, never exhausts the divine *Logos* (think of all the worlds that God could, but never will, create). We may therefore distinguish *Logos* with a capital "L" (that is, the divine *Logos* in its fullness without self-limitation) from *logos* with a small "l" (that is, a specific divine word spoken to achieve a particular end).

Lacking a capitalization convention, the Greek New Testament employs *logos* in both these senses. At the beginning of John's Gospel, we read that "the [*Logos*] was made flesh, and dwelt among us" (John 1:14). Here the reference is to the infinite divine *Logos*, the second person of the Trinity, incarnated in Jesus of Nazareth. Later in John's Gospel, Jesus tells his disciples, "Now ye are clean through the [*logos*] which I have spoken unto you" (John 15:3). Here the reference is to a definite spoken word from Jesus by which the disciples' hearts are purified (sometimes the New Testament conveys this sense of *logos* also with the Greek word *rhema*).

Because a particular spoken word always excludes other spoken words, speech constitutes self-limitation. To say "I do" at your wedding means to say "I don't" to all others. Likewise, every divine spoken word constitutes a divine self-limitation. Accordingly, no divine spoken word can ever fully encompass the divine *Logos*. It follows that creation itself, as a divine spoken word, can never fully encompass the divine *Logos* either. This is why idolatry—worshipping the creation rather than the Creator—is so misconceived, for it assigns ultimate value to something inherently incapable of achieving ultimate value. Creation, especially a fallen creation, can at best reveal God's glory. Idolatry makes the creation rather than the Creator ultimate.

For the ancient Greeks, *logos* was never merely a linguistic entity. Today, when we think "word," we often visualize a string of symbols written on a sheet of paper. This is not what the Greeks meant by *logos*. *Logos* for them was a much broader concept. Consider its following meanings from Liddell and Scott's Greek-English Lexicon:

- the word by which the inward thought is expressed (speech)
- the inward thought or reason itself (reason)

- reflection, deliberation (choice)
- account, consideration, regard (inquiry)
- relation, proportion, analogy (harmony, balance)
- calculation, reckoning (mathematics)
- a reasonable ground, a condition (evidence, truth)

Logos is therefore an exceedingly rich notion, encompassing the entire life of the mind.

The etymology of *logos* is revealing. *Logos* stems from the Indo-European root *l-e-g*. This root appears in the Greek verb *lego*, which in the New Testament typically means "to speak." Yet the primitive meaning of *lego* is "to lay"; from there it came to mean "to pick up and gather"; then "to select and put together"; and hence "to select and put together words," and therefore "to speak." According to Marvin Vincent, in his study of New Testament words, "*logos* is a *collecting* or *collection* both of things in the mind, and of words by which they are expressed. It therefore signifies both the outward form by which the inward thought is expressed, and the inward thought itself, the Latin *oratio* and *ratio*: compare the Italian *ragionare*, 'to think' and 'to speak.' "[1]

The root *l-e-g* has several variants. It appears as *l-o-g* in *logos*. But it also appears as *l-e-c* in *intellect* and *l-i-g* in *intelligent*. This should give us pause. The word *intelligent* actually comes from the Latin rather than from the Greek. It derives from two Latin words, the preposition *inter*, meaning "between," and the Latin (not Greek) verb *lego*, meaning "to choose or select." The Latin *lego* stayed closer to its Indo-European root meaning than its Greek cognate, which came to refer explicitly to speech. According to its etymology, intelligence therefore consists in *choosing between*. In the act of creation, God chose between which worlds to create. The creation of the world is thus an act of divine intelligence.[2]

To say that God creates through a spoken word leaves unanswered the motivation for creation. Why create? Why does God create? Why do we create? Although creation is always an intelligent act, it is much more than an intelligent act. The impulse behind creation is always to offer oneself as a gift. Creation is a gift. Moreover, it is a gift of the most important thing we possess, namely, ourselves. Creation is the highest act of giving. In creation, a creator—whether divine, human, or otherwise—gives oneself unreservedly in self-revelation.[3]

But why give? What is the motivation for giving? Giving, as psychologist Erich Fromm noted, is an

> expression of potency. In the very act of giving I experience my strength, my wealth, my power. The experience of heightened vitality fills me with joy. I experience myself as overflowing, spending, alive, hence as joyous. Giving is more joyous than receiving, not because it is a deprivation, but because in the act of giving lies the expression of my aliveness.[4]

To live is to give, and to give supremely is to create because in the act of creation we give ourselves. Orthodox theologian Christos Yannaras illustrated this truth with reference to the person and work of Vincent van Gogh:

> We know the person of van Gogh, what is unique, distinct and unrepeatable in his existence, only when we see his paintings. There we meet a reason (*logos*) which is his only and we separate him from every other painter. When we have seen enough pictures by van Gogh and then encounter one more, then we say right away: This *is* van Gogh. We distinguish immediately the otherness of his personal reason, the uniqueness of his creative expression.[5]

Creation invests the creator's life in the thing created. When God creates humans, he breathes into them the breath of life—God's own life. At the end of the six days of creation, God is exhausted—not fatigued, as we might be, but exhausted in the sense of having drawn out of himself everything needed for the creature to be what it was intended to be. Having given the creature everything it needs, God can now rest. Rest, however, does not signify the cessation of activity. In particular, God is not done interacting with creatures after he has created them. Rather, the whole point of rest is for the Creator and the creature to enjoy each other in a covenant relation of trust and love.[6]

The impulse to create and give oneself in self-revelation need not be grand; it can be quite humble. The important thing about the act of creation is that it reveal the creator. The act of creation always bears the signature

[99]

of the creator. The creation of the world by God is the most magnificent of all acts of creation. Creation and the redemption of humanity through Jesus Christ are the two key instances of God's self-revelation. If you want to know who God is, you need to know God through both creation and redemption. According to Scripture, the angels praise God for these two things: God's creation of the world and God's redemption of the world through Jesus Christ. Humanity can do no better than follow the angels' example.

THIRTEEN

BEING AS COMMUNION

BECAUSE the divine *Logos* is the prime instrument of creation, the world is not a buzzing confusion but an orderly composition; it is a *cosmos* rather than a *chaos*. The divine *Logos* guarantees the world's intelligibility. In particular, it guarantees the ability of human language to make sense of the world and to speak meaningfully of God—hence our confidence that our words can speak truly about reality. Human language is therefore not an evolutionary refinement of grunts and stammers once uttered by apelike ancestors. We are creatures made in the divine image. Human language is a divine gift for understanding the world and therewith God himself. This is not to deny that human languages change or, in some sense, evolve.[1] Nor is it to say that we ever fully comprehend God, as in achieving fixed, final, and exhaustive knowledge of God. But it is to say that human language does enable us to express accurate statements about God.

This conception of language stands against the view that biblical language about God is hopelessly anthropomorphic. "Reimagining God" is a dominant theme in contemporary theological discussions.[2] The rationale for "reimagining God" is that all our references to God are human constructions; thus, they can and should be changed as human needs require new constructions. The ancients imagined God one way. Times have changed, so we need to reimagine him another way. Certain feminist theologians, for instance, object to referring to God as father. God as father, we are told, is an outdated patriarchal way of depicting God that, given contemporary challenges, needs to be changed. "Father," we are told, is a metaphor, co-opted from human experience and pressed (unnaturally) into theological service. Ironically, those who claim to oppose anthropomorphism do not offer a less anthropomorphic view, only a different one, and usually an impoverished one.[3]

Let me suggest a radically different view. The concept of *father* is not an anthropomorphism, nor is referring to God as father a metaphor derived from pressing ordinary language into theological service where it does substandard or misleading work. It's not that we are taking human father-hood and idealizing it into a divine father image (as in the critiques of religion by Ludwig Feuerbach or Sigmund Freud). Instead of committing an *anthropomorphism* by referring to God as father, we are committing a *theomorphism* by referring to human beings as fathers. We are never using the word *father* as accurately as when we ascribe it to God. As soon as we ascribe "father" to human beings, our language becomes analogical and derivative.

All instances of fatherhood therefore reflect the fatherhood of God. Scripture confirms this. Indeed, ask yourself why Jesus would tell us to call no one father except God (Matt 23:9). Certainly Jesus is not telling us never to refer to any human as "father." All of us have human fathers, and we rightly refer to them as such. But human fathers reflect a more profound reality, the fatherhood of God. This is not to say that we have a direct intuition of God's fatherhood. Our experience of human fatherhood is the *occasion* for our knowledge of God's fatherhood (this places tremendous responsibility on human fathers and also explains the tremendous damage that results when fathers fail in their responsibility). Precisely because God created the world to reflect his glory, human fatherhood gives us accurate insight into divine fatherhood. Nonetheless, the essence of fatherhood is found not in human but in divine fatherhood.

In the same vein, consider how Jesus responded to a rich young ruler who addressed him as "good Teacher." "Why do you call Me good?" asked Jesus. "No one is good but One—God" (Mark 10:18 HCSB). Goodness properly applies only to God. It's not an anthropomorphism to call God good. The goodness we attribute to God is not an idealization of human

[102]

goodness. God defines goodness. When we speak of human goodness, it is only as a reflection of divine goodness.

Contemporary thinkers are often offended at the inadequacy, as they see it, of language used to describe God. In consequence, they regard preferred metaphors traditionally used to describe God (e.g., God's fatherhood) as subject to change. Thus, according to Cambridge theologian Janet Soskice, our metaphors for God must be "responsive to the needs and perceptions of religious adherents."[4] I would turn this around. The metaphors traditionally used to describe God are themselves divinely inspired, drawn as they are from a determinate world that was created by God to reflect his character and glory.

So when Soskice asks, "What happens when a set of metaphors stops being authoritative and starts to repel?"[5] the proper reply is that this question, if directed at the guiding metaphors of the Christian faith, is inadmissible. One might as readily ask, "What happens when the Ten Commandments or the Sermon on the Mount stops being authoritative and starts to repel?" Once you get to that place in your thinking, you need to start looking for a new belief system—Christianity is no longer for you. The guiding metaphors of the Christian faith are non-negotiable. We need these metaphors to understand God aright. To change these metaphors is, in fact, to deny God.[6]

To view human language as a divine gift for understanding the world and thereby God is powerfully liberating. It means that we don't live in a Platonic world of shadows from which we must escape if we are to discern the divine light. It means that we don't live in a Kantian world of experience (Kant's "phenomena") that bars access to the underlying reality (Kant's "noumena"). It means that we don't live in a naturalistic world that rules out any meaningful divine interaction. It means, rather, that we live in a world where everything is a sacrament, radiating God's glory. In this way, language becomes a gift for celebrating that glory by enabling us to speak truly about God and what God has wrought in creation.

The view that creation proceeds through a divine spoken word has profound implications not only for the study of language, but also for the study of knowledge, or what philosophers call *epistemology*. For naturalism (the view that the physical world is all that exists), epistemology's main problem is unraveling Einstein's dictum: "The most incomprehensible thing about the world is that it is comprehensible."[7] How can we have any knowledge about the world at all? Why should what goes on in our heads have any rational connection with what goes on in the world?

Within a naturalistic worldview, no solution exists to this riddle. Naturalistic epistemology attempts to ground human knowledge in nature and, specifically, in an evolutionary process said to be responsible for our cognitive apparatus. The problem with naturalistic epistemology, however, is that it ends in complete skepticism, destroying the very possibility of knowledge. G. K. Chesterton perhaps said it best:

> Reason is itself a matter of faith. It is an act of faith to assert that our thoughts have any relation to reality at all. If you are merely a sceptic, you must sooner or later ask yourself the question, "Why should *anything* go right; even observation and deduction? Why should not good logic be as misleading as bad logic? They are both movements in the brain of a bewildered ape?" The young sceptic says, "I have a right to think for myself." But the old sceptic, the complete sceptic, says, "I have no right to think for myself. I have no right to think at all."[8]

Later writers have developed Chesterton's insight into a full-blown evolutionary argument against naturalism: if we evolved through blind natural processes, which put a premium on survival and reproduction, then our cognitive apparatus was formed by a process that did not put a premium on knowing truth. Whence, then, the confidence that our cognitive apparatus can know the truth about anything and, in particular, about naturalism and evolution? Naturalistic epistemology is thus seen to be self-referentially incoherent—it cannot pass its own test.[9]

Theism, happily, can avoid such radical skepticism. For theism the problem is not how we can have knowledge but why our knowledge is so prone to error and distortion. The Judeo-Christian tradition attributes the problem of error to the Fall. At the heart of the Fall is alienation. Beings are no longer properly in communion with other beings. We lie to ourselves. We lie to others. And others lie to us. Appearance and reality, though not divorced, are out of sync. The problem of epistemology within the Judeo-Christian tradition isn't to establish that we have knowledge but instead to root out the distortions that try to overthrow our knowledge.

On the view that creation proceeds through a divine spoken word, not only does naturalistic epistemology fail, but so does naturalistic ontology. Ontology asks, what are the fundamental constituents of reality? According to naturalism (specifically, the scientific naturalism that currently dominates Western thought), the world is fundamentally an interacting system of mindless entities (be they particles, strings, fields, or whatever). Mind therefore becomes an emergent property of suitably arranged mindless entities. But naturalistic ontology is all backwards. If creation and everything in it proceeds through a divine spoken word, then the entities that are created don't suddenly fall silent at the moment of creation. Rather, they continue to speak.

A blade of grass speaks to you. In the light of the sun, it tells you that it is green. If you touch it, you learn that it has a certain texture. It communicates something else to a chinch bug intent on devouring it. It communicates something else still to a particle physicist intent on analyzing its atomic and subatomic constituents. But a blade of grass is more than the arrangement of particles that constitute it, and it is capable of communicating more than is inherent in any such arrangement. Indeed, its reality derives not from its particulate constituents but from its capacity to communicate with other entities in creation and ultimately with God himself.

Ontology's fundamental problem, the problem of being, now receives a straightforward solution: To be is to be in communion, with God and with the rest of creation. It follows that the fundamental science, indeed the science that needs to ground all other sciences, is communication theory and not, as is widely supposed, an outdated mechanistic science of particles or other mindless entities, which then need to be built up to ever greater orders of complexity by equally mindless principles of association, known typically as natural laws.

Communication theory has come into its own only in the last half century. Its object of study is not particles but the information that passes between entities.[10] The problem with mechanistic science is that it has no resources for recognizing and understanding information.[11] That is a particularly pressing problem just now because we live in an information age.[12]

The science of the last millennium sidestepped the primacy of information. The science of the new millennium will not be able to avoid it.

Indeed, information makes the world go around—the information that God speaks to create the world, the information that continually proceeds from God in sustaining the world and acting providentially in it, and the information that passes among God's creatures. Information, of course, is just another name for *logos*. All the information in the universe is, in the end, mediated through the divine *Logos*, who is before all things and by whom all things consist (Col 1:17).

Because the divine *Logos* is active in creation, the world is a sacrament. As a sacrament, the world reflects God's glory—if we but have the eyes to see it. What undermines the sacred is not the nature of the world (created, as it is, by God) but the power of evil to disrupt the world and darken our understanding. The point of redemption, then, is to overcome the distorting effects of evil by clarifying our vision, purifying our imagination, and, ultimately, establishing a new heaven and earth in which righteousness dwells. Whereas the sacred is for now largely hidden, when Christ restores all things, it will be self-evident.

FOURTEEN

CREATION AS DOUBLE CREATION

I N *The Seven Habits of Highly Effective People*, leadership expert Stephen Covey offers an insight into creation that is at once obvious and profound: "*All things are created twice*. There's a mental or first creation, and a physical or second creation to all things."[1] Creation always starts with an idea and ends with a thing. Anything achieved must first be conceived. Creation is thus a process bounded by *conception* at one end and *realization* at the other. This dual aspect of creation is so obvious that it is often unstated. Plato underscored it in the *Timaeus* when he had the Demiurge (Plato's world architect) structure the physical world so that it conformed to patterns residing in the abstract world of ideas. But anyone who forms a plan to accomplish a purpose operates by this principle of double creation.

Covey, as a businessman, applied the principle of double creation to business: "If you want to have a successful enterprise, you clearly define what you're trying to accomplish. You carefully think through the product or service you want to provide in terms of your market target, then you organize all the elements—financial, research and development, operations, marketing, personnel, physical facilities, and so on—to meet that objective."[2] All this is unproblematic so long as the second creation fulfills the promises of the first. But what if the two creations don't match up? What if the second creation doesn't achieve anything like the goal set by the first creation? Covey addresses this possibility: "Most business failures begin in the first creation, with the problems such as undercapitalization, misunderstanding of the market, or lack of a business plan."[3]

Covey here shifts the blame for failure to the first creation—that the plan was inadequate for achieving the goal. But that raises an interesting theological question. God, who is perfect, cannot make mistakes in the first creation. The first creation is creation as a conceptual act and is therefore completely under divine control. In the first creation, as we saw in chapter 10, the entire Trinity acts: God the Father forms an intention, God the Son articulates it, and God the Holy Spirit empowers it. Thus, if divine creation miscarries, it has to miscarry at the second creation. But how can a perfect first creation end in failure at the second creation? This question, not a concern for Covey because he is thinking of human creation, must be answered for divine creation if we are to understand God's goodness in creation. The short answer, of course, is rebellion of the creature—in a word, the Fall. Rebellion of the creature sabotages the second creation by preventing the first creation from fulfilling its purpose.

G. K. Chesterton showed how a perfect first creation can issue in an imperfect second creation. First he noted that all creation entails separation—in creating a thing, one necessarily gives it a separate existence and therefore "divorces" oneself from it. Then he delivered the punch line:

> It was the prime philosophic principle of Christianity that this divorce in the divine act of making (such as severs the poet from the poem or the mother from the new-born child) was the true description of the act whereby the absolute energy made the world. According to most philosophers, God in making the world enslaved it. According to Christianity, in making it, He set it free. God had written, not so much a poem, but rather a play; a play he had planned as perfect, but which had necessarily been left to human actors and stage-managers, who had since made a great mess of it.[4]

Chesterton's metaphor of creation as a play whose production does not match the quality of the text raises an intriguing question: What do you do if you've written a perfect play but the actors can't perform it properly? There you are watching your masterpiece butchered by hacks. If you hope to salvage anything from this mess, you must either get the actors to shape up and do their parts right or rewrite the play and give the actors something they can perform properly. In the latter case, hiring completely new actors is not an option—in the creation of the world, God has, as it were, "pooled" all available actors. Assuming the actors are hopeless (as is our situation in consequence of the Fall), then a rewrite is the only option. I'm not sure such a rewrite has ever occurred in the theater (actors have demanded that material be rewritten to suit them, but that's different). Such rewrites, however, have happened in music. For instance, William Walton's *Duets for Children* were originally written as solo piano pieces for his niece and nephew. When they had difficulty playing them, he rewrote them as duets, which his niece and nephew were then better able to perform.[5]

Now there's a big difference between us rewriting a play or piece of music so that it can be performed properly and God rewriting cosmic history. In our case, we see a botched performance, rewrite the material, and give the performers a chance to redeem themselves by giving a better performance the second time around. That's possible because the performance is separate from the rest of our lives: for any humanly produced play, the fictional world of the play is separate from the nonfictional world that the actors normally inhabit. But when God creates a world in which we are players, the fiction/nonfiction (or performance/nonperformance) distinction breaks down. God places us in precisely one world, and everything we do takes place in it.[6]

We have but one life to live and one world in which to live it. Unlike actors who can step outside their roles to improve their acting skills, we have no other world than this one in which to improve our life skills. We can't step off the world, fix what's broke, and step back on once everything is right again with the world. Here's a joke that makes the point:

> A mechanic was removing a cylinder head from the motor of
> a Harley motorcycle when he spotted a well-known heart sur-
> geon in his shop. The surgeon was there waiting for the service
> manager to come take a look at his bike when the mechanic
> shouted across the garage, "Hey, Doc, can I ask you a question?"
> The surgeon, a bit surprised, walked over to where the mechanic
> was working on the motorcycle. The mechanic straightened up,
> wiped his hands on a rag. "So Doc, look at this engine. I open

its heart, take the valves out, repair any damage, and then put them back in, and when I finish, it works just like new. So how come I get such a small salary and you get the really big bucks, when you and I are doing basically the same work?" The surgeon paused, smiled, leaned over, and whispered to the mechanic, "Try doing it with the engine running."[7]

God writes our story and, when we fall, rewrites it—but with the engine running and thus with no break in the action. Moreover, as unbound by time, God is under no compulsion merely to rewrite the future of the world from the moment of the Fall (as assumed by young-earth creationism). Rather, God can rewrite our story while it is being performed and even change the entire backdrop against which it is performed—that includes past, present, and future. An infinite God who transcends time can redeem a botched performance by acting across time. In particular, God could make effects of the Fall evident in creation so that those effects, though attributable to the Fall, come temporally prior to it. In other words, the effects of the Fall can be retroactive.

A retroactive view of the Fall was one of several Christian options proposed in the nineteenth century to explain prehuman suffering and death. Thus J. Jay Dana, writing in 1853, before the Darwinian revolution but after the revolution in geology (which assigned a much older age to the Earth than customarily associated with Genesis), continued to affirm the Fall as the *cause* of animal death but dissociated it from the temporal *appearance* of death: "If sin could be pardoned in view of a *foreseen* offering which should atone for its guilt, then a foreseen offence may be made a reason for accommodating the physical conformation of things to such an event."[8]

Thus, just as the death and Resurrection of Christ is responsible for the salvation of repentant people throughout all time, so the Fall of humanity in the Garden of Eden is responsible for every natural evil throughout all time (future, present, past, and distant past preceding the Fall). Conrad Wright traced this view in the work of nineteenth-century biblical geologists (who were concerned with reconciling the Bible and geology). How, according to the biblical geologists, did death enter the world?

Genesis declares that it was because of Adam's sin; geology reveals long ages when plants flourished and died before the creation of Adam. But God knew that man would sin, and so he created a world in which death would exist. "Death . . . entered into the original plan of the world in the divine mind, and was endured by the animals and plants that lived anterior to man." *By anticipation, the sin of Adam was the cause of death for all prior creation.*[9]

Thus, by explaining prehuman suffering and death as a consequence of the Fall, the biblical geologists sought to preserve theological orthodoxy regarding the Fall and scientific orthodoxy regarding geology. Their resolution of the problem of natural evil seems not to have caught on. For instance, Nicolaas Rupke, a well-known historian of geology with a long-standing interest in its theological implications (he was at one time a young-earth creationist), asks, "How could death be a punishment for man's sin if it already existed in prehuman geological history?"[10] Yet, in the review article where he poses this question, he fails to cite the biblical geologists or their proposed resolution. Even Charles Hodge, who was America's premier theologian during the second and third quarters of the nineteenth century, didn't advert to, much less develop, the biblical geologists' retroactive view of the Fall when he published his substantial three-volume systematic theology in the 1870s.[11]

Why didn't the biblical geologists' retroactive view of the Fall catch on? The short answer is that they never developed a coherent account of how God could act across time or, as we might say, *transtemporally.* For their solution to be more than an empty proposal requires some such account. I will analyze divine transtemporal action in the sequel as I flesh out the biblical geologists' proposal. In closing this chapter, however, I want merely to note how their proposal meshes neatly with creation as double creation. God, in Genesis 1, creates a perfect world. In Stephen Covey's terms, this is the "first creation." As a conceptual act by a perfect God, it cannot help but be perfect. In Genesis 2–3, we find the "second creation," which starts off great but quickly ends in ruin. Thus, once humanity falls in Genesis 3, God must act to undo the damage.

Within young-earth creationism, all divine compensatory action to redress humanity's sin occurs forward in time from the Fall. But why should God be limited in that way? Even we are not limited in that way. Granted, our foreknowledge of events is partial. But actuaries, for example, are remarkably accurate at forecasting expected patterns of events. To be sure, God's ability to forecast excels ours. We only see "through a glass darkly" (1 Cor 13:12). The actuary cannot know when and where two cars will collide. God knows that and infinitely many other things besides. His foreknowledge is complete and not partial. But even partial foreknowledge enables insurance companies to respond to future events by setting rates that take into account an expected number of total writeoffs from auto collisions in a given year.

To assume that God must respond to the Fall only with actions that take effect afterward is thus doubly mistaken. First, it commits an unwarranted anthropomorphism by treating God as time-bound in the same way that we are. Second, it fails to recognize that though we ourselves are time-bound creatures, we often respond to events before they occur. God, as unbound by time, can therefore respond to events before, during, and after their occurrence. In particular, he can respond to the Fall by changing not only the history that comes after it but also the history that comes before it.

FIFTEEN

MOVING THE PARTICLES

C HRISTIAN theism has traditionally viewed God's action in the world as effectual and even vigorous. God is said to act through miracles, answer specific prayers, and inspire prophecies that accurately predict future events. The current mental environment rejects this traditional view. Instead, it regards the world as a closed causal nexus operating by unbroken natural laws. Causal closure is thus seen to rule out any real-time divine interaction with us and our world.

Insofar as the current mental environment is comfortable speaking about divine action at all, it focuses on God's role in "sustaining" the world. Granted, every contingent thing that continues to exist does so because God sustains it, and no contingent thing has the power in itself to continue its existence. But appealing to God's sustaining activity can become merely a device for sidestepping the charge of deism, saying little more about how God relates to the world than that God makes sure the world behaves itself properly and does nothing too out of the ordinary (such as by going out of existence or radically changing its character). By contrast, Christian orthodoxy views the God-world relationship as confined not merely to creation and sustenance. It also regards the God-world relationship as one of ongoing providence, with providence being both general (as in God's overseeing the weather) and particular (as in God's answering specific prayers).

Our mental environment rejects that God can act effectually and vigorously in the world. Behind this rejection stands a worry. Paul Davies articulated this worry at a symposium he convened in 1999. The symposium, at which I participated, was titled "Complexity, Information, and Design: A Critical Appraisal."[1] For me the most significant moment at this event occurred when Davies, though acknowledging evidence for design in nature, nonetheless rejected that the God of classical Christian theism could be the Designer. Such a God would be outside nature and thus, in his view, incapable of interacting coherently with nature. As he put it, "But at some point God has to move the particles."[2]

Davies's worry is not universally shared. Christians through the ages have not had a problem with God, or with angelic beings for that matter, moving particles. In general, Christians have resisted attempts to limit God. History is on their side, even the recent history of science. Scientists who, in the name of science, have tried to limit God have not fared well. For instance, Albert Einstein, in criticizing the apparent incompleteness of quantum mechanics, asserted, "God does not play dice with the universe." To this Niels Bohr replied, "Albert, stop telling God what to do."[3] Quantum physics has since vindicated Bohr at Einstein's expense. Bohr's words apply equally to Davies: like Einstein, Davies is inappropriately telling God what he can and can't do. Why should Davies's limited conception of God (all our conceptions of God are limited) impose any actual limits on God?[4] Davies is too squeamish about divine action. Nonetheless, in the remainder of this chapter I propose, for the sake of argument, to take Davies's worry seriously. In doing so, we will discover that even if God refrains from moving particles, he can still interact effectually and vigorously with the world.

Although Davies rejects a particle-moving God, he is happy to affirm a God who acts in and through law-governed physical processes. Such a God poses no challenge to science. Indeed, atheists are happy to break bread with theists who demand no more of their God than that he act consistently with natural laws.[5] But must all God's actions be consistent with natural laws? Can God make a discernible difference in the physical world that is not reducible to natural laws? For God to make a discernible difference in the physical world, God, according to Davies, needs to move particles. Yet, in our ordinary experience, physical objects move because other physical objects make them move. In other words, they move not from the top down but from the bottom up. How, then, does God get his divine fingers into the world?

The world consists of physical stuff, and for God to make a difference in the world seems to require that God intervene in, meddle with, or in some way coerce physical stuff. What's wrong with this picture of divine action? The problem is not flat contradiction with the results of modern science. Take, for instance, the law of conservation of energy. Although the law is often stated as "energy can neither be created nor destroyed," in fact all we have empirical evidence for is the much weaker claim that "in an isolated system energy remains constant." Thus, a supernatural action that moves particles or creates new ones is beyond the power of science to disprove because one can always claim that the system under consideration was not isolated.

No logical contradiction exists here. Nor does a "god-of-the-gaps" necessarily follow. The "gaps" in the god-of-the-gaps objection to supernatural agency denote putative gaps in human knowledge (i.e., ignorance) about underlying physical causes. A supernatural agent, however, might act so that the resulting discontinuity in the chain of physical causes could never be removed by appealing to ordinary physical explanations. We may know everything there is to know about the physical causes underlying an event and yet find that no story we tell about such causes plausibly explains the event. Such "gaps" would constitute discontinuities in the actual chain of physical causes and thus remain forever beyond the capacity of ordinary physical explanation. In short, natural causes operating according to natural laws might provide an *incomplete* account of what nature actually does.

Although a nonmaterial God who "moves particles" is not logically incoherent, such a being nonetheless remains problematic for many scientists. The problem is that natural causes are fully capable of moving particles. Thus for God also to move particles can seem like an arbitrary intrusion. God is merely doing something that nature is already doing, and even if God is doing it better, why didn't God make nature better in the first place so that it can move the particles better? Scientists want a nature they can respect. And if they believe in God, they want God to respect her as well. Yet that seems to preclude God from moving particles.

[115]

But what if God is not in the business of moving particles but of imparting information? In that case nature moves its own particles, but an intelligence nonetheless guides the arrangement that those particles assume. When a system is responsive to information, its dynamics vary sharply with the information imparted and are largely immune to purely physical factors (e.g., mass, charge, or kinetic energy). For instance, the energy needed to punch in a nuclear launch code is minimal, but the energetic output, given the correct code, is enormous. Information, though embodied in matter and capable of directing the behavior of matter, is itself nonmaterial (see chapter 11). Thus Norbert Wiener, one of the founders of modern information theory, could write, "Information is information, not matter or energy. No materialism which does not admit this can survive at the present day."[6]

How much energy is required to impart information? We have sensors that can detect quantum events and amplify them to the macroscopic level (the eyes of certain frogs can register single photons). What's more, the energy in quantum events is proportional to frequency or inversely proportional to wavelength. And since there is no upper limit to the wavelength of electromagnetic radiation, there is no lower limit to the energy required to impart information. By taking these limits to their extremes, God could therefore impart information into the universe without inputting any energy at all.

Such "extreme limits," however, are never attained in practice. Granted, an embodied intelligence may use arbitrarily small amounts of energy to impart information. But an arbitrarily small amount of energy is still a positive amount of energy, and any intelligence employing positive amounts of energy to impart information is still, in Davies's phrase, "moving the particles." The question remains how God, who is unembodied and therefore not composed of particles, can influence the natural world without imparting any energy whatsoever. An indeterministic universe provides one way to answer this question. Although we can thank quantum mechanics for the widespread recognition that the universe is indeterministic, indeterminism has a long philosophical history, and appears in such diverse places as ancient materialism (e.g., Lucretius) and American pragmatism (e.g., William James).

Older models of the universe drawn from classical physics tend to be informationally closed. That's because classical physics is deterministic, and determinism precludes novel information from getting into a system.[7] Indeterministic models of the universe, such as given by quantum mechanics, are by contrast more informationally open. Such a universe will produce (seemingly) random events and can thus produce patterns of events that stand out against the backdrop of randomness. Such patterns, if intended by God, would constitute information. Accordingly, in an indeterministic universe, divine action could impart information into matter without disrupting ordinary physical causality.

At this point skeptics are likely to charge theists with evading the question of how God introduces information into the world. Surely there must be some physical mechanism by which the information is imparted. Surely there are thermodynamic limitations governing the flow of information. Thermodynamic limitations do apply if we are dealing with embodied information sources that need to output energy to transmit information. But nothing prevents God, who is immaterial, from enlisting (seemingly) random processes and imparting to them information. If divine action takes this form, the problem of "moving the particles" simply does not arise. Indeterminism means that God can substantively affect the structure and dynamics of the physical world by imparting information and yet without imparting energy.

To say that the physical world is indeterministic is not to reject the principle of sufficient reason. Often indeterminism is taken to imply acausality, so that an event that is attributed to a random or indeterministic process is regarded as having no cause or at best an incomplete cause (i.e., whatever we are calling a cause does not provide a complete account of the event in question). If one views chance as fundamental and patterns in nature as anomalies of chance, then this view follows. But one can also view the patterns in nature as fundamental (indeed, God-given) and treat chance as derivative from those patterns. In my paper "Randomness by Design," I took this line of reasoning to its logical end, arguing that chance and randomness do not even make sense apart from underlying patterns and information.[8]

So far I have argued that an indeterministic universe is informationally porous and thus open to action by a deity who can impart information without moving particles. Quantum mechanics seems to present such a picture of the universe, allowing God free play at the quantum level. I personally find this picture appealing. Many scientists, however, find divine activity at quantum interstices unappealing. The current mental environment conceives of the world as a closed causal nexus operating by unbroken natural laws. A deity who acts through quantum events, even though such a God does not strictly speaking "move the particles," is to many scientists unacceptable. For them, causal closure seems to preclude any real-time divine interaction with the physical world.

Yet surprisingly, causal closure places no restriction on God's activity in the world. To see this, consider the following thought experiment. Imagine that you are alone in a room with ten boxes laid out in a row. You open the first box and in it is a slip of paper with the words, "How are you today?" You say, "Pretty good, except that I misplaced my checkbook and need to pay some bills." You then open the second box, and in it is a slip of paper with the words, "You laid it on the mantle above the fireplace when you were distracted changing your baby's diaper." You say, "Yes, that's right. But how did you know that?" You open the third box, and in it is a slip of paper with the words, "This is God, and I have some matters of urgency to discuss with you." And so on, moving sequentially through the ten boxes, you find yourself holding a coherent, real-time conversation of tremendous importance to your life.

The question I now want to address is not the identity of your interlocutor (who claims to be God) but rather this: When were those slips of paper inserted into the boxes? After you've read the slip in the last box, you are puzzled. You examine the boxes but find no pneumatic tubes capable of inserting the slips at appropriate points in the conversation. So too, you find no evidence of microphones or other listening devices. Indeed, when you examine the room, you find that it is entirely low-tech and self-contained. Thus, there is no chance that slips were being inserted into the boxes while you were in the room. More surprisingly still, you find that when you examine the boxes and the slips, the best scientific evidence suggests that the slips were written and placed in the boxes hundreds of years before your birth. It appears, then, that the information in those boxes, though meant to take effect when you entered the room today, was actually fully in place hundreds of years ago.

This thought experiment illustrates how a world that is a closed causal nexus operating by unbroken natural laws could, in principle, still allow for real-time interaction from outside. Because of causal closure, such a world will preclude what may be called "counterfactual intervention." In other words, it precludes God from overriding the causal structure of the world by stopping effects that would have happened (hence the reference to "counterfactual"—the effects were stopped, so they didn't happen and therefore are "contrary to fact"). Moreover, it precludes God from substituting other effects in their place (hence the reference to "intervention"—the substituted effects would not have happened unless God intervened). A world barring counterfactual intervention, however, cannot preclude God from prearranging the constitution and dynamics of the world so that desired material effects are achieved even if they appear extraordinary and bespeak a deity active in the particulars of the moment. All that is required is that God build in the necessary information from the start so that it gets expressed at appropriate times and places.

This, actually, is an old idea. It comes up in Augustine's *Literal Commentary on Genesis*, where God is said to implant nature with seeds that come to fruition at appointed times and places.[9] It is implicit in Leibniz's ideas about concurrence and preestablished harmony, in which divine purposes and material effects precisely track one another.[10] Charles Babbage, the inventor of the modern digital computer, updated these ideas by arguing that God imbued nature with computational programs that kick in when the time and place are right. Babbage put forward this view in his *Ninth Bridgewater Treatise*, which predated Darwin's *Origin of Species* by more than 20 years.[11]

Philosopher of science Michael Polanyi went even further in analyzing how the physical world processes information. According to Polanyi, the laws of nature assume certain general mathematical forms for which fundamental constants and free parameters then need to be specifically calibrated. But, in addition, for any such laws to describe nature effectively, they must also take into account boundary conditions. For instance, Newton's law of gravity describes the behavior of objects in a gravitational field. But to describe the actual behavior of a ball released from a tower, we need to know the height of the tower. The height of the tower constitutes a boundary condition. All such boundary conditions are highly contingent and, depending on the precise arrangement they take, can bring about vastly different effects—most of them ordinary, but some of them extraordinary. The information inherent in such effects reflects the information embedded in these boundary conditions.[12]

Accordingly, even in a world that is causally closed, God, by carefully arranging the world from the start, could achieve all intended effects, up to and including acts of particular providence that appear to require direct, real-time intervention (though, in fact, they have been "front loaded"). The most vivid illustration I know of careful prearrangement leading to extraordinary results is a commercial by the automobile manufacturer Honda. This commercial, a two-minute film called *Cog,* records a complicated chain reaction of events (like dominoes falling, only much more spectacular). The film begins with a transmission bearing, which rolls into a synchro hub, which rolls into a gear wheel cog, which falls off a table and lands on a camshaft, and so on.[13] The amazing thing about this film is that each event occurs exactly as it appears to occur—the sequence of events is unaltered, unretouched, and not simulated. After a month for script approval, two months of concept drawings, and a further four months to develop and test the concept, the actual filming took 605 failed takes before the chain-reaction worked as intended.

Although the prearranged chain reaction in *Cog* suggests full physical determinism, God's front-loading of information in the universe requires nothing of the sort. If for every possible situation God knows each course that the world would take (what philosophers call "middle knowledge"), then God could arrange for the world to produce those and only those situations in which random as well as freely chosen events precisely fulfill his will. Here we would have an indeterministic universe in which humans exercise libertarian free will (i.e., act intentionally and have the ability to do otherwise) and in which God has arranged the world so that everything is divinely guided but nothing requires "supernatural additions."[14]

Note that even a full-bodied physical determinism need not obviate libertarian free will: given a mind-body dualism, God could have arranged the physical world to reflect the freely made choices of spiritual agents that have physical bodies. The very structure of the physical world, which seemingly determines the movements of our bodies, would then itself be arranged by God to reflect our freely chosen actions as spiritual beings linked to physical bodies. If you will, our bodies do what they do because of the way in which the universe was constituted at the Big Bang, but God constitutes the universe at the Big Bang to ensure that our bodies do what our spirits would freely have them do. In this way God would coordinate physical determinism with human freedom, making the former subservient to the latter.

The lesson to be drawn about causal closure is therefore counterintuitive: a world open to direct, real-time divine intervention could be empirically indistinguishable from a causally closed world that operates by unbroken natural laws, provided that God, from the start, is able to precisely arrange the unfolding of events. The Enlightenment view that we must choose between a world whose causal structure is ruled by unbroken natural laws or a God who supernaturally intervenes in the world is thus seen to be doubly mistaken. Divine concurrence, in which God acts through ordinary events, has always been a feature of Christian theology.[15] In particular, God is able to work through natural laws (they are, after all, his creation). More important for this discussion, however, is that what appears to be supernatural intervention could just be ordinary events suitably coordinated to achieve extraordinary results.[16]

To sum up, God has plenty of ways of getting information into the world and thereby accomplishing his will. He can, if he likes, get information into the world by moving particles (the one who created particles can certainly move them). The lesson of this chapter, however, is that God can also get information into the world without moving particles. The world is informationally open.

PART IV

RETROACTIVE
EFFECTS OF THE FALL

SIXTEEN

CHRONOS AND *KAIROS*

T O see how the Fall can affect not only the future but also the past, we need to understand how God acts across time, or transtemporally. Scripture teaches that creation is a progression of effected words spoken by God.[1] In creating the world, God says one thing, then another, building on what he just said, and so on. This progression has an inherent logic because the effect of one word depends logically on the prior effect of others (e.g., the creation of fish presupposes the creation of water).

This logic has traditionally been called the *order of creation*.[2] We can think of the order of creation as history from the vantage of divine intention and action. In this top-down view of history, certain divine intentions and actions are logically prior to others. Logical priority rather than temporal priority defines history for God. History from the divine perspective therefore contrasts with our ordinary, bottom-up view of history, which we may refer to as *natural history*.[3] Natural history confines history to space and time and sees the logic of history as determined by physical causality rather than by divine intention.

This distinction between the order of creation and natural history reflects a fundamental distinction in the nature of time. In English, we have just one word for time. But the Greek of the New Testament had two: *chronos* and *kairos*.[4] According to Arndt and Gingrich's standard lexicon of New Testament Greek, *chronos* denotes mere duration whereas *kairos* denotes time with a purpose (especially a divine purpose). Thus, in defining *kairos*, Arndt and Gingrich characterize it as "a welcome time," "the right, proper, favorable time," and "the time of crisis."[5] The special role of *kairos* in fulfilling divine purposes is reflected in the liturgy of the Eastern Orthodox Church, which begins with the deacon calling to the congregation, "It is time [*kairos*] for the Lord to act," signifying that in worship temporality and eternity intersect.[6]

Paul Tillich highlighted the distinction between *chronos* and *kairos* in his theology. In his lectures on the history of Christian thought, he remarked,

> [*Kairos* describes] the feeling that the time [is] ripe, mature, prepared. It is a Greek word which, again, witnesses to the richness of the Greek language and the poverty of modern languages in comparison with it. We have only the one word "time." The Greeks had two words: *chronos* (still used in "chronology," "chronometer," etc.): it is clock time, time which is measured. Then there is the word *kairos*, which is not the quantitative time of the watch, but is the qualitative time of the occasion: the "right" time. "It is not yet *kairos*," the hour; the hour has not yet come. (Cf. in the Gospel stories. . . .) There are things in which the right time, the *kairos*, has not yet come. *Kairos* is the time which indicates that something has happened which makes an action possible or impossible. We all have in our lives moments in which we feel that now is the right time for something: now I am mature enough for this, now everything around me is prepared for this, now I can make the decision, etc.: this is *kairos*. In this sense, Paul and the early Church spoke of the "right time," for the coming of the Christ. The early Church, and Paul to a certain extent, tried to show why this time in which the Christ appeared was the right time, why it is the providential constellation of factors which makes His appearance possible.[7]

The distinction between *chronos* and *kairos* can be understood in light of the New Testament distinction between the visible realm (i.e., the physical world or *kosmos*) and the invisible realm (i.e., the heavenly world or *ouranos*).[8] Time operates differently in these two realms. According to the apostle Paul, "the things which are seen are temporal; but the things which are not seen are eternal" (2 Cor 4:18). The visible realm thus operates according to *chronos*, the simple passage of time. But the invisible realm, in which God resides, operates according to *kairos*, the ordering of reality according to divine purposes.

Of the two forms of time, *kairos* is the more basic. *Chronos* is the time of physics, and physics has only been around as long as the cosmos. But *kairos* is God's time, and God has been around forever. The *chronos-kairos* distinction underwrites such scriptural assertions as, "One day is with the Lord as a thousand years, and a thousand years as one day" (2 Pet 3:8). Yet *chronos* and *kairos* are not utterly separate. When the visible and invisible realms intersect, *kairos* becomes evident within *chronos*. The creation of the world and the incarnation of the second person of the Trinity are the preeminent instances of this intersection.

Given that time means different things from an earthly and a heavenly vantage point, Genesis 1–3 confronts us with the problem of reconciling natural history *(chronos)* with the order of creation *(kairos)*. To this problem, young-earth creationism offers a straightforward solution: it equates natural history with the order of creation. This solution is, to be sure, theologically neat. Yet, in our current mental environment, informed as it is by modern astrophysics and geology, the scientific community as a whole regards young-earth creationism as scientifically untenable.

Instead of conflating *chronos* and *kairos*, as young-earth creationism does, I propose to detach them. Covey's distinction between first and second creation (see chapter 14) is illuminating in this regard: God first creates in *kairos* and then implements this first creation as a second creation in *chronos*. Once humanity falls, he acts to restore the second creation. Yet, as unbound by time, God can restore the original creation by acting across time. Thus God responds to the Fall by acting not simply after it, as held by young-earth creationism, but also by acting before it. But how can God act transtemporally in this way? To see how, we turn to a result known as Newcomb's Paradox and explore its implications for divine action.

SEVENTEEN

NEWCOMB'S PARADOX

A T the end of *Miracles*, C. S. Lewis reflects on the reasonableness of praying for things that are past and thus, seemingly, already decided. Lewis believes in efficacious prayer—prayer to which God responds by making a difference in the world. Usually, however, we pray that God will act to affect the future. The question Lewis considers is whether prayers offered retroactively can be efficacious:

> When we are praying about the result, say, of a battle or a medical consultation, the thought will often cross our minds that (if only we knew it) the event is already decided one way or the other. I believe this to be no good reason for ceasing our prayers. The event certainly has been decided—in a sense it was decided "before all worlds." But one of the things taken into account in deciding it, and therefore one of the things that really cause it to happen, may be this very prayer that we are now offering. Thus, shocking as it may sound, I conclude that we can at noon become part of causes of an event occurring at ten a.m.[1]

If Lewis's view that retroactive prayers can be efficacious seems paradoxical, it is because we are time-bound creatures who cannot return to the past to change it. God, who is not time bound, on the other hand, suffers no such limitation. Indeed, it is as easy for God to respond to an event before it has occurred as after. Moreover, in responding before and thus anticipating an event, God can modify its impact. And, of course, God can prevent an event that would otherwise have occurred. It follows that we are not as time-bound as we might think: since prayer gives us access to a trans-temporal God, prayer lifts us out of our temporal existence and enables us to participate in God's transtemporal existence. Einstein's remark that "the distinction between past, present, and future is only a stubbornly persistent illusion"[2] is therefore truer than he may have realized.

Retroactive prayer, if it works, would materially affect the past.[3] But does it work? To see how it might work, we turn to Newcomb's Paradox (it is also called Newcomb's Problem). Newcomb's Paradox analyzes how things that happen in the present could materially affect the past. Physicist William Newcomb devised this paradox in the 1960s.[4] The late Harvard philosopher Robert Nozick then popularized it by applying it to decision theory.[5]

The paradox runs as follows: Imagine two boxes, one black and the other white. The black box always contains $1,000. The white box contains either $1,000,000 or nothing. The contents of neither box are visible. You can choose to take the sum of money in both boxes or the money that's in the white box alone. Suppose an agent with perfect foreknowledge (i.e., with perfect knowledge of future contingent propositions) informs you that $1,000,000 will be put into the white box today *if* you choose only the white box tomorrow but that no money will be put into the white box today if you choose both boxes tomorrow.

Tomorrow rolls around. What do you do? You can adopt either of two strategies: a one-box strategy or a two-box strategy. According to the two-box strategy, whatever money is in the white box has already been placed there. So you may as well choose both boxes. To choose only the white box leaves you necessarily $1,000 poorer. You'll get what's in the white box regardless (hopefully $1,000,000), and you'll be sure to get the $1,000 in the black box.

On the other hand, you can adopt the one-box strategy. In adopting this strategy, you reason as follows: The agent has perfect foreknowledge (let's assume this ability has been verified on numerous occasions). If you choose both boxes, it's guaranteed that the white box will be empty. Therefore, to choose both boxes leaves you necessarily $999,000 poorer. Sure, you'll get the $1,000 in the black box, but you'll miss out on the $1,000,000 that would have been placed in the white box if only you hadn't gotten greedy and decided to go for both boxes.

Newcomb's Paradox was much discussed in the philosophical literature of the 1970s and 80s. One-boxers and two-boxers debated the merits of their preferred decision procedure and divided pretty evenly. The key unresolved issue was what sort of agent could in fact possess knowledge of future contingent propositions. William Lane Craig's article "Divine Foreknowledge and Newcomb's Paradox" appeared in 1987, near the end of intense debate among philosophers over this paradox.[6] There Craig argued that divine foreknowledge does not preclude human freedom: if God foreknows what I shall choose, then I shall not choose otherwise; it doesn't follow, however, that I can't choose otherwise. As Craig put it, "my freely chosen actions . . . supply the truth conditions for the future contingent propositions known by God."[7]

In that paper Craig also detailed how efforts to show that knowledge of future contingent propositions is incoherent had all failed. Of course, this failure of philosophers and theologians to discount such knowledge doesn't prove that it exists or can rightly be ascribed to any agent. Nonetheless, it leaves a door wide open to the classical Christian view of divine foreknowledge, which holds that God possesses comprehensive knowledge of future contingent propositions.[8]

The overwhelming reason that current theological discussions (especially among openness and process theologians) limit divine foreknowledge is to help justify why God should not be faulted for evil. In theodicies of divine limitation, God is absolved from having to remove evils for the simple reason that he is incapable of removing them. But why engage in such theodicies at all? No sound arguments have ever shown that divine foreknowledge is logically inconsistent (i.e., collapses in self-contradiction), and plenty of scriptural evidence supports that God actually possesses such knowledge. To argue against God's ability to know future contingent propositions invariably involves questionable assumptions about how the world, though created by God, might nonetheless impede God's knowledge of the future.[9]

In contrast to theodicies that attempt to justify God's goodness by limiting God, I'm going to argue that full divine foreknowledge of future contingent propositions in fact helps to reconcile God's goodness with the existence of evil. By taking a retroactive approach to the Fall, which traces all evil in the world back to human sin (even the evil that predates human sin), the theodicy I develop preserves the traditional view that natural evil is a consequence of the Fall. To see how the Fall can have such retroactive effects, however, we need to understand the two logics by which creation operates. This is our next topic.

EIGHTEEN

TWO LOGICS OF CREATION

C HRISTIAN theism has traditionally regarded God as omniscient in the sense of possessing perfect knowledge of future contingent propositions and as omnipotent in the sense of being able to act effectively in the world to bring about any result that is not logically impossible. Combined with Newcomb's Paradox, divine omniscience and omnipotence means that God is able to anticipate events and human actions by acting in response before they occur. Thus, when they do occur, God is able to bring good out of them. In fact, it would display a lack of love and care for the world if such an omniscient and omnipotent creator God did not act by anticipating its course.

Embedded as we are in the world's nexus of cause and effect, such anticipatory acts strike us as counterintuitive. Because we are part of the world's causal nexus and limited in our knowledge, all our actions have unanticipated consequences. Thus, our power of anticipation is extremely limited, based not on precise knowledge of the future but on probabilities (which can amount to completely unsubstantiated guesses). As creatures confined to space and time (time here conceived as *chronos*), our activities and those of the rest of physical creation are subject to a *causal-temporal logic* that treats time as linear and sees events as unfolding in tightly linked chains of cause and effect. The totality of these causal chains, the causal nexus of nature, has an integrity that does not permit willy-nilly changes.

Change the causal nexus at one place, and other changes in cause-effect relations will ramify throughout space and time.

For beings like us embedded in the causal nexus of nature, the logic of cause and effect seems inviolable. In contrast, God, as omnipotent and omniscient, transcends the physical world and therefore is not bound by this logic. This is not to say that in acting in the world God violates the causal-temporal logic. To violate it, he would need to be under its jurisdiction. (As C. S. Lewis notes, it is a "false picture of Providence" that "represents God and Nature as being both contained in a common Time."[1]) But as the creator of nature's causal nexus and therefore as the originator of its causal-temporal logic, God can act in ways that transcend this logic. For if this logic restricted divine action, then God would be subject to nature and creation would be other than ex nihilo.

Because God knows the future and can act on this knowledge by anticipating events and directing their course, divine action follows not a causal-temporal logic but an *intentional-semantic logic*. This logic treats time as nonlinear (cf. *kairos*) and sees God as acting in the world to accomplish his purposes in accord with the meaning or significance of events. The causal-temporal logic underlying the physical world and the intentional-semantic logic underlying divine action are not at odds—they neither contradict nor are reducible to each other.[2] Notwithstanding, the intentional-semantic logic is ontologically prior to the causal-temporal logic. God has always existed and acted on the basis of intentions and meanings. The world, by contrast, has a beginning and an end. It operates according to the causal-temporal logic because God, in an intentional act, created it that way. Divine action is therefore a more fundamental mode of causation than physical causation. Intoxicated as it is with nature, our current mental environment resists this conclusion.[3]

The causal-temporal logic and the intentional-semantic logic constitute the two logics of creation. The causal-temporal logic is bottom-up and looks at the world from the vantage of physical causality. The intentional-semantic logic is top-down and looks at the world from the vantage of divine purpose and action. The causal-temporal logic that underlies the physical world is the organizing principle for natural history (*chronos*). The intentional-semantic logic that underlies divine action is the organizing principle for the order of creation (*kairos*).

C. S. Lewis distinguished these logics in terms of "facts" (for the causal-temporal logic) and "meaning" (for the intentional-semantic logic). The problem with materialism, for Lewis, is that it attempts to reduce all of reality to the causal-temporal logic. Anyone who does this is, according to Lewis, like to a dog who

> cannot understand pointing. You point to a bit of food on the
> floor; the dog, instead of looking at the floor, sniffs at your
> finger. A finger is a finger to him, and that is all. His world is
> all fact and no meaning. And in a period when factual realism
> is dominant we shall find people deliberately inducing upon
> themselves this doglike mind. . . . The extreme limit of this self-
> binding [*sic*] is seen in those who, like the rest of us, have con-
> sciousness, yet go about to study the human organism as if they
> did not know it was conscious. As long as this deliberate refusal
> to understand things from above [cf. the intentional-semantic
> logic], even where such understanding is possible, continues, it
> is idle to talk of any final victory over materialism. The critique
> of every experience from below [i.e., in terms of the causal-
> temporal logic], the voluntary ignoring of meaning and concen-
> tration on fact, will always have the same plausibility. There will
> always be evidence, and every month fresh evidence, to show
> that religion is only psychological, justice only self-protection,
> politics only economics, love only lust, and thought itself only
> cerebral biochemistry.[4]

Lewis here underscored the temptation to explain away the top-down causation of the intentional-semantic logic by reducing all causation to the bottom-up causation of the causal-temporal logic. In the metaphysics of evil, this temptation is the most fundamental of all temptations. Rather than find meaning and purpose in creation as put there by the Creator, the temptation here is to invent meaning and purpose on one's own without re- course to the Creator. This is the essence of evil. Interestingly, the etymol- ogy of our English word *evil* captures this essence. Evil, as it traces back to the original Sanskrit, denotes something that wells up from beneath.[5] Evil is the lower asserting itself against the higher and attempting to usurp the rightful place of the higher.

This conception of evil is evident throughout Scripture. Certainly we see it in the New Testament teachings of Jesus where he emphasizes the necessity of subordinating the lower to the higher, the flesh to the spirit, the kingdoms of this world to the kingdom of God. But we see it most clearly in the Old Testament teachings about Satan, notably in Isaiah 14 and Ezekiel 28.[6] Thus in Isaiah we read,

> How art thou fallen from heaven, O Lucifer, son of the morning! how art thou cut down to the ground, which didst weaken the nations! For thou hast said in thine heart, I will ascend into heaven, I will exalt my throne above the stars of God. I will sit also upon the mount of the congregation, in the sides of the north: I will ascend above the heights of the clouds; I will be like the most High. Yet thou shalt be brought down to hell, to the sides of the pit. (Isa 14:12–15)

And in Ezekiel we read,

> Thus saith the Lord GOD: Thou sealest up the sum, full of wisdom, and perfect in beauty. Thou hast been in Eden the garden of God; every precious stone was thy covering, the sardius, topaz, and the diamond, the beryl, the onyx, and the jasper, the sapphire, the emerald, and the carbuncle, and gold: the workmanship of thy tabrets and of thy pipes was prepared in thee in the day that thou wast created. Thou art the anointed cherub that covereth; and I have set thee so: thou wast upon the holy mountain of God; thou hast walked up and down in the midst of the stones of fire. Thou wast perfect in thy ways from the day that thou wast created, till iniquity was found in thee. By the multitude of thy merchandise they have filled the midst of thee with violence, and thou hast sinned: therefore I will cast thee as profane out of the mountain of God: and I will destroy thee, O covering cherub, from the midst of the stones of fire. Thine heart was lifted up because of thy beauty, thou hast corrupted thy wisdom by reason of thy brightness: I will cast thee to the ground, I will lay thee before kings, that they may behold thee. Thou hast defiled thy sanctuaries by the multitude of thine iniquities, by the iniquity of thy traffick; therefore will I bring forth a fire from the midst of

thee, it shall devour thee, and I will bring thee to ashes upon the earth in the sight of all them that behold thee. All they that know thee among the people shall be astonished at thee: thou shalt be a terror, and never shalt thou be any more. (Ezek 28:12–19)

In both Isaiah and Ezekiel, evil displays a clear direction of movement. It starts with a vertical ascent (the lower rises up and attempts to usurp the higher) and ends with a vertical descent (the lower, having exalted self, is cast down precipitously, never to rise again). The evil here is pride. Pride, by definition, is the exaltation of self above rightful authority. Small wonder that Christian theology has traditionally regarded pride as the deadliest of the deadly sins, for it alone among sins denies that God is God. Pride does not merely disobey God. Pride also entertains the grand ambition of replacing God. And why replace God? Because, says Pride (now writ large), it can do a better job than God. This was Eve's sin—she thought she knew better than God what was best for her.

Orthodox theologian Alexander Schmemann saw into the heart of evil when he wrote, "It is not the immorality of the crimes of man that reveal him as a fallen being; it is his 'positive ideal'—religious or secular—and his satisfaction with this ideal."[7] The heart of evil is pride. Pride always comes with a self-righteous agenda. It finds fault and knows better. It is intensely moralistic and becomes indignant as soon as its pretensions are exposed. The tax collectors and prostitutes of Jesus' day had many faults, but pride was not high on the list. They realized their lack of standing before God. As a result, Jesus could offer them hope. Although the tax collectors and prostitutes were widely regarded as the worst sinners in Jewish society, Jesus never condemned them. That distinction he reserved for the Pharisees and Sadducees, who paid lip service to God, but whose real interest lay in glorifying themselves. Their sin, preeminently, was pride.

Today's Pharisees and Sadducees are no longer religious but secular. Bent on controlling our mental environment in the name of science and technology, our secular elite trumpets the bottom-up causation of the causal-temporal logic as the only form of causation that applies to the world, dismissing the top-down causation of the intentional-semantic logic by which God interacts with the world as irrelevant and even superstitious.[8] In the techno-utopia they envision, the living God, who makes a real difference in the real world, need not apply. Theirs is a domesticated

God who does nothing, demands nothing, deserves nothing. As theologian Leslie Zeigler put it:

> This God who tells Moses "I am Who I am," who enters into contingent relationships with human beings at particular times and in particular places, who approves of certain actions and not of others, has always been, to say the least, hard to live with. Human beings have always preferred gods for whom they can write the job descriptions themselves.[9]

The Judeo-Christian tradition is not alone in distinguishing the top-down intentional-semantic logic from the bottom-up causal-temporal logic. Any religion or philosophy that sees end-directedness (i.e., teleology) as a fundamental feature of the world draws this distinction. Take Plato's philosophy. In his dialogue the *Phaedo*, Plato's teacher Socrates argues for the irreducibility of intention to anything other than intention. Thus Socrates contends that it is absurd to reduce the conversation he is having with his friends to "causes such as sound and air and hearing and a thousand others."[10] Yes, these physical causes (following the causal-temporal logic) play a role. But their conversation is not merely these physical causes. In addition, intentions and meanings (following the intentional-semantic logic) give shape to these physical causes.

Platonic philosophy saw a deep connection between the macrocosm (the universe as a whole) and the microcosm (smaller aspects of the universe, especially the human body). Patterns present in the universe as a whole were, for Plato, reflected at smaller scales. Macrocosm and microcosm were thus mutually illuminating. Hence, in Plato's *Philebus*, Socrates notes that both the human body and the universe are composed of the same basic physical elements. Yet Socrates rejects that the "universe is controlled by a power that is irrational and blind, and by mere chance"; instead, he accepts that "it is governed by reason and a wondrous regulating intelligence."[11] But what operates in the macrocosm operates in the microcosm, so reason and intelligence also govern the human body. And just as intentions can mobilize an entire human body, setting bones and sinews (not to mention billions of neurons) to achieve certain ends, so intentions can mobilize the entire universe, coordinating all its various components to achieve its ultimate end. Accordingly, the intentional-semantic logic is the deep structure of the world; the causal-temporal logic is merely the stage on which this deeper logic plays out.

In summary, God has employed both the intentional-semantic and the causal-temporal logic in creating the world. The essence of evil is to assert the all-sufficiency of the causal-temporal logic, allowing it to swallow up the intentional-semantic logic. To understand creation aright, we need to understand how both these logics figure into creation. Specifically, we need to understand how the order of creation (which follows the intentional-semantic logic) relates to natural history (which follows the causal-temporal logic). Young-earth creationism attempts to make natural history match up with the order of creation point for point. By contrast, divine anticipation—the ability of God to act upon events before they happen—suggests that natural history need not match up so precisely with the order of creation and that the two logics of creation can proceed on independent, though complementary, tracks.

NINETEEN

THE INFINITE DIALECTIC

A N omniscient and omnipotent God, by anticipating human actions, can respond in advance to humanity's Fall. To glimpse how
this might work, suppose you knew with certainty that someone would
commit a crime—as in the film *The Minority Report*. You could, as in the
film, restrict the prospective criminal's freedom prior to committing the
crime. The problem with such preemptive restrictions, however, is that
until the crime is committed, the person is literally innocent (i.e., has done
no harm). To preempt by restricting the freedom of the would-be criminal
is therefore to base legal practice on the presumption of guilt rather than
innocence. Moreover, if carried out consistently, this approach, depending
on how many potential criminals are in the society, will require constantly
putting people in restraints to prevent them from committing crimes. This
hardly makes for a joyous and vibrant society.

An alternative approach that avoids these difficulties is to take steps
prior to the crime to ensure that once it is committed, the criminal is
dealt with effectively. With this approach, getting the proper structures
in place *before* the crime is committed (e.g., legal procedures, law en-
forcement, and jail cells) becomes a moral imperative lest the crime
go unredressed. Just what form those anticipatory structures take will
depend on the purposes of those in authority. If, for instance, their aim
were not punishment but rehabilitation, they might take steps to ensure

that the means for rehabilitation were in place before the crime was committed.

How, then, does God act to anticipate the Fall? To answer this question, we need to consider a wrinkle not addressed by Newcomb's Paradox but implicit in the intentional-semantic logic by which God acts in the world. In Newcomb's Paradox, an agent either places or refrains from placing $1,000,000 in a white box depending on what a box chooser is going to do. The agent's very act of placing money inside the box, however, does not in any way affect the box chooser or, for that matter, the rest of the world—until, that is, the boxes are opened. The agent's act of placing the money is therefore causally isolated and does not ramify throughout the world as long as the boxes remain unopened.

The problem with this idealized situation is that, in the real world, there are no causally isolated events. Everything hangs together with everything else.[1] The slightest change in one thing changes everything. Thus, by the luck of a draw, a young Dostoevsky is spared execution and becomes the greatest of Russian novelists. Thus, by a butterfly flapping its wings in Brazil, a hurricane is averted in Miami. Thus, by a chance encounter, two people fall in love, marry, and produce children who would otherwise not have existed.

Sweep the floor and miss a speck of dust. No big deal. At least, that's how we ordinarily think of such cases. But the lesson of chaos theory and nonlinear dynamics is that even the slightest physical changes ramify and eventually change the history of the entire world.[2] We tend to distinguish important from negligible events. With important events, nothing is ever the same again if they happen. With negligible events, nothing would be different if they didn't happen. But this distinction is false. Hitler's birth was an important event. Yet Hitler's conception was determined by countless seemingly insignificant events. Disrupt any of these "negligible" events, and the Hitler of history would never have been.

The causal structure of the world is robust—nature tends to operate in certain settled ways (see chapter 6). But the causal history of the world is extremely fragile. Indeed, the slightest change in any event makes everything different (if not immediately, then soon enough). That's why films like *It's a Wonderful Life*, *Frequency*, and *Timecop* (in decreasing order of excellence), which chart different possible futures but keep too many features of the world constant, make for entertaining fiction but are completely unrealistic. As with such films, Newcomb's Paradox, in its original formulation, does not factor in the fragility of the world's causal history (the $1,000,000 cannot just magically materialize in the white box but must be placed there, and that placement changes the causal history of the world). When we factor in this fragility and then explore what it would mean for God to act by anticipating future events, we come face to face with what I call the *infinite dialectic.*

Think of the infinite dialectic as follows: Suppose God acts to anticipate certain events. So long as divine action is not a hollow concept, God's actions make a difference in the world and therefore induce novel events (all change in the physical world being mediated through events). But this requires that God act to anticipate novel events induced by God's prior actions (priority here conceived not temporally or causally [*chronos*] but in terms of the intentional-semantic logic [*kairos*] by which God orders the creation). Such actions by God now induce still further novel events. And so on. This up and back between divine action and creaturely causation proceeds indefinitely. It constitutes an infinite dialectic. In the infinite dialectic, God does not so much act *in* the world as *across* the world (*across* both space and time).

Because the causal history of the world is extremely fragile, the infinite dialectic is ever in danger of spinning out of control, degenerating into positive feedback loops in which divine anticipation needs to rectify problems provoked by (logically) prior acts of divine anticipation. Consequently, only an infinitely powerful and infinitely wise God can pull off the infinite dialectic. Both wisdom and power are indispensable here. Power is needed because otherwise divine action is but an empty phrase. Yet wisdom must temper power because otherwise power will rip the fabric of creation and overthrow God's ultimate purpose, which is to unite all creation to God through the redemption in Christ (see 1 Cor 15:28).

The infinite dialectic renders divine action at once real-time and eternal. It bridges immanence and transcendence.[3] In the infinite dialectic, God acts on the whole of creation at all times and in all places, acting not as a cause among other causes (God does not moonlight as a physical cause) but as a *cause of causes* (God causes physical causes to fulfill his purposes). As a cause of causes, God's action in the infinite dialectic is not merely ontological, in the sense of giving being to the world (cf. Paul Tillich's "ground of being"). Nor is it merely providential in a general sense, as might be subsumed under the regularities of nature (cf. God maintaining seasonal weather patterns).

In the infinite dialectic, God acts providentially to guide the world in its particulars, taking an active interest in the details of this world and making a difference at all levels of the created order. Good managers know the precise details of the systems they are managing but intervene sparingly, giving the systems as much autonomy as they need to flourish. God is a wise manager, not a micromanager. He has not created the world to be his prosthesis or puppet. At the same time, even though God has granted the world a measure of autonomy, the world's autonomy is not absolute. Just as an orchestra needs the conductor's continual guidance, so too does the world require God's continual guidance. That guidance is neither dispensable nor coercive. It is real and powerful, and it takes the form of an infinite dialectic. Because of the infinite dialectic, Jesus can say that God knows our name, numbers the hairs on our head, and monitors the sparrows that fall to the ground (see John 10:3 and Matt 10:29–30).

TWENTY

A KAIROLOGICAL READING
OF GENESIS 1–3

W E are now in a position to offer a reading of Genesis 1–3 that reconciles a traditional understanding of the Fall (which traces all
evil in the world to human sin) with a mainstream understanding of geology and cosmology (which regards the earth and universe as billions of
years old, and therefore makes natural evil predate humanity). The key to
this reading is to interpret the days of creation as natural divisions in the
intentional-semantic logic of creation. Genesis 1 is therefore not to be interpreted as ordinary chronological time (*chronos*) but rather as time from
the vantage of God's purposes (*kairos*).

Accordingly, the days of creation are neither exact 24-hour days (as in
young-earth creationism) nor epochs in natural history (as in old-earth creationism) nor even a literary device (as in the literary-framework theory).[1]
Rather, they are actual (literal!) episodes in the divine creative activity.
They represent key divisions in the divine order of creation, with one episode building logically on its predecessor. As a consequence, their description as chronological days falls under the common scriptural practice of
employing physical realities to illuminate spiritual truths (cf. John 3:12).
The physical world, as a divine creative act, provides a window into the
life and mind of God, who created it. This is not just, as John Calvin saw it,
God "condescending" to our limited understanding. Yes, our understanding

is limited. But God has precisely ordered the physical world to enlighten our minds about him. Creation elucidates the Creator.

Because the Genesis days represent key kairological divisions in the intentional-semantic logic of creation, a widely cited reason for treating the days of creation as strict 24-hour periods dissolves. Young-earth creationists sometimes insist that the author of Exodus, in listing the Ten Commandments, could only be justified in connecting Sabbath observance to the days of creation if the days of creation were successive 24-hour chronological days (see Exod 20:11, where Sabbath observance is justified in terms of God's creation of the world in six days and then resting on the seventh[2]).

Yet if the days of creation are kairological, referring to basic divisions in the divine order of creation, then Sabbath observance reflects a fundamental truth about the creation of the world. Specifically, since days form a basic division in the way humans experience time, Sabbath observance enables us, who are made in the image of God, to understand the proper place of human work in light of God's work. Creation is not all work. It is also play—the enjoyment of that work once it is finished. Without this sabbatarian perspective, we cannot understand the proper place of work or rest in human life.

From a purely chronological perspective, however, there is nothing particularly fitting or distinctive about God's creating the world in six 24-hour days. God could presumably have created the same world using very different chronologies. For instance, in *The Literal Meaning of Genesis*, Augustine entertains the possibility that God created everything simultaneously.[3] Given a chronological interpretation of the Genesis days, Sabbath observance reflects purely contingent facts about the chronology of creation (a chronology that God could have altered in any number of ways to accomplish the same outcomes and purposes). By contrast, given a kairological interpretation of the Genesis days, Sabbath observance reflects the basic structure of reality. In that case, Sabbath observance underscores fundamental divisions in the divine order of creation.

A kairological interpretation of the six days of creation is unashamedly anthropocentric. Genesis clearly teaches that humans are the end of creation. For instance, Genesis describes the creation as merely "good" before humans are created but describes it as "very good" only after they are created. God's activity in creation is therefore principally concerned with forming a universe that will provide a home for humans. Although this anthropocentrism sits uneasily in the current mental environment, it is not utterly foreign to it. Indeed, the intelligibility of the physical world through our intellects and, in particular, through such intellectual achievements as mathematics suggests that we live in a meaningful world whose meaning was placed there for our benefit.[4]

To entertain anthropocentrism in theological discussions often elicits the charge that we are creating God in our own image. Although there is a danger here, contemporary theological discussions have vastly exaggerated it. Precisely *because* humans are made in the image of God and *because* humans are the end of creation and *because* the second person of the Trinity was incarnated as a human being, our humanity (especially in light of Christology) provides our best window into understanding God. This is not to say that we ever exhaustively comprehend God, but it is to say that knowledge of our humanity provides accurate insight into the Godhead.[5]

A kairological interpretation of the creation days in Genesis now proceeds as follows: On the first day the most basic form of energy is created: light. With all matter and energy ultimately convertible to and from light, day one describes the beginning of physical reality.[6] With the backdrop of physical reality in place, God devotes days two and three to ordering the earth so that it will provide a suitable home for humanity. On these days God confines the earth's water to appropriate locations and forms the plants on which humans and other animals will depend for their sustenance.

On day four God situates the earth in a wider cosmic context. On day five animals that inhabit the sea and sky are created. And finally, on day six animals that inhabit dry land are created, most notably humans. Finally, on day seven, God rests from his activity in creation. Clearly Genesis 1 omits and abbreviates many details of creation. Nor, on this reading, does it specify how the divine purposes of creation were implemented chronologically. Genesis 1 summarizes the order of creation viewed kairologically.

Where is the Fall in this kairological view of creation? To answer this question, we need to recognize that Genesis 1 describes God's *original* plan for creation. The Fall and its consequences, in subverting that plan through human rebellion, elicits no radically new creative activity from God. The Fall represents the entry of evil into the world, and evil is always parasitic, never creative. Indeed, all our words for evil presuppose a good that has been subverted. Impurity presupposes purity, unrighteousness presupposes righteousness, transgression presupposes a boundary that has been "stepped across," deviation presupposes a way (i.e., a *via*) from which we've departed, sin (the Greek *hamartia*) presupposes a target that was missed, etc. To see evil as parasitic is not to deny or trivialize it but rather to see it for what it is. Evil does not create. It only deforms.

God's immediate response to the Fall is therefore not to create anew but to control the damage. (Though note, God's ultimate response to the Fall is, at the Cross, to undo its damage and then, at Christ's Second Coming, to create a new heaven and earth.) In the Fall humans rebelled against God and thereby invited evil into the world. The challenge God faces in controlling the damage resulting from this original sin is to make humans realize the full extent of their sin so that, in the fullness of time, we can fully embrace the redemption in Christ. Only in this way can we experience full release from what Thomas Dubay describes as "the deformed, repulsive, and loathsome pool of human sinfulness: hatreds, cruelties, betrayals, avarice, arrogance, lust, and sundry dishonesties, together with their roots and their offspring."[7]

To make us realize the full extent of human sin, God does not merely allow personal evils (i.e., the disordering of our souls and the sins we commit as a result) to run their course *subsequent to* the Fall. In addition, God allows natural evils (e.g., death, predation, parasitism, disease, drought, floods, famines, earthquakes, and hurricanes) to run their course *prior to* the Fall. Thus, God himself wills the disordering of creation, *making it defective on purpose*. God wills the disordering of creation not merely as a matter of justice (to bring judgment against human sin as required by God's holiness) but, even more significantly, as a matter of redemption (to bring humanity to its senses by making us realize the gravity of sin—see chapter 4).

It's helpful here to recall a classic patristic insight into the nature of God's will. According to the Church Fathers, God's will takes three forms: it can be active, providential, or permissive.[8] To accomplish his active will, God acts directly to bring about a desired state of affairs. The call of Abraham illustrates God's active will (Genesis 12). To accomplish his providential will, God orders the creation and gives it a determinate character so that it consistently displays the patterns and movements for which it was designed. Seasonal weather patterns display God's providential will (Gen 8:22).[9] Finally, to accomplish his permissive will, God lets "agents or circumstances take their course."[10] God permitting Satan to test Job illustrates God's permissive will (Job 1 and 2).

All three forms of God's will seem to be involved in the disordering of creation via natural evil. Genesis 3:17–18 suggests that God actively wills thorns and thistles (which symbolize the material effects of the Fall). Once thorns and thistles are here, however, they perpetuate themselves through natural processes of reproduction. This suggests that God is also providentially willing thorns and thistles. We might say, therefore, that the arrival of thorns and thistles reflects God's active will, their survival reflects his providential will. In addition, nature consequent to the Fall exhibits a nastiness and perversity that seem hard to attribute to the active will of a loving God. Vipers, viruses, and vermin seem more appropriately attributed to God's permissive will, the permission going to Satan. On this view Satan ravages the earth prior to the Fall but is permitted to do so because of his success in tempting the first humans, a temptation that itself required God's permission.

Throughout the rest of this chapter, I refer to "Adam and Eve." As humanity's progenitors, Adam and Eve are usually taken to be a single male-female pair. This clearly is how the Bible portrays them and how creationists of all stripes have historically understood them. The theodicy developed in this book is certainly compatible with a literal Adam and Eve. But it does not require a literal Adam and Eve. What it does require is that a group of hominids, however many, had their loyalty to God fairly tested (fairness requiring a segregated area that gives no evidence of natural evil—the Garden); moreover, on taking the test, they all failed. Notwithstanding, many evolutionists now accept that modern humans trace their ancestry back to a single male-female pair.[11]

Would God be unjust to bring natural evil on the whole created order in response to the sin of Adam and Eve? Denis Alexander, who heads the Faraday Institute for Science and Religion, thinks so:

> If the suffering of animals really started with the human Fall,
> then God would remain morally responsible for linking the two
> things. Why, for example, should deep sea fish begin to suffer as

a result of a human sin far away and on land? In a sense it would be less of a problem if animal suffering were linked to a whole system of creation designed to eventually lead to a new principle of morality [for Alexander, this is evolution], than if animal suffering were arbitrarily linked in this way to human action.[12]

Many contemporary theologians, following Alexander, shift responsibility for natural evil to limitations inherent in a natural evolutionary process. Evolution, as they see it, confers benefits (by bringing about free moral agents, like us) but also incurs unavoidable costs (notably, by allowing natural evil). In their approach the sin of Adam and Eve does not spill over to nature as a whole but is confined to the human race.

By contrast, I submit that the link between human sin and natural evil is far from arbitrary. In the approach I am advocating, God is fully justified in linking the two. The broad principle that justifies linking human sin and natural evil is humanity's covenant headship in creation. Humans are the priests of creation, offering a world given by God back to God. God, having placed humanity in this position, holds creation accountable for what its covenant head does. God's dealings with creation therefore parallel his dealings with humanity. If God's relation with the covenant head goes awry, so does his relation with all that the covenant head represents (in this case, the world).

Scripture supports the view that God deliberately makes Adam and Eve's sin the basis for natural evil. Consider the apostle Paul's teaching on God's subjection of creation to "futility" and creation's eventual release from "the bondage of corruption":

> For the creation was subjected to futility—not willingly, but
> because of Him who subjected it—in the hope that the creation
> itself will also be set free from the bondage of corruption into the
> glorious freedom of God's children. For we know that the whole
> creation has been groaning together with labor pains until now.
> (Rom 8:20–22 HCSB)

The Church Fathers overwhelmingly interpreted this passage as describing the impact that human sin had on creation, with humanity's headship in creation as the reason for natural evil. Thus John Chrysostom, in commenting on this passage in his *Homilies on Romans*, wrote: "Paul means by this that the creation became corruptible. Why and for what reason? Because of you, O man! For because you have a body which has become mortal and subject to suffering, the earth too has received a curse and has brought forth thorns and thistles."[13]

Rather than question God's justice for bringing about natural evil in response to human sin, I would turn the question around: Wouldn't God be unjust if he didn't subject the world to natural evil so that it reflects the evil in human hearts? Sin has ignited a raging fire in our hearts. God uses natural evil to fight fire with fire, setting a comparatively smaller fire (natural evil) to control a much larger fire (personal evil). Modern firefighters do, in fact, light smaller fires to contain larger fires:

> A *backfire* or *back burn* is a fire which is set deliberately in the path of an oncoming fire. As the backfire burns, it consumes fuel, thereby depriving the primary fire of tinder when it reaches the site of the backfire. When the technique is executed correctly, it stops a wildfire in its tracks, or confines it, making it much easier to control. . . . When the decision to set a backfire is placed, it is an acknowledgment that the primary fire is getting out of control, and that it needs to be arrested before it becomes significantly larger. Setting backfires requires some consideration and calculation. The fire must be far away enough from the primary fire that it creates a dead zone of consumed tinder, rather than merely adding to the larger fire. It must also be optimally positioned, which requires thinking about [i.e., anticipating] the movement of the fire through the course of several hours.[14]

God's response to the "big fire" of the Fall is like the anticipatory action of firefighters in setting backfires.[15]

What's the alternative to fighting fire with fire? The Swedish government at one time proposed placing criminals on a cruise ship, arguing that it would teach them community values.[16] (No doubt, it was also cheaper to send them on a cruise than to house them in prison.) Imagine that God followed the Swedish government's example: Would housing fallen humans who have rebelled against their maker on a cosmic cruise ship be doing us any favors? If the aim is rehabilitation and if rehabilitation demands understanding the truth about our deeds and attitudes, then a world that includes natural evil seems necessary. As it is, sending criminals on cruises did not catch on in Sweden—public outcry scuttled the proposal.[17] It would appear that God also scuttled the proposal to keep the world on a cosmic cruise ship—Adam and Eve were, after all, forced to leave Paradise, a cosmic cruise ship if ever there was one.

Leaving a cosmic cruise ship is one thing. Entering a sanitized prison is a step down but perhaps still tolerable. Plunging into a world of natural evils that are downright perverse, however, is another matter. Darwin saw such perverseness throughout the animal world. In an 1860 letter to Asa Gray, Darwin wrote, "I cannot persuade myself that a beneficent and omnipotent God would have designedly created the Ichneumonidae [certain parasitic wasps] with the express intention of their feeding within the living bodies of Caterpillars."[18]

Biologists have since discovered even nastier critters. I leave to the reader to study the emerald cockroach wasp (which stings the brain of a cockroach twice, first turning it into a zombie and then into a vegetable) and the toothpick fish, or candirú, of the Amazon (which can swim up a urethra and, short of surgery or castration, be impossible to dislodge). Or take the microsyringe known as the type-three secretory system that occurs in certain bacteria. In *Yersinia pestis*, the bubonic plague bacterium, this microsyringe served as a poison delivery system that killed a third of the population of Europe in the fourteenth century. Or, finally, take the rabies virus, which looks like a bullet and seems perfectly designed to implode a mammalian nervous system.

Did God, in making the creation defective on purpose, specifically design such features into the natural world? Did God, for instance, actively toggle the genes needed for the type-three secretory system to induce the bubonic plague? Or did God merely permit evils like these systems to form? One possibility worth exploring is to what extent such instances of perverseness in nature can be explained as the subversion (by Satan? by evolution?) of an originally good design. For instance, the type-three secretory system seems to have devolved from a motor-driven propeller known as the bacterial flagellum, which moves bacteria through their watery environment. Unlike the type-three secretory system, whose object is to deliver poison, the bacterial flagellum seems harmless enough.[19]

Explaining the "evil" type-three secretory system in terms of the "good" bacterial flagellum has a certain plausibility. Unfortunately, it does not suggest a general strategy for explaining natural evil as the subversion of an original good. We don't seem able consistently to identify the original good behind a present evil. Indeed, doing so is the exception rather than the rule. Yes, drugs meant to alleviate pain may become sources of addiction, and knives meant to cut bread may be used to injure people, but some things are simply bad from the start—for example, a torture chamber. And even if a bad thing can be traced to an initially good thing, ingenuity is often required to subvert a good thing into a bad thing.

The worry now arises whether the "genius" who subverts an original good into a natural evil is God. Theological determinists, who think that every detail of the world is planned and executed by God, counter this worry by simply admitting that any such subversion of an original good must be God's doing. Theistic evolutionists, by contrast, attempt to meet this worry by ascribing any perverseness in nature to evolution. Similarly, C. S. Lewis attempted to meet this worry by ascribing any perverseness in nature to Satan. Theistic evolutionists and C. S. Lewis are here invoking God's permissive will to diminish divine responsibility for natural evil.

Even so, invoking God's permissive will can never fully eliminate divine responsibility for natural evil (at least not if one's conception of God is classical and thus includes omnipotence as one of his attributes). As philosopher John Lucas notes, "No theist would want to deny that God is omnipotent, and that he could intervene to prevent any particular event's occurring, and therefore his non-intervention is a necessary condition for each event."[20] It is painful to accept that God bears at least some responsibility for natural evil and that he brings it about (whether actively or by permission) in response to human sin. But acceptance of this bitter pill includes the promise of redemption. God brings about natural evil not to be gratuitously nasty but to free us from the more insidious evil in our hearts. Alternative approaches to natural evil that divorce it from human sin are worse than a bitter pill and constitute theological suicide, distorting the Christian doctrines of both creation and redemption.

To sum up, a kairological reading of Genesis preserves the young-earth creationist emphasis on tracing all evil in the world to human sin: God creates a perfect world, God places humans in that world, they sin, and the world goes haywire. Yet this reading, unlike young-earth creationism's reading of Genesis, must do more than merely connect the world's going haywire to human sin. It must also account for how the world could go haywire *before* human sin. The challenge, therefore, is to make sense of the Fall chronologically. Humans do not merely exist kairologically in the divine mind. They also exist chronologically in space and time, and the Fall occurred in space and time.

To understand how the Fall occurs chronologically and how God nonetheless allows natural evils to rage before it, we need to take seriously that the drama of the Fall unfolds in a *segregated area*. Genesis 2:8 refers to this area as a garden planted by God (i.e., the Garden of Eden). Now, ask yourself why God would need to plant a garden in a perfect world untouched by natural evil. In a perfect world, wouldn't the whole world be a garden? And why, once humans sin, must they be expelled from this garden and live outside it, where natural evil is present?

Proponents of the Documentary Hypothesis for the Pentateuch (often called "JEDP," referring to the four purported source documents) describe the juxtaposition of Gen 1:1–2:3 and Gen 2:4–3:24 as a kludge of two disparate and irreconcilable creation stories circulating among the ancient Hebrews (the days of creation vs. humanity's creation and fall in the Garden).[21] But in fact, the second creation account, depicting the Garden, is just what's needed for *kairos* and *chronos* to converge in the Fall. It constitutes the "second creation" in the sense of chapter 14 of this book.

If we accept that God acts to anticipate the Fall, then, in the chronology leading up to the Fall, the world has already experienced the consequences of human sin in the form of natural evil. This seems to raise a difficulty, however, because humans who have yet to sin come into a world where natural evil is already raging. Starting their material existence in such a world puts them at a disadvantage, tempting and opposing them with evils for which they are not (yet) responsible. The Garden of Eden, as a segregated area in which the effects of natural evil are not evident (one might think of it as a tropical paradise), provides the way out of this difficulty.

The essential point of the Fall is not the precise physical backdrop against which Adam and Eve play out their drama in the Garden but rather their phenomenological experience (i.e., how it feels to them from the inside) of willfully turning against God. To understand this, think of the movie *The Matrix*. People inside the Matrix are fed experiences.[22] The experiences are not real, but they feel real. And because they feel real, actions taken within the Matrix can be as morally significant as those taken outside of it.[23] Thus, when Cypher betrays Morpheus, it's by plugging himself into the Matrix and meeting with the nefarious agents of the Matrix in that virtual environment. Now, I'm not saying that Adam and Eve were plugged into a matrix when they fell (though that's an interesting possibility). What I am saying is that even in a world ravaged by natural evil, God could create an island of sanity—the Garden of Eden—in which natural evil was not felt and thus Adam and Eve's love for God could be fairly tested (i.e., the test could occur without any evident natural evil and thus without any excuse to question God's love).

Another way to think about the Garden of Eden uses the hardware-software distinction from computer science. Different computer hardware (cf. different possible physical backdrops for creation) can run the same software (cf. the phenomenological experience of willfully turning against God). Perhaps one piece of hardware is state-of-the-art whereas the other is old and unreliable. Nonetheless, for a given software application, they may both run equally well, performing the required operations accurately. The same software running on different hardware is an instance of multiple realizability considered in chapter 11—the same information gets expressed in different media. Likewise, different physical backdrops could "run" the same drama of Adam and Eve in the Garden.

This computer analogy now applies to the Fall as follows: Imagine a perfect creation that has a segregated area in which Adam and Eve turn willfully against God and for which everything, both inside and outside that area, is perfect prior to the Fall (cf. the state-of-the-art computer). Alternatively, imagine an imperfect creation that has a segregated area in which Adam and Eve have exactly the same phenomenological experience of turning willfully against God as in the perfect creation, but for which only this segregated area is perfect—the perfection in this case being strictly in the phenomenological sense of no evil overtly tempting or opposing Adam and Eve (cf. the old unreliable computer that nonetheless can perform at least one software application well).

[152]

In the Garden of Eden, Adam and Eve simultaneously inhabit two worlds. Two worlds intersect in the Garden. In the one world, the world God originally intended, the Garden is part of a larger world that is perfect and includes no natural evils. In the other world, the world that became corrupt through natural evils that God brought about in anticipation of the Fall, the Garden is a safe haven that in the conscious experience of Adam and Eve (i.e., phenomenologically) matches up exactly with their conscious experience in the perfect world, the one that God originally intended.[24]

This duality, in which the Garden of Eden simultaneously touches heaven and earth, is mirrored in myth and legend. Eldorado, Shangri-La, and the Fountain of Youth all capture this quality of the terrestrial but not merely the terrestrial. Clearly, the Judeo-Christian religious tradition captures this intersection of heaven and earth in its vision of Paradise, which traditionally is identified both with the Garden of Eden and with heaven (as when Jesus remarks to the thief on the Cross that, upon their deaths, they shall meet in Paradise—Luke 23:43). The Islamic view of Adam and Eve in the Garden presents an interesting twist: it teaches that the Garden of Eden was actually in heaven but that Adam and Eve were cast down to earth when they fell.[25]

In the Garden of Eden, the originally intended perfect world borders the Fall-corrupted imperfect world. In the originally intended world, there are no pathogenic microbes and, correspondingly, there is no need for Adam and Eve to have an immune system that wards off these microbes. In the imperfect world, whose imperfection results from God's acting to anticipate the Fall, both pathogenic microbes and human immune systems exist. Yet, in their Garden experience, Adam and Eve never become conscious of that difference. Only after they sin and are ejected from the Garden do they become conscious of the difference. Only then do they glimpse the world they might have inhabited but lost, a world symbolized by the Tree of Life. Only then do they realize the tragedy they now face by being cast into a world full of natural evil and devoid of a tree that could grant them immortality.

Why doesn't God grant Adam and Eve immortality despite the Fall? The ancient myth of Tithonus and Eos provides an answer. Eos (Latin Aurora), the goddess of dawn, marries Tithonus, who is human and mortal. She asks Zeus to make Tithonus immortal but forgets to ask that Zeus

[153]

also grant him eternal youth. As a consequence, Tithonus grows older and older, and ultimately becomes completely decrepit. The lesson is that immortality reinforces corruption. When God imposes mortality on humans by ejecting them from a Garden that contains their only known source of immortality (i.e., the Tree of Life), he limits human corruption. Moreover, in the protoevangelium (Gen 3:15, where God foretells that the woman's seed [Jesus] will come and destroy the serpent), God promises a way out of that corruption. Yes, death is the last enemy to be destroyed (1 Cor 15:26). But given our corruption through sin, death also becomes a grace and benefit as we await the final redemption in Jesus Christ.[26]

A question remains: How did the first humans gain entry to the Garden? Physician Paul Brand provides an interesting angle on this question. Genesis 2:7 reads, "And the LORD God formed man of the dust of the ground and breathed into his nostrils the breath of life; and man became a living soul." In reflecting on this passage, Brand writes,

> When I heard that verse as a child, I imagined Adam lying on the ground, perfectly formed but not yet alive, with God leaning over him and performing a sort of mouth-to-mouth resuscitation. Now I picture that scene differently. I assume that Adam was already biologically alive—the other animals needed no special puff of oxygen, nitrogen, and carbon dioxide to start them breathing, so why should man? The breath of God now symbolizes for me a spiritual reality. I see Adam as alive, but possessing only an animal vitality. Then God breathes into him a new spirit, and infills him with His own image. Adam becomes a living soul, not just a living body. God's image is not an arrangement of skin cells or a physical shape, but rather an inbreathed spirit.[27]

Regardless of how we explain human origins (whether through special creation or through an evolutionary process), the reading of Genesis 1–3 that I'm proposing here requires that whatever makes humans distinctly human (thereby separating them from the rest of the animals and infilling them with God's image) must happen at the precise point when they enter the Garden. For if the world outside the Garden of Eden exhibits the effects of the Fall (which, chronologically speaking, has yet to happen), then as fully God-conscious humans, they would be experiencing the punishing effects of the Fall while they were still, literally, innocent. And this eventuality is precisely what the theodicy developed here attempts to forestall.

Any evils humans experience outside the Garden before God breathes into them the breath of life would be experienced as natural evils in the same way that other animals experience them. The pain would be real, but it would not be experienced as divine justice in response to willful rebellion. Moreover, once God breathes the breath of life into them, we may assume that the first humans experienced an amnesia of their former animal life: Operating on a higher plane of consciousness once infused with the breath of life, they would transcend the lower plane of animal consciousness on which they had previously operated—though, after the Fall, they might be tempted to resort to that lower consciousness.

The constant opposition between flesh and spirit in Jesus' and Paul's teaching mirrors this duality in the creation of humans. Our entire moral life mirrors this duality as well, constantly impressing on us that "what is" (the world outside the Garden) doesn't match up with "what should be" (the Garden). Animal life is exclusively concerned with "what is"; human life, made in the divine image, is additionally concerned with "what should be."[28] According to Paul Brand, humans are initially created as animals but then further created to be much more than animals. Humans therefore enter the Garden created in God's image; they leave the Garden still in God's image but now also as sinners in need of redemption.

PART V

LOOSE ENDS

TWENTY-ONE

WHAT ABOUT EVOLUTION?

W HAT were humans doing before they received the divine image and entered the Garden of Eden? Creationists and theistic evolutionists answer this question differently. For creationists (whether young-earth or old-earth), humans bearing the divine image were created from scratch in the Garden of Eden. On this view, hominids with fully human bodies but lacking the divine image never existed. For theistic evolutionists, by contrast, primate ancestors evolved over several million years into hominids with fully human bodies. What happened next? In the theodicy I am proposing, these hominids initially lacked the cognitive and moral capacities required to bear the image of God.[1] Then, at the moment they entered the Garden, they received God's image and became fully human.

Which of these options, the creationist or the evolutionist, is preferable? It's not my purpose here to argue for the superiority of one over the other.[2] My concern, rather, is to show what form evolution must take if the theodicy developed in this book is to apply. Also, I want to show why the evolutionist option does not make the task of theodicy any easier than the creationist option. Theistic evolutionists tend to argue that the creationist option makes the task of theodicy impossible and that Christian theism, properly conceived, in fact requires evolution. Denis Alexander, for instance, goes so far as to speculate whether biological evolution "really *is* the only way in which truly free humans can be formed and fashioned in such a way that they can respond freely to God's love and know him forever."[3] Creationists, who historically have regarded evolution as a hindrance to Christian faith, find promoting evolution to aid orthodoxy ironic. In any case, I'm going to argue that when it comes to theodicy, evolution has no advantage over good old-fashioned special creation.

For the theodicy I am proposing to be compatible with evolution, God must not merely introduce existing human-like beings from outside the Garden. In addition, when they enter the Garden, God must transform their consciousness so that they become rational moral agents made in God's image. On the assumption that humans evolved, this transformation of human consciousness by God when they enter the Garden is essential to the kairological reading of Genesis outlined in the previous chapter. For if the first humans bore the full image and likeness of God outside the Garden prior to the Fall, they would have been exposed to the natural evils present there—evils for which they were *not yet* responsible. This would be problematic since humanity's responsibility and culpability in the Fall depends on the Fall occurring without undue temptations or pressures. These temptations and pressures are absent from the Garden but not from the environment outside it.

Is such a transformation of consciousness compatible with biological evolution as it is understood by the scientific world? Yes and no. Evolutionary geneticist Jerry Coyne defines biological evolution as follows:

> There is only one going theory of evolution, and it is this: organisms evolved gradually over time and split into different species, and the main engine of evolutionary change was natural selection. Sure, some details of these processes are unsettled, but there is no argument among biologists about the main claims.[4]

This is the standard definition of biological evolution—it is textbook orthodoxy. According to it, biological evolution rests on two pillars: *common descent*, the historical claim that all organisms trace their lineage back to a common ancestor; and the *Darwinian mechanism*, the theoretical claim that natural selection acting on random variations accounts for biological diversification.

Nothing about biological evolution, as characterized by Coyne, prevents God from endowing hominids with the cognitive and moral capacities required to bear the image of God. Nor does this transformation of consciousness necessarily require a miracle in the traditional sense. For instance, the image of God might be an emergent property of human brains that attain a certain level of complexity. This assumes a monism in which the human is viewed as essentially material (though also as a creature of God).[5] Alternatively, a dualism in which the human is viewed as essentially a union of matter and spirit is also compatible with Coyne's characterization of biological evolution.[6] In this case, spirit would be added to the human body to impress on it the image of God. Nancey Murphy is a proponent of the monistic view;[7] Francis Collins is a proponent of the dualistic view.[8] Each confidently affirms both evolution and Christian faith.

Coyne's textbook definition of biological evolution gives God plenty of room to maneuver in endowing humans with the divine image. Nonetheless, many evolutionists resist any fundamental discontinuity between the consciousness of humans and the consciousness of our putative primate ancestors. Charles Darwin himself rejected a fundamental divide between human cognitive and moral capacities and those of the rest of the animal world. In *The Descent of Man*, he wrote,

> The difference in mind between man and the higher animals,
> great as it is, certainly is one of degree and not of kind. We have
> seen that the senses and intuitions, the various emotions and
> faculties, such as love, memory, attention, curiosity, imitation,
> reason, etc., of which man boasts, may be found in an incipient,
> or even sometimes in a well-developed condition, in the lower
> animals.[9]

Some theistic evolutionists agree with Darwin that humans are in every way continuous with the rest of the animal world. For instance, Karl Giberson writes,

> Once we accept the full evolutionary picture of human origins,
> we face the problem of human uniqueness. The picture of natural
> history disclosed by modern science reveals human beings evolv-
> ing slowly and imperceptibly from earlier, simpler creatures.
> None of our attributes—intelligence, upright posture, moral
> sense, opposable thumbs, language capacity—emerged suddenly.
> Every one of our remarkable capacities must have appeared

gradually and been present in some partial, anticipatory way in our primate ancestors. This provocatively suggests that animals, especially the higher primates, ought to possess an identifiable moral sense that is only *quantitatively* different from that of humans. Not surprisingly, current research supports this notion.[10]

Unfortunately, scientific research can be suitably slanted to support just about anything. Giberson goes on to make a case against human uniqueness based on primate research. In *The Design of Life*, Jonathan Wells and I make a case for human uniqueness based on linguistics, mathematics, and cognitive psychology.[11] Let the reader decide who has the better argument.[12] The theodicy I am proposing gladly acknowledges that important similarities exist between humans and primates. But it insists that far-reaching differences also exist, especially differences in cognitive and moral capacities, and that these represent a difference in kind and not, as Darwin and many contemporary evolutionists hold, merely a difference in degree.[13]

Giberson's hard-core Darwinism leads him to reject the theodicy I am proposing, even when this theodicy is adapted to evolution:

Clearly, the historicity of Adam and Eve and their fall from grace are hard to reconcile with natural history. The geological and fossil records make this case compellingly. Nevertheless, scholars have proposed many convoluted and implausible ways to resolve these tensions in the past couple centuries. One could believe, for example, that at some point in evolutionary history God "chose" two people from a group of evolving "humans," gave them his image, and then put them in Eden, which they promptly corrupted by sinning. But this solution is unsatisfactory, artificial, and certainly not what the writer of Genesis intended.[14]

But if our concern is with what the writer of Genesis intended, then we probably shouldn't be trying to graft a theory of evolution onto it. When the writer of Gen 1:21 and 1:25 stated that organisms were created "after their kind," it's hard to imagine that he intended the fluidity of all species as required by evolution. Nonetheless, as soon as one decides to read Genesis from an evolutionary perspective, I would argue that the theodicy proposed in this book becomes both satisfactory and natural—provided, that is, one is serious about preserving the Fall.

Giberson, unfortunately, is not serious about preserving the Fall. The very passage just quoted, where he rejects theodicies such as mine, occurs in a section titled "Dissolving the Fall." Giberson rejects any traditional conception of the Fall.[15] Indeed, his understanding of sin is simplistic and heterodox. He sees the essence of sin as selfishness. And coincidentally, "selfishness," for Giberson, "drives the evolutionary process."[16] Simply put, we are selfish because evolution is selfish, and we are a product of evolution. Salvation for him, then, is transcending our evolutionary past. By contrast, in the theodicy I am proposing, our evolutionary past would itself be a consequence of sin (i.e., evolution would be a retroactive effect of the Fall). In this theodicy, we are saved not from what evolution has produced in us but from what we have done to ourselves in willfully sinning against a holy God.

I want next to turn to the charge made by some theistic evolutionists that Christian theism requires God to create indirectly by evolution rather than directly by intervention (as in special creation). Theistic evolutionists worry that a God who creates by direct intervention renders the problem of evil insoluble. Such a God would be responsible for all the botched and malevolent designs we find in nature. By letting Darwinian natural selection serve as a designer substitute, theistic evolutionists can refer all those botched and malevolent designs to evolution. This, in their view, is supposed to resolve the problem of natural evil and thereby help validate Christian theism.[17]

Well-known evolutionist and former Catholic priest Francisco Ayala makes precisely such an argument: "A major burden was removed from the shoulders of believers when convincing evidence was advanced that the design of organisms need not be attributed to the immediate agency of the Creator, but rather is an outcome of natural processes." According to Ayala, "if we claim that organisms and their parts have been specifically designed by God, we have to account for the incompetent design of the human jaw, the narrowness of the birth canal, and our poorly designed backbone, less than fittingly suited for walking upright."

In Ayala's view, right-thinking Christians need to "acknowledge Darwin's revolution and accept natural selection as the process that accounts for the design of organisms, as well as for the dysfunctions, oddities, cruelties, and sadism that pervade the world of life. Attributing these to specific agency by the Creator amounts to blasphemy." Charging Christian opponents of evolution with blasphemy may seem unduly harsh. Ayala therefore attempts to soften this charge by granting that those who oppose evolution and support special creation "are surely well-meaning people who do not intend such blasphemy." Ayala's concession (and condescension) here is to the intellectual feebleness, as he sees it, of those who cling to the old naive creationist outlook and have yet to wrap their minds around the stark truth of evolution. In any case, he doesn't retract the charge of blasphemy: "this is how matters appear to a biologist concerned that God not be slandered with the imputation of incompetent design."[18]

In turning the table on special creation, Ayala has in fact turned it 360 degrees. The table is therefore back to where it was before, and the problem he meant to shift to special creation confronts him still. Ayala worries that a God who creates by direct intervention must be held accountable for all the bad designs in the world. Ayala's proposed solution is therefore to have God set up a world in which evolution (by natural selection) brings about bad designs. But how does this address the underlying difficulty, which is that a creator God has set up the conditions under which bad designs emerge? In the one case, God acts directly; in the other, indirectly. But a creator God, as the source of all being, is as responsible in the one case as in the other.

We never accept such shifting of responsibility in any other important matter, so why here? What difference does it make if a mugger brutalizes someone with his own hands (i.e., uses direct means) or employs a vicious dog on a leash (i.e., uses indirect means) to do the same? The mugger is equally responsible in both cases. The same holds for a creator God who creates directly by intervening or indirectly by evolution. Creation entails responsibility. The buck always stops with the Creator. That's why so much of contemporary theology has a problem not just with God intervening in nature but also with the traditional doctrine of creation ex nihilo, which makes God the source of nature.

The rage in theology these days is to diminish the power and ultimacy of God so that God is fundamentally constrained by the world and thus cannot be held responsible for the world's evil (recall chapter 3). Process theology, which sees God as evolving with the world and the world as having an autonomy beyond God's reach (thereby enabling God to shed responsibility for evil), is a case in point. As process theologian Robert Mesle elaborates,

> since God cannot control the evolutionary process, there is no reason even to assume that God was aiming that process specifically at us. The history of evolution has been filled with more crucial events than we can dream of, and God could not control them. God and the world have been involved in a continuous dance in which God must continually take the decisions of the creatures and work with them—whatever they may be. For better or worse, each decision of each creature plays some role in the world's process of becoming. And God works to create something good out of what the world makes possible. Evolution, then, is an ongoing adventure for God, as it is for the world.[19]

In my view, process theology unleashes a raging pack of new problems and thus is not a suitable replacement for the traditional doctrines of God and creation. But let's grant, for the sake of argument, that it resolves the problem of dysteleology (bad designs) resulting from natural selection. The problem is that Ayala and fellow theistic evolutionists are not arguing for process theology (or some other diminished deity) but for the compatibility of evolution with classical Christian theism. We are told, "Embrace evolution and you can still be a good Christian."[20]

Ayala is therefore in no position to require that Christian believers revise their doctrine of God in light of evolution. In particular, he cannot require that believers in divine omnipotence and creation *ex nihilo* revise these beliefs to suit a more evolution-friendly theology. Christians who hold to a traditional doctrine of creation and accept natural selection as God's method of creating organisms therefore confront the problem of evil with the same force as believers who hold the identical doctrine of God but reject natural selection and accept special creation. Indeed, for the Christian it does nothing to resolve the problem of evil by passing the buck to a naturalistic evolutionary process (a process, in that case, created by God). A theodicy that passes the buck in this way is inadequate and simplistic. It fills one hole by digging another.

Although many theistic evolutionists see evolution as assisting in the task of theodicy, many agnostic and atheistic evolutionists see it as under-cutting that task. What sort of God, they ask, would create life by so brutal and wasteful a process as evolution? Darwin himself continually referred to evolution as "the great battle of life" and "the war of nature."[21] He elaborated: "From the war of nature, from famine and death, the most exalted object which we are capable of conceiving, namely, the production of the higher animals, directly follows."[22] The struggle for life is absolutely central to evolution. Herein lies evolution's creative potential.

Darwin's most famous work is his *Origin of Species*, often simply called the *Origin*. Few remember the full title: *On the Origin of Species by Means of Natural Selection or the Preservation of Favoured Races in the Struggle for Life*. Favored races? Doesn't that mean superior races? And don't superior races imply inferior races? Within evolutionary theory, it is the destiny of inferior races to be rooted out and destroyed. Thus, in *The Descent of Man*, the sequel to the *Origin*, Darwin noted,

> At some future period, not very distant as measured by centuries, the civilised races of man will almost certainly exterminate, and replace, the savage races throughout the world. . . . The break between man and his nearest allies will then be wider, for it will intervene between man in a more civilised state, as we may hope, even than the Caucasian, and some ape as low as a baboon, instead of as now between the negro or Australian and the gorilla.[23]

Just so there is no doubt, Darwin saw, as a consequence of his theory, that whites (whom he regarded as "superior") would exterminate blacks (whom he regarded as "inferior").

To soften evolution's harshness, Denis Alexander asks us to imagine that God, when creating by evolution, is a "great artist in the studio, with energy, creativity and paint flying in all directions, out of which process emerges the richness and diversity of the created order."[24] It hardly follows from this analogy to an artist's studio that creativity must, as a matter of course, be messy and wasteful. Having at one point in my career been an art dealer (the family business consisted in buying and selling oil paintings), I can testify that the studios of artists can be reasonably neat and that neatness seems not to have impaired their creativity. Nor does history bear out that great artists have tended to be slobs. Even so, it's not clear what waste or mess would mean to an omnipotent God of unlimited resources. Let's therefore grant, for the sake of argument, that Alexander is correct in not faulting God for any presumed waste or mess in the evolutionary process.

The charge that evolution is inherently cruel now poses a more difficult problem for reconciling theism and evolution. Some evolutionists have tried to soft-pedal the cruelty inherent in evolution by suggesting that cooperation plays as important a role in it as competition.[25] But cooperation, far from eliminating or mitigating evolution's cruelty, is merely an outgrowth of it. That's because organisms tend to cooperate when other organisms are competing against and trying to destroy them—in other words, they cooperate when a competitor is being cruel to them. Cruelty from an out-group is, we might say, evolution's way of making us nice to our in-group.[26]

The preferred way that theistic evolutionists deal with nature's cruelty, however, is denial and rationalization. Sure, natural selection involves pain; but, as Darwin stressed, the pain is worth it: "As natural selection works solely by and for the good of each being, all corporeal and mental endowments will tend to progress towards perfection."[27] Thus Darwin sanctified evolution and deified natural selection. It's just too bad that natural history had to be littered with casualties "from the war of nature, from famine and death."[28] But to make an omelet, you have to break a few eggs, and evolution certainly knows how to break eggs.

Besides rationalization, there's denial. Thus we are told that cruelty is not really cruel unless conscious moral agents (like us) are suffering it: "Whilst cruel rats and malevolent weasels might exercise such wicked designs in the pages of children's books," writes Denis Alexander, "to the best of our knowledge the real animal world is amoral and has no ethics."[29] But Alexander here fails to distinguish between cruelty as a conscious motivation (which is culpable in us but lacking in other animals) and cruelty as it is experienced by us (such cruelty comes against us as much from nature as from the malevolent intentions of fellow humans). The fossil record— as a history of predation, parasitism, disease, death, and extinction—is seen by us as cruel even if the animals in it cannot properly be said to have cruel motivations. In any case, ask yourself which requires rationalization: affirming nature's cruelty or denying it. Clearly, denying it.[30]

Does evolution therefore undermine the theodicy I am proposing? Not at all. Although I personally think that the scientific evidence supports only limited forms of evolutionary change, evolution in the grand sense ("monad to man") would simply underscore natural evil in the world and thus constitute a further way that God makes the world reflect the corruption in the human heart as a consequence of the Fall. On this view evolution is not so much a method of creation (though it can be that also) as a method of judgment by which God impresses on the world the radical consequences of human sin. In Genesis 1 and 2, God gives humanity a perfect world. In Genesis 3, God removes humanity to a less than perfect world. A world dominated by evolution is certainly less than perfect but may perfectly reflect the imperfection of human hearts as a consequence of the Fall.[31]

TWENTY-TWO

BEYOND GENESIS 1–3

22.1 Christology

Genesis 1–3 fits within a wider biblical context. I want in this chapter to address several exegetical and theological concerns that my kairological reading of Genesis 1–3 is likely to raise. Let's begin with Christology, the theological study of Christ and his work. Though not a big fan of neo-orthodoxy, I take seriously Karl Barth's injunction that the whole of Christian theology must ultimately be viewed through the lens of Christology. Indeed, Christ's preeminence demands it (Col 1:18). The theodicy I propose, however, might seem to leave Christ as an afterthought: God creates the world, humans sin, God by anticipation introduces natural evil to expose the gravity of human sin, and somewhere down the line God sends Christ to undo the mess that humans have made. It's as though God sees Adam and Eve eat the forbidden fruit and only then realizes that the second person of the Trinity must be incarnated to save humanity.

But, in fact, nothing in my kairological reading of Genesis 1–3 requires so low a view of Christology. Quite the contrary. The theodicy I propose is entirely compatible with the exalted view of Christ in Rev 13:8, which describes him as "the Lamb slain before the foundation of the world" (cf. 1 Pet 1:18–21). To see that they are compatible, ask yourself why God would create this world rather than another. The intentional-semantic logic defined in chapter 18 applies specifically to *this* world, characterizing its order of creation. But it does not account for *why* God created this world—he could well have created others. Following Leibniz, God may have chosen to create this world because the good to be achieved through Christ's death on the Cross surpassed the good achievable in other worlds. Or perhaps God, as poet and artist, found this world above all others most beautiful. Or perhaps God's purposes are inscrutable, and we shall never understand why he chose to create this world rather than another.

In any case, God intended the Cross before the foundation of the world. The intentional-semantic logic of creation that is the basis for the theodicy developed in this book is itself logically downstream from the Cross. Rightly construed, the theodicy developed here presupposes the Cross. According to this theodicy, the effects of the Fall (in enslaving the world to sin) work not only proactively (i.e., forward in time) but also retroactively (i.e., backward in time). Likewise, the effects of the Cross (in saving the world from sin) work both proactively and retroactively. In this theodicy, natural evil prior to humans results from human sin at the Fall. So too, in the theology of the Cross, people who lived before Christ experience salvation from their sins through his Cross. God allows the effects of the Fall to work themselves out across history because he intends the ultimate good for creation that only the Cross can bring. The theodicy developed here is therefore entirely compatible with the primacy of Christology and the Cross.

22.2 Genesis 4–11

Throughout this book my focus has been on Genesis 1–3. Nonetheless, the young-earth position, which has been my principal foil, receives its support not only from Genesis 1–3 but also from Genesis 4–11. The latter chapters present a chronology that appears to allow only around 6,000 years from the creation of Adam and Eve to the present. What are we to make of these chapters? First, note that the theodicy I have presented attempts to account for evil and vast ages of the earth prior to the creation of Adam and Eve but places no restriction on what happens thereafter. Thus, in principle, the theodicy developed here is compatible with an old earth and a recent humanity (i.e., a kairological reading of Genesis 1–3 and a chronological reading of Genesis 4–11).

That said, the present theodicy attempts to make peace between our understanding of Genesis and the current mental environment. That makes a face-value reading of Genesis 4–11 and the chronology presented there difficult. Genesis 12–50, by contrast, does not face the same chronological difficulties. In Genesis 12, Abraham enters the picture. The story of his life and family in succeeding chapters contains elements that can be confirmed through independent archeological and anthropological evidence. Genesis 4–11, on the other hand, lacks such evidence. Moreover, a face-value chronological reading of these chapters requires, among other things, acceptance of the following highly dubious claims (dubious, that is, in the current mental environment):

- that Noah's flood occurred around 1600 years after the creation of Adam and thus roughly 2400 BC (at a time when known civilizations were flourishing);
- that an ark much smaller than many cruise ships housed all animals (and how many plants?) for a year without access to outside food (unless Noah and his sons were also fisherman or could harvest sea plants), quite likely without access to outside drinking water (the oceans presumably were salty back then), and with very limited sunlight (what did lizards that need to bask in sunlight do on the ark to keep alive?);
- that eight people (Noah, his wife, their three sons, and three daughters-in-law) populated not just the earth but whole civilizations within 400 years of the Flood, with Noah's death and Abraham's birth virtually coinciding;
- that a mere 200 years before Abraham was born the Tower of Babel incident occurred, before which all humans spoke exactly one language.

How, then, to interpret Genesis 4–11? That's a topic for another book. Briefly, however, Noah's flood, though presented as a global event, is probably best understood as historically rooted in a local event (e.g., a catastrophic flood in the Middle East). Such an interpretation may be less of a problem exegetically than it might first appear. To see this, consider that scriptural claims to universality are often hyperbolic or eschatological, and thus not fully realized in the present. For instance, Paul in Rom

10:18 describes "their sound" (i.e., the preaching of the gospel) as having gone "into all the earth, and their words unto the ends of the world." So far as we know, the preaching of the gospel in Paul's day did not extend beyond the Mediterranean basin, the Middle East, and perhaps India. It certainly did not extend to the New World. I don't mean to suggest that fancy hermeneutic footwork will resolve all interpretive questions about Genesis 4–11. There is work to be done. But in my view these chapters invite a certain latitude of interpretation (on both exegetical and historical grounds) that the later chapters of Genesis seem to rule out.

22.3 The World That Never Was

Given that God responds to human sin across time (both retroactively and proactively), there never was a chronological moment when the world we inhabit was without natural evil (or a disposition toward it; it is, for instance, not apparent how, at the moment of the Big Bang, the universe could have exhibited natural evil). That raises the question of what the world would have looked like if Adam and Eve had not sinned and, in turn, God had not needed to act in anticipation of their sin.

It may seem pointless to speculate about what would have happened if there had been no Fall. Still, our minds naturally gravitate toward such speculation. If humans could not have avoided the Fall, it seems that the guilt of the Fall cannot properly be ascribed to humans. Guilt presupposes responsibility, and responsibility presupposes live options (at least so we are told, though see the next chapter). Moreover, if God is able to respond in anticipation of the Fall, he surely is able to respond in anticipation of its absence. In fact, Christian theology teaches that there are angels who never fell. God presumably anticipated that these angels would not fall and thus arranged a suitable environment for their nonfallen state.

What environment would God have arranged for us if Adam and Eve had not sinned? We don't know. Our inability to answer this question, however, does not empty it of interest. Even without a clear answer, this question raises a practical worry, namely, how could our world avoid being overrun by organisms if, in the absence of sin, death does not limit reproduction? Without death, life, as we know it, increases exponentially. If humans never sinned and if death in this physical world only arises as a consequence of human sin, a world of runaway overpopulation seems unavoidable. And that's the case even if we set aside the death of plants and microbes as unproblematic (their consumption being necessary for the life of organisms that would not die).

Let me suggest that this concern about overpopulation is misplaced and results from an invalid extrapolation of reproductive trends in a fallen world. In a nonfallen world, there need be no imperative for organisms to reproduce once they adequately fill an environmental niche. In Genesis 1, God tells humanity and the other organisms to reproduce and fill the earth. Once the earth is adequately filled with a given type of organism, and supposing organisms of that type do not die, what is the point of continued reproduction? It makes sense to think that a homeostatic mechanism activates when a population has adequately filled an environmental niche, maintaining the stability of population numbers and thus preventing overpopulation. Indeed, that is precisely what does happen even in this fallen world; but the process includes disease, death, and among those organisms capable of it, suffering.

Speculations about worlds that never were are interesting as far as they go. But they ought not to distract us from the world that we actually inhabit. Our world is dynamic and messy. There never was any other, so far as we are concerned. In the mind of God, creation always presupposed the Cross, humans always sinned, and divine anticipation always ensured that the Fall had retroactive effects. To be sure, in the intentional-semantic logic by which God creates and organizes the world—not chronologically but kairologically—evil is always logically downstream. In that logic God creates a good world, it becomes even better once humans are created, and then it goes haywire once humans sin. Seen chronologically, however, the world has always been haywire. Hence the need for a new heaven and a new earth.

22.4 Texts of Terror

In *Texts of Terror*, feminist theologian Phyllis Trible examines four Old Testament women who experienced terrible abuse: Hagar, Tamar, the unnamed dismembered woman in Judges 19, and the daughter of Jephthah.[1] Trible's study is moving and leads one to ponder why the Old Testament is so filled with violence, some of it evidently sanctioned by God. God commands whole towns to be destroyed, killing everything that's alive in them—both human and animal (Josh 6:21). On other occasions God commands that the entire male population of a town be destroyed and only the virgins be kept alive as slaves (Num 31:17–18). When Korah, Dathan, and Abiram rebel against Moses, God has the earth, in judgment, swallow and kill not only them but also their entire families, including small children (Num 16:23–33). And yet, in Ezek 18:20, we read that children are not liable for their parents' sins.

Atheists use texts of terror to portray the God of the Old Testament as a monster. I'm not sure there's any way to put an entirely positive spin on these texts, but when reading them, several considerations must be borne in mind:

1. We need to distinguish clearly between God's acts and acts that the text does *not* suggest were ordered or approved by God.[2]

2. In the ancient Near East, where all these Old Testament narratives take place, if you were not in a covenant relationship with someone, you were a *zero*—you had no claims on anyone's mercy (for instance, see Joshua 9, which depicts the desperation of the Gibeonites to establish a covenant with Israel).

3. In John 1:17 we read "the law was given by Moses, but grace and truth came by Jesus Christ." The new covenant in Christ fundamentally transforms God's relationship with humanity from one of wrath because God's law has been violated to one of mercy because Christ has sacrificed himself for our sins.

4. The violence described in the Old Testament was endemic to the ancient Near East and remains endemic to much of the world today. Although our refined Western sensibilities recoil from these violent passages, in fact the Old Testament is to be credited for presenting the human condition in all its starkness (see the imprecatory psalms).

5. God has to deal with a sin-ridden world and all the messiness that entails. There are no neat solutions for dealing with a fallen world. Even God faces difficult decisions.

To say that God faces difficult decisions is not to question his omnipotence. God has no problem in understanding the full range of decisions before him or in executing any of them. The problem is that in a fallen world, no decision, when executed, has perfect consequences. A fallen world is a world of costs and benefits. It is a world of tradeoffs and compromise. The challenge for God is to pick the best compromise among competing objectives that procures the greatest good. The cosmic calculus by which God forms such decisions will, most likely, forever elude us. Nevertheless, human experience gives some glimpse into the magnitude of the difficulties that God faces.

In 1945, the American government faced a difficult decision. Unlike Germany, Japan just was not going to realize it was beaten and surrender. For cultural reasons Japanese civilians were prepared to fight to the death or commit mass suicide—and that had already happened in certain locations. In some cases they were incited by false tales of Allied atrocities. Now, the Americans, as it happened, had developed a way to force Japan's surrender, and they used it at Hiroshima and Nagasaki. To this day the conventional cant is that they did it because they were evil and vicious. In fact, their express purpose was to reduce the number of casualties by forcing the Japanese high command to tell the people it was all over and they should stop resisting. In a fallen world God faces similar choices. It is easy to portray the evil that is done or permitted, less easy to portray the one averted. The one thing we know as Christians is that God, through the Cross of Christ, did not hesitate to take evil upon himself.

In any case, readers who fault God for the violence of the Old Testament are unlikely to embrace my proposal that God introduces natural evil in anticipation of the Fall. Both will seem like bitter pills to swallow. And yet alternatives that play down the suffering of our age or God's role in it introduce problems of their own, both exegetically and theologically. Ultimately we should want the truth. If the truth hurts, so be it. The promise of the Christian faith is that this life presages a glorious new life that will make present pains seem negligible: "I reckon that the sufferings of this present time are not worthy to be compared with the glory which shall be revealed in us" (Rom 8:18).

22.5 The Problem of Good

Throughout this book I have focused on the problem of evil. To resolve the problem of evil, I proposed a kairological reading of Genesis that looks to the intentional-semantic logic by which God acts in creation.

According to this logic, God is able to act in the world by anticipating events and especially human actions. In so acting, God does not hinder the exercise of human freedom but rather anticipates its consequences. The kairological reading of Genesis described in this book preserves the classic understanding of Christian theodicy, according to which all evil in the world ultimately traces back to human sin at the Fall. Moreover, having preserved this classic understanding of the Fall, this reading of Genesis also preserves the classic Christian understanding of God's wisdom and particular providence in creation.

In focusing on divine anticipation as God's way of controlling the Fall's damage, I have stressed the active role God played in bringing about natural evil prior to the Fall. Natural evil mirrors the personal evil in our souls brought on through the distorting power of sin. Accordingly, a world that exhibits natural evil becomes an instrument for revealing to us the gravity of sin. In particular, the emergence of living forms through a violent and competitive historical process (be it through a series of special creations or through a more continuous evolutionary development) does itself exhibit natural evil attributable to the Fall. The theodicy proposed in this book therefore does nothing to soft-pedal natural evil. It is as stark as the Darwinian view, which regards evolution as a "great battle for life" (Darwin's own choice of words) and nature as "red in tooth and claw" (words of Darwin's compatriot Alfred Lord Tennyson).[3] Indeed, as I showed in the previous chapter, it can assimilate the Darwinian view.

Yet the theodicy I propose here also allows God's grace and mercy to break through into nature. Although divine anticipation can account for natural evils that occur prior to the Fall, it is not limited to that. The world is a cosmos, an ordered arrangement meant to reflect the glory of God. The natural evil that God (by anticipation) introduced into the world on account of the Fall clouds the world's ability to reflect God's glory but can never entirely block it. Indeed, God's original intention for creation always has a way of shining through, regardless of the pervasiveness of personal and natural evil. Moreover, in responding to the Fall before it happens chronologically, God does not merely bring about natural evil but also, as a matter of common grace, stems its influence. Yes, pathogenic microbes constitute a natural evil brought on by God in response to the Fall. But God doesn't just leave us at the mercy of these microbes. Our immune system is an amazing work of common grace by which God, acting in anticipation, limits the harm these microbes would otherwise cause.[4]

With God, evil never has the final word. The Tree of Life, which Adam and Eve could no longer reach because they were expelled from the Garden, appeared again 2,000 years ago as a cross on a hill called Golgotha.[5] Through the Cross of Christ, the immortality that eluded humanity in the Garden is restored. Evil is but a temporary feature of the world. Created as it is by God, the world is destined to fulfill God's good purposes.

More than any other problem, people have used the problem of evil to distance God from themselves and even to rationalize that God doesn't exist. In response, Boethius posed the following paradox: "If God exists whence evil; but whence good if God does not exist?"[6] The problem of evil is part of a much larger problem, namely, how a benevolent God can restore a prodigal universe to himself. This is the problem of good, and it subsumes the problem of evil.

TWENTY-THREE

THANKING GOD FOR ALL THINGS

IN ordinary life, theodicy isn't so much a matter of justifying God's action in the distant past (as when God brings about natural evil prior to the Fall). Rather, it is a matter of justifying God's action (or perhaps seeming inaction) in the present. Why, we ask, does God allow certain evils to happen here and now? What was God's role in a catastrophe, and could he have prevented it? Where is the responsibility for the immediate evils that assail us? How much of the responsibility lies with God? Above all, what should be our attitude toward God in the midst of evils?

In Eph 5:20, the apostle Paul provides a startling answer to this last question: "[Give] thanks always for all things unto God and the Father in the name of our Lord Jesus Christ." The preposition "for" in this verse is striking. It translates the Greek *hyper*, which means "on behalf of." Is Paul serious about giving thanks to God *on behalf of* all things? Can he, and the Holy Spirit writing through him, really intend that our thanksgiving is to encompass not just the good that comes our way but also the bad?

To see that God really does intend us to be grateful *for* all things, we need to reflect on what keeps us from giving God thanks. The original sin consisted in humans disobeying God to achieve knowledge of good and evil. In the Fall we set ourselves up as judges of good and evil. Henceforth, the good would be an object of gratitude, the evil an object of ingratitude.

But how do we know what is good and what is evil? Can we, as fallen beings, reliably distinguish the two?

Consider a Chinese parable. A series of unexpected events occurs in the life of a farmer and his son. The local residents comment on each of the events, calling them either good or bad. When the residents say "good," the farmer asks, "How do you know it is good?" When they say "bad," he asks, "How do you know it is bad?" The story is so contrived that events that initially seem good later appear bad, and vice versa.

Here is one telling of the parable: The farmer has a bumper crop and can thus afford to buy a donkey. That, according to neighbors, is supposed to be good. His son, riding the donkey, breaks his leg and becomes disabled. That is supposed to be bad. A local warlord comes through the region looking for conscripts. Because of his injury, the son is exempted. All the other young men from that region die in battle. And so things turn out all right for the farmer and his son. But do they?

An obvious lesson from this story is that silver-lined clouds and disguised blessings may not be immediately evident. A deeper lesson is that classifying the events of life as either good or bad is inherently unreliable. What if we did not end the story here? What if the leg of the farmer's son did not heal properly and the complications slowly and painfully killed him over the course of several years? What if during this time the son reflected on the far less painful death of his friends in battle and wished that he had suffered their fate instead? In that case, events that the farmer and son previously regarded as a blessing would now seem like a cruel joke.

The problem with classifying the events of life as either good or bad is that it enslaves us to life's circumstances. The world not only confronts each of us with many things but also writes the labels "good" or "bad" on them. If we let these labels stick, we become helpless. And that's the case even if most of the things that come our way have "good" written on them. Victims of pleasure are as much victims as victims of pain. The world divides humanity into winners and losers. The winners are those to whom the world sends things mainly with "good" written on them. Substitute "bad" for "good," and those are the losers. Through our efforts we can try to make the world's "goods" outweigh its "bads." But that's all we can do—we can *try*. The world—and we are part of the world—is always ready to overrule our best efforts.

But even when our best efforts are rewarded with success, the anticipated benefits may elude us. The satirist Juvenal, writing at a time when
Rome was the dominant world power, remarked, "We are now suffering
the evils of a long peace; luxury, more deadly than any foe, has laid her
hand upon us and avenges a conquered world."[1] Rome seemed to have it
all, and yet it was losing its former virtue. The very things we yearn for
most and regard as our highest good (wealth, fame, power, luxury, leisure,
and even scientific insight) can be our undoing.

Alexander Schmemann saw the clearest demonstration of humanity's
predicament (recall chapter 18) not in such obvious evils as immorality
and crime but in humanity's "positive ideal—religious or secular" and,
he stressed, its "satisfaction with this ideal."[2] Humanity's fallenness, for
Schmemann, was most evident not in what it regards as evil but in what
it regards as its highest good. For Adolf Hitler, it was the German people;
for Karl Marx, it was the classless society; for today's neo-atheists, it is a
materialistic, reductionistic science. Humanity's positive ideal is its god,
and for an unrepentant humanity this god is invariably false.

Our positive ideal determines what we value most. And what we value
most shapes and compels us, regardless of whether it should shape and
compel us. There's only one way out of Schmemann's predicament, and
that is by valuing not things but the one who brings good out of things—
the living and true God. Reposing ultimate value in things is, of course, the
essence of idolatry. This is what it means to violate the First Commandment, which proscribes false gods. Reposing ultimate value in the God
who brings good out of things, on the other hand, is the essence of true
worship. Only then do we line up with the First Commandment. Only then
do we experience genuine human freedom.

What is real freedom? In a culture that values absence of restraint, we
are apt to think of freedom in terms of options and intentions. The more
options we have and the more fully the option we choose expresses our
intentions, the freer we are. Alternatively, to the degree that our options are
diminished and the option we choose fails to express our intentions (for
instance, if we are coerced into doing something we'd rather avoid), the
less free we are. Insofar as we have only one option or our choices do not
express our intentions, we are not free at all and therefore not responsible
for our actions.

[179]

This is not the biblical view of human freedom. Nor is it compelling on its own terms. The problem is that it fails to account for how the agent sorting among options arrives at his or her intentions. Indeed, what accounts for those intentions? To a corrupt human heart, the intentions by which we sort among options are themselves corrupt. The biblical view sees corruption of the human heart as fundamentally undermining human freedom. The Bible calls this being a "slave to sin" (Rom 6:16–17). Martin Luther called it "the bondage of the will."[3] Freedom consists in having one's heart renewed and mind transformed so that one's actions conform to God's will. Freedom, in the biblical view, is obedience to God.[4]

To see that this is in fact the biblical view, recall Jesus' oft-quoted statement, "And ye shall know the truth, and the truth shall make you free." In context, the statement reads, "If ye continue in my word, then are ye my disciples indeed. And ye shall know the truth, and the truth shall make you free" (John 8:31–32). Freedom here consists in knowing the truth of God's Word and doing it. By contrast, those who "believed not the truth, but had pleasure in unrighteousness" (2 Thess 2:12) are not free. Yet, though lacking freedom, they are fully culpable: "this is the condemnation, that light is come into the world, and men loved darkness rather than light, because their deeds were evil" (John 3:19).

As creatures made in God's image, we know enough to know that we have turned against our Creator. Thus Rom 1:18–20 speaks of the ungodly as those

> who hold [i.e., suppress] the truth in unrighteousness; because
> that which may be known of God is manifest in them; for God
> has shewed it unto them. For the invisible things of him from the
> creation of the world are clearly seen, being understood by the
> things that are made, even his eternal power and Godhead; so
> that they are without excuse.

In our rebellion against God, we see the world as so dark that we have no obligation to seek and serve God. But in fact we see more than we let on. As Jesus remarked to the Pharisees, "If you were blind, you would have no sin; but now you say, 'We see.' Therefore your sin remains" (John 9:41 NKJV).

The destruction of human freedom is to know enough truth to be accountable for denying it and yet to deny it by pretending that not enough truth is evident. By contrast, the triumph of human freedom is to know the truth of God revealed in Christ and to embrace it, not just intellectually but with one's whole heart. This requires repentance, in which one turns away from sin and to God, and faith, in which one trusts God in a living relationship. Only in this way is our heart renewed and our mind transformed so that the intentions by which we make our life choices are free.

God sets us free because he loves us. Indeed, the Bible teaches that God is love (John 4:8). But what is love except unconditionally seeking the good of the other? And for humans, created as we are in God's image, our ultimate good is found only in God. Once we repose ultimate value in the God who is unconditionally committed to bringing good out of things, we are freed to give thanks *for* all things. Why? Because our focus then is not on things as such but on the divine activity that works in all things to bring about good.[5] Given this perspective, our tendency to thank God for the things that we deem good but not for the things that we deem bad is seen to be misconceived. God, who always acts in love, is at every instant working all things out for good regardless of how we, in particular circumstances, judge some things to be good and others bad.

The call of our humanity is to liberty. This liberty depends not on life's circumstances but on God's power acting through us and in the world to bring good out of circumstances. Bernard Malamud's novel *The Fixer* illustrates the liberty that transcends circumstances. Yakov Bok, a Jewish handyman in prerevolutionary Russia, leaves his small town and heads off to the big city (Kiev). Unknown to him, trials await him there. Why does he go? He senses the risks. But he asks himself, "What choice has a man who doesn't know what his choices are?"[6] However limited our choices may seem, the one choice we always have is this: We can choose not to limit our choices.

Later in the novel, Bok is imprisoned and humiliated. With choice after choice removed, he has one remaining choice: he can refuse to confess to a crime he did not commit, and he can thereby prevent a pogrom. In refusing to betray the Jewish community, Bok must first embrace liberty for himself, and in doing so, he enables it for others. As he learns, "the purpose of freedom is to create it for others."[7] Though bound in prison, Bok is still free to create freedom for others. His liberty consists not in controlling life's circumstances but in giving meaning to them and thereby bringing good out of them. Such a liberty cannot be removed by circumstances because it was not created by circumstances. Only a liberty that transcends circumstances can be real and enduring.

To say that our liberty transcends circumstances is not to minimize circumstances. We live in this world and must make the best of things. We must play the cards that we are dealt, and no one is dealt a perfect hand. It follows that regardless of the cards we are dealt, we must play them creatively. What does this mean practically? First off, it means that we must be clear about what our choices actually are. Invariably, we have more choices than we think we have.

Just as we must not take the circumstances of life at face value, so too we must not take the choices that those circumstances seemingly permit at face value. A weakness of our humanity is that we tend to take any choice whatsoever as a sign of freedom. This weakness is readily exploited. Manufacturers, for instance, realize that to sell more of their "target brand" it is helpful to introduce a "decoy brand." To be effective, the decoy brand must be at a higher price and of lower quality than the target brand. Obviously, with respect to the target, the decoy presents no actual choice at all (it is in every way an inferior product). As a matter of human psychology, however, we imagine that we have a real choice and congratulate ourselves on getting a good deal. In fact, the manufacturer is cynically manipulating the buyer and only using the decoy to drive interest to the target.[8]

In dealing creatively with the circumstances of life, we face three challenges: first, knowing what choices we actually have; second, settling on which choice to make; and third, following through with the choice we make. The third requires perseverance and courage. The second requires wisdom and clarity. The first requires inspiration and insight. This is where the creative potential of life resides, in refusing to be bullied by an artificially constricted set of choices and understanding instead our true range of choices.

Viktor Frankl exemplified this form of liberty. In *Man's Search for Meaning*, Frankl described his life as a prisoner in a Nazi concentration camp.[9] According to Frankl, the hardest trial that he and other prisoners endured was to maintain a sense of meaning and purpose in the face of

Nazi cruelty. He could see in prisoners' eyes when they lost their purpose. And having seen their purpose die, he knew that they too would soon be dead.

How did Frankl maintain his sense of purpose in the face of Nazi cruelty? There's no general formula for meeting the assaults that would rob our life of meaning and purpose. In Frankl's case, what kept him going was the thought that Nazi cruelty at Auschwitz was an unexampled evil and that by surviving he could give voice to its victims and solace to those who had to deal with its aftermath. Frankl lived a long and fruitful life after his concentration camp experience (he died in 1997 at age ninety-two), and through his work as a psychotherapist helped many to recover their sense of purpose in living.

Though the Nazis murdered Frankl's family, and though he himself experienced the full brunt of Nazi cruelty, one detects no bitterness in his writings. Instead, he constantly emphasized the power of purpose to bring peace, hope, love, and healing. For the one who would be neither victim nor victimizer but experience true freedom, there is no place for bitterness, anger, and unforgiveness. To succumb to these impulses because of life's injustices is, unhappily, to perpetuate the hold these injustices have on the victim and turn victimhood into a full-time occupation.

Writing out of his Christian experience more than 1,500 years ago, the Church father John Cassian described the underlying problem with anger and its related emotions:

> No matter what provokes it, anger blinds the soul's eyes, preventing it from seeing the Sun of righteousness. Leaves, whether of gold or lead, placed over the eyes, obstruct the sight equally, for the value of the gold does not affect the blindness it produces. Similarly, anger, whether reasonable or unreasonable, obstructs our spiritual vision."

Cassian concluded that the only legitimate use of anger is to "turn against our own impassioned or self-indulgent thoughts."[10]

The problem with anger, bitterness, and the unforgiveness that regularly accompany them is that they are born of frustration. Unforgiveness says, "You had the power to frustrate my purposes, and I resent you for it." It assumes that a properly structured life is one that determines its own purposes and then single-mindedly pursues them. Insofar as one's purposes are accomplished, that is good; insofar as they are frustrated, that is bad. If we were godlike beings who could determine the course of nature and the destinies of people, we might be justified in this attitude. But we have no such power. We are human beings, made of the same dust (humus) that lies beneath our feet.

In consequence, our only hope of true freedom is to deny circumstances the power to decide the purpose of our lives and, instead, reserve purpose as the supreme gift that God has given to us and that we, in turn, as priests of God, transmit to creation. This is not just sound theology and philosophy but also sound medicine and psychotherapy. Bernie Siegel, whose message of hope has so blessed cancer patients, stresses the need for inner peace if genuine healing is to take place. At the heart of this inner peace, he finds "an increasing tendency to let things happen rather than to make them happen."[11]

Siegel here underscores a curious inversion. The person who "makes things happen" seems so much more energetic and engaged than the person who merely "lets things happen." The one seems so active, the other so passive. But, in fact, the person who lets things happen and then creatively endows what happens with meaning is the active participant in life. Ironically, the person who is constantly making things happen by forcing life's circumstances into preset molds stunts creativity. The busy life is not the creative life.[12] The world attempts to keep us busy by foisting its purposes on us and thereby denuding us of our creativity. Our challenge is to maintain our creativity by giving purpose to the world's incursions. William Blake put it this way: "I must create a system or be enslaved by another man's. I will not reason and compare; my business is to create."[13]

In the act of creation, we endow raw materials with purpose. To be sure, the raw materials that the world sends us are not always pleasant or pliable. But, inevitably, they present us with an opportunity to be creators, making us into givers of purpose rather than slaves of another's purpose. In this way, we become co-creators with the ultimate Creator, whose gift of purpose to us is our ability to give purpose to the world. As a consequence, we are not just creators but also priests, offering back to the Creator a transformed world, formerly profane, but now rendered sacred through the gift of purpose.

The biggest temptation we face is to refuse this obligation to be creators. Specifically, we are tempted to take the raw materials of life at face value and stop there. Initially, we cannot help but take the raw materials of life at face value. That's how we first experience life. But the point of redemption is not to stop there but to urge a prodigal universe back to its Creator. Redemption is painful business. Indeed, its business is bringing good out of evil, and, invariably, this requires grappling with evil and being hurt by it. The Nazis intended Viktor Frankl harm. Their purpose was to destroy him, body and soul. That was the face value of Frankl's experience. But he did not let the Nazis have the final word. Redemption is God having the final word.

Redemption presupposes a community of purpose that works concertedly to overthrow unjust, enslaving, and incapacitating structures. Often we point to some key figure who symbolizes redemption, and we might even refer to this person as a *redeemer* (Joan of Arc, William Wilberforce, and Martin Luther King Jr. spring to mind). But redemption is always a joint effort, and those outside the limelight are as necessary for bringing about redemption as those in it. As the structures that oppress increase in scope, so do the communities of purpose needed to unseat those structures. The logic here entails a universal community of purpose whose purpose-giver is the Redeemer, writ large, who happens also to be the Creator, again writ large. The Creator-Redeemer is Christ. Christians refer to this universal community of purpose as the Church.

Redemption is concerned not simply with release from moral evils. Natural evils, such as disease, famine, and earthquakes, also require redemption, and some of our best and noblest communities of purpose are dedicated to alleviating natural evils. But whether a community of purpose is dedicated to unseating moral evil or alleviating natural evil, neither the pain of evil nor the need to overcome it is ever absent.

Perhaps the most poignant passage in Harold Kushner's *When Bad Things Happen to Good People* is where he reflects on the death of his son Aaron, who died of progeria, a premature aging disease. Kushner sees clearly that without his son's tragedy his effectiveness in helping others deal with similar tragedies would have been significantly diminished. And yet, when Kushner reflects on all he has learned as a result of his son's death and on all the good that has come from it, he states that he would still rather have his son alive and healthy:

> I am a more sensitive person, a more effective pastor, a more sympathetic counselor because of Aaron's life and death than I would ever have been without it. And I would give up all of those gains in a second if I could have my son back. If I could choose, I would forego all the spiritual growth and depth which has come my way because of our experiences.[14]

Oh, that we had never been put in the position of having to bring good out of evil! This is the pain that gnaws at the hearts of all who work for redemption. Redemption in this world is never complete. That's why ultimately we must look not to redemption *in* the world but to a final redemption *of* the world in which the pain of redemption is once and for all healed and the tears of redemption are once and for all wiped away.

The good news of Christianity is that this great redemption is ours in Christ. Our great Redeemer, the Lord Jesus, has accomplished this redemption by bringing good out of the Cross. As Christians, we thank God for the Cross. Yet, if we can thank God for the Cross, the ultimate instrument of torture and death, for what can we not thank God? The living God, who brings good out of the Cross and is able to bring good out of all life's circumstances—regardless of how we, from our fallen vantage, regard them as good or evil—is always worthy of our thanks and praise. That is why Paul can write: "Give thanks always *for* all things to God the Father in the name of our Lord Jesus Christ."

TWENTY-FOUR

LUMINOUS WITH PURPOSE[1]

P OISED between the Garden of Eden and the future Paradise, we can be like fugitives stranded in a no-man's land without a sense of purpose. We know of a primordial state of bliss we lost and of a perfected state of bliss toward which we are moving, but in the meantime we are here, on this earth, with its perplexing mix of beauty and tragedy. Though banished from the Garden with its gate forever barred, the memory of that perfect union with God keeps alive the hope of Paradise. When we let that memory fade, this earth is a place of exile. But when we remember that the divine image is in each of us, this earth becomes an arena of purpose. Then our vision is liberated. The divine images in all of us shine and collectively illumine the way—a way of purpose.

What is the divine image that generates purpose? God, the Divine, is Love. Thus our divine image, our defining feature, is love. Tertullian says: "And this therefore is to be considered as the image of God in man, that the human spirit has the same motions and senses as God has."[2] What are the "motions" of God? As a means of drawing all of us back to himself, God moved down into this earthly arena. Here, his crowning achievement was his "passion," his death. *Passion* shares its etymological root with the word *passive,* which means "able to be moved." The ultimate expression of our divine image is to allow ourselves to be moved to the point of sacrifice, with the motive of moving others toward a perfected state of bliss, toward

Love. This sense of purpose makes life on this earth no longer hellish but a wondrous place of duty.

Many faiths share the motif of voluntary self-sacrifice to enable a greater life. The biblical teaching is that "except a corn of wheat fall into the ground and die, it abides alone: but if it dies, it brings forth much fruit" (John 12:24). It brings the fruit of love. In similar vein, the ancient Eleusinian mystery rites ritually reenacted the slaying, dismembering, and scattering of Osiris, and celebrated afterward his resurrection in the green wheat that sprang anew. The initiate was made to understand that the sacrifice of the individual opened up new and larger vistas of life.

Those of us who profess to have no faith still follow the impulse to move toward something greater than the self. Consider, for instance, the disillusioned youth. Perhaps he never learns that his defining feature is to give himself over to something that extends beyond himself. The youth, his instincts still ardent, must expend himself in some way. A life devoid of high calling repels him. Saint Augustine, at the age of 17, expressed this sentiment: "I wanted something to love but knew not what to love. I hated a life of security and with no snares for my feet."[3] And a youth today may still feel this godly impulse. With no channels to guide his movements, he may give himself over to indiscriminate movements such as those found in the use of drugs. The vocabulary of drug abuse in particular is laden with imagery showing the need to move beyond one's present state. One takes "uppers," "downers," drugs to "get high," or to "take a trip." Such movements cannot bring forth fruit; because such movements are erratic expressions of being lost, they miscarry.

Movements might become even more abortive. When we lose the image of God beyond ourselves and in ourselves, our sense of purpose is mutilated. This, in turn, can naturally lead us to mutilate others or ourselves. Man, the only creature capable of despair, is also the only creature who can out of this despair move to end his own life. In such a case, one sees no purpose in one's life and therefore no purpose in continuing one's existence. This calls for a retraining of the imagination, a divine guidance that illumines the true nature of the images of God in this world. Such was the divine guidance of Beatrice, who in *The Divine Comedy* drew out the lost and disenchanted Dante. She took him through the *inferno* and the *purgatorio,* wherein he began to see and have compassion for the plight of the images of God. She purged his vision to see the world as it really was. At last she delivered him into *paradiso*, where he gazed upon the very movements of God in the great cosmic wheel:

> Lift up then, Reader, to the lofty wheels
>> With me thy vision straight unto that part
>> Where the one motion on the other strikes,
> And there begin to contemplate with joy
>> That Master's art, who in himself so loves it
>> That never doth his eye depart therefrom.[4]

We are irresistibly drawn through this world; time itself dictates that we change. But the image of God in us does not change. That image was by no means destroyed by the Fall but only distorted. Thus acts of hate are in fact acts of love gone awry. The image of God remains but is misdirected. Therefore our purpose is misdirected. Actions then "miss the mark," which is the biblical definition of sin. This is the only perspective from which to understand the missteps of others and the misguided movements of ourselves. The essence of humility is to realize that we're all made of the same essence, the same dusty *humus* into which divinity is breathed. Knowing this, our purpose becomes the redirection and soothing of all who have lost our way. We embrace others and ourselves. While on earth, our way may seem precarious, but we all still bear the beautiful image of God. As W. H. Auden puts it in his 1937 poem "Lullaby,"

> Lay your sleeping head, my love,
> Human on my faithless arm;
> Time and fevers burn away
> Individual beauty from
> Thoughtful children, and the grave
> Proves the child ephemeral:
> But in my arms till break of day
> Let the living creature lie,
> Mortal, guilty, but to me
> The entirely beautiful.[5]

This understanding of humanity refines and burns away all sense of shame and accusation. We acknowledge that we are faithless and that we and others are guilty. Yet the image of God shines its aureole, and we see that our bond elevates the fleeting moment into something holy. No single moment of life is ever insignificant but is instead luminous with purpose.

Such an understanding focuses on the small, forgotten moments, but it also widens its focus to take in the large picture. It does not deny that time and fevers burn away beauty. Nor does it deny the fact of the grave. To deny the cruelties of life is cruel. Struggling to explain the place of evil, some have conceived of it as provisional for an ultimately good purpose. To the one suffering, this explanation can ring hollow. At such times, only trust in divine love—perhaps in the form of fellow sufferers bearing the divine image—can make the suffering bearable.

The stoic philosopher Epictetus possessed this understanding. Epictetus was brought up as a slave in the home of a freedman of Nero. As such, he never had "freedom" as most people conceive of it. Yet his spirit was free because it was informed by a lofty sense of purpose. Epictetus said: "For everything that happens in the world it is easy to give thanks to Providence, if a person has but these two qualities in himself: a habit of viewing broadly what happens to each individual, and a grateful temper."[6] We can have a broad perspective and a grateful heart if we recognize that a divine Providence has a purpose.

In 1772, William Cowper was blessed with a sudden and unexpected view of the Providence of God. Despairing, he decided one day to jump into the Thames River and end his life. But because of the dense fog that day, coupled with his suicidal disorientation, he repeatedly lost his way to the river. Weary, he decided that he could go no further and, looking up, found that his footsteps had brought him back to the safety of his own front door. In that moment he recognized that God indeed had a purpose for his life. He dedicated the rest of his life to helping others understand the purpose of their own lives. One means of doing this was to write the hymn "God Moves in a Mysterious Way":

> Deep in unfathomable mines of neverfailing skill,
> He treasures up His bright designs and works His sovereign will.
> Ye fearful saints, fresh courage take; the clouds ye so much dread
> Are big with mercy and shall break in blessings on your head.
> His purposes will ripen fast, unfolding every hour;
> The bud may have a bitter taste, but sweet will be the flower.[7]

In his 1959 prose poem "Archangel," John Updike illustrates the way in which the seemingly small forgotten moments have yet been guided by a sacred purpose. In this poem an archangel liberates a man's perception to perceive the image of God in all created things, in one's loved ones, and in oneself. *Everything* is luminous with purpose. The archangel conjures up a boyhood memory, allowing the man to see how every fleeting second dilates into eternity. The archangel whispers,

> Certain moments, remembered or imagined, of childhood. Three-handed pinochle by the brown glow of the stained-glass lampshade, your parents, out of their godliness silently wishing you to win. . . .
>
> Such glimmers I shall widen to rivers; nothing shall be lost, not the least grain of remembered dust, and the multiplication shall be a thousand thousand fold; love me.[8]

The man now sees that it was the image of divinity in his parents which enabled them to love and sacrifice for their child.

When this man received the visitation from the archangel, it is as when God allows us to see the sacramental nature of everything that has being. We then realize that to perceive a beautiful object merely as beautiful object is to miss the mark, or to sin. Augustine said that the very "queen of colours," in and of itself, is transitory, and therefore could leave him "dispirited."[9] But when he recognized God in all lovely things, he said, "You shone upon me; your radiance enveloped me, you put my blindness to flight"[10]

Such is an instance of the promise in Zech 14:20–21 (NRSV): "On that day there shall be inscribed on the bells of the horses, 'Holy to the LORD.' And the cooking pots in the house of the LORD shall be as holy as the bowls in front of the altar; and every cooking pot in Jerusalem and Judah shall be sacred to the LORD of hosts." On that day there is no arbitrary separation between the sacred and the profane. For while *profane* means "before or outside the temple," on that day *everything* is part of the temple. And just as each detail of the temple had a specific, essential purpose, on that day we see that everything around us, every person around us, has a specific, essential purpose.

An old catechism poses its first question as, "What is the chief end of man?" And the answer given is, "To glorify God and to enjoy him forever."[11] One definition of *glorify* is "to multiply the splendor." Our purpose is to see the glory of God in its multiplicity, to see that even mundane things are splendid. Zechariah 14:20 confirms that this is to be our liberated vision. Our purpose is to see that nothing is without purpose. During such an "epiphany," that is, with light shining all around, we see that each object is beautiful and luminous with the divine imprint.

Ancient philosophers have intuited this connection between beauty and the Divine. Plato taught that the love of beautiful things leads one to the love of Beauty, of Good, itself. Aristotle spoke of "great-souled" men such as Anaxagoras and Thales, who yearned for beautiful but useless things. These men gazed upon the "remarkable, admirable, difficult, and divine," but they were judged by others to be "ignorant of what is to their own advantage."[12] The purpose of these men was not focused upon taking care of themselves. Such a focus would have fulfilled only the acquisitive portion of their souls and would ultimately have fragmented their souls. These men were "great-souled" because their focus was on the divine, thereby filling their *whole* soul.

Consider the example of Achilles in the *Iliad*, who was transformed from the greatest of all ancient heroes into something greater than a hero: a full-souled human being. Before his transformation, Achilles identified himself only with his goddess mother Thetis, scorning his human father Peleus. He refused to break bread with his human companions, instead eating ambrosia, which means "*not* human bread." But after his wrathful hubris burns itself away, Achilles' purposes change. His purpose now becomes to immerse himself in the common lot of humanity and serve others, for he now cherishes the divine image in humanity all around him. He washes and drapes the body of Hector, the archenemy he had killed and dragged triumphantly through the dirt. He roasts a sheep and serves it to Hector's father and the enemy king, Priam. He shows compassion for his own father Peleus, saying he will stand by him in his old age. This story of service is an echo of another story: that of Jesus washing the feet of his disciples, putting himself at the service of humanity. To do so was to align himself with the sacred purposes of the cosmos. He was the fully divine embodiment who reinstated the creative order. He presented an image of what our creative purposes are to be.

Jungian psychoanalyst Erich Neumann depicts our creative role as beings in the divine image. The Creator God demands that man also participate in creation and thus fulfill his purpose. Neumann says:

> This drive to realization, which is a living factor in everything creative, belongs to the essential nature of unitary reality, which manifests itself alike in the creativity of nature and in that of the psyche, and urges man on to unite them both. Creative man . . . must also obey the trend to realization of the unitary reality itself, which impinges upon him from within and without. This forces him to "transcend"—i.e., to break through the partial worlds— and by so doing to achieve the "Great Experience."[13]

Neumann here uses verbs describing movement, such as "transcend" and "break through the partial worlds." The dynamic is a refraction of the Christian concept of movement toward a state of bliss, as discussed earlier. Neumann describes an expressly creative purpose of moving toward Love, which he terms "unitary reality." It is our sacred purpose to place our own creative nature in consonance with the divine creative nature—to "unite them both." It is our means of becoming a co-creator. It is a means of having dominion over all the earth, of being fruitful and multiplying. When we direct our purposes to be creative in this way, we reflect a feature of the divine Creator. To do so is to obey the drive toward "unitary reality." Such a supreme unifying force has been recognized throughout times and cultures as Love. The Christian faith describes this Love as God himself, from whom all things proceed, to whom all things are drawn, and who charges all movements of humanity with purpose.

Wallace Stevens was one of the great twentieth-century poets. He was fascinated with the sacred purposes of the cosmos. His work is preoccupied with ideas of order, with origins, with passageways that allow entrance into a never-defined realm of transcendental spirit. His poetry is lyric in the classical sense of the word, for his poetic ear listens for the lyre of the gods. That is, Stevens understands that man's senses in this physical world are to be attuned in a suprasensual way to a divine realm. Although his poetry shows that he was always yearning to understand the divine order, Stevens did not become a Christian until his deathbed. He lay the last two weeks of his life in a hospital, asking questions while the nuns on the hospital floor prayed for him. He was at last baptized.

Wallace Stevens illustrates his longing to perceive the divine order, the divine purpose, in his 1935 poem "The Idea of Order at Key West."[14] Here he depicts one seeing the beauty of the divine and in turn rendering the world around him as infused with the divine. The poem describes this dynamic: the divine draws the poet to a state of contemplation, wherein his world is illumined. This allows the poet to see divine purpose reflected in human purpose. This draws the poet more deeply into the heart of the divine. It is a circle of love that never ends.

The poem climbs to a state of exaltation as the poet perceives that each mundane thing opens a window into infinity. Each created thing shines out, clear and full of purpose. The poem begins with "She sang beyond the genius of the sea." The "she" here is an archetypal anima, that which represents the feminine, chthonic part of the soul, that which is endowed with generative powers. "Genius" signifies exceptional generative powers, while "the sea" connotes energy of unbounded mystery and depth. Yet "she" sang even beyond this. Thus the poet understands that her song extends to the material world but is unconstrained by it. "She" is the idea, an image of creative divinity.

The anima expresses herself in the material world. The poet relates that she "Made constant cry, caused constantly a cry." She yearned to reveal herself to the poet below. The poet goes on to describe the anima in terms of light: "the outer voice of sky"; "Theatrical distances, bronze shadows heaped / On high horizons, mountainous atmospheres / Of sky and sea." He describes her as an austere geometrician who measures the light: "It was her voice that made / The sky acutest at its vanishing." This calls to mind the belief of the ancient Pythagoreans, who held that geometry explained the structure and purpose of the cosmos.

The poet relates that he and his friend "beheld her striding there alone," and were transformed by her presence. They had been surrounded by the effusions of the divine, illuminating their vision to see the presence of the divine in everything around them, including mundane human endeavors. Their vision has been transmuted. They do what the medieval alchemists attempted to do: their vision turns base elements into gold. They engage in *poesis,* for in a sense they remake the natural order. The poet pleads with his friend to help him understand the divine mystery:

> . . . tell me, if you know,
> . . . tell why the glassy lights,
> The lights in the fishing boats at anchor there,
> As the night descended, tilting in the air,
> Mastered the night and portioned out the sea,
> Fixing emblazoned zones and fiery poles,
> Arranging, deepening, enchanting night.
>
> Oh! Blessed rage for order, . . .
> The maker's rage to order words of the sea,
> Words of the fragrant portals, dimly-starred
> And of ourselves and of our origins, . . .[15]

Thus the poet now turns his attention from the light of the transcendent anima to the "glassy lights" of the fishing village. The light of the divine has opened his eyes, and he now sees that all loving human endeavors reflect the light of the holy. Their purposes may be like the glassy lights—they may be fragile, prone to break if not gently held—but they still spread light. And not only do they spread light; they do so in a way that enhances the structure of the cosmos. Their lights master the night and portion out the sea. They arrange and deepen the enchantment of the night. Each glassy light is *true* in the sense of truth given by Thomas Aquinas: "the truth of a thing as the possession of the existence established for it."[16] That is, each glassy light fulfills its purpose. The fishing village is vulnerable as it sways on the edge of the dark sea, yet it too shines with eternal purpose. And since the village contributes to the symmetry of the cosmos, its lights are beautiful, cosmetic—in the sense that *cosmos* and *cosmetic* are derived from the same ancient root word for order.

"Oh! Blessed rage for order, . . . The maker's rage to order words of the sea." For it is indeed a blessed thing to be consumed with fulfilling our part of the divine order, with fulfilling our purpose. Then we are drawn closer to the fragrant portals of eternity. Though the glass is dark, it is luminous, and we begin to see through it. And we see that we are being drawn more deeply into Divine Love.

NOTES

Introduction

1. Simon Blackburn, *Being Good: A Short Introduction to Ethics* (Oxford: Oxford University Press, 2001), 1.

2. Ibid.

3. A mental environment differs from a worldview. A mental environment applies corporately to a group, population, or culture. On the other hand, a worldview is, in the first instance, held individually, though it can be shared and therefore held corporately. Thus we may speak of "the Christian worldview." Your worldview is the set of beliefs that you hold about what the world is like. As such, it doesn't distinguish between beliefs that are held intensely and those that are taken more lightly. A mental environment, by contrast, emphasizes the deeply entrenched cognitive and moral structures by which we make sense of life. A mental environment therefore tends to be far more influential than a worldview. Born again Christians, for example, hold, as part of their worldview, that marriage is sacred. Yet divorce among them is as prevalent as elsewhere in the culture. Nor do they attach to it much of a stigma. The prevalence and widespread acceptance of divorce in our culture, and even among born-again Christians, reflects less on our worldviews than on our mental environment. For the divorce rate among born again Christians, see The Barna Group, "Born Again Christians Just As Likely to Divorce As Are Non-Christians," September 8, 2004, available online at http://www.barna.org/FlexPage.aspx?Page=BarnaUpdateNarrow&BarnaUpdateID=170 (accessed February 13, 2009).

4. For a critique of how science is abused to justify atheism, see John Lennox, *God's Undertaker: Has Science Buried God?* (Oxford: Lion Hudson, 2007).

5. Richard Dawkins, *The God Delusion* (New York: Houghton Mifflin, 2006); Christopher Hitchens, *god Is Not Great: How Religion Poisons Everything* (New York: Hachette, 2007); Sam Harris, *The End of Faith: Religion, Terror, and the Future of Reason* (New York: W. W. Norton, 2004).

6. The neo-atheists have many faults, but apathy is not one of them. According to psychologist Rollo May, "Hate is not the opposite of love; apathy is." In that case, we've made considerable progress since my MIT days. The quote by May is from *Love and Will* (New York: Norton, 1969), 29.

7. William Dembski and Jonathan Wells, *The Design of Life: Discovering Signs of Intelligence in Biological Systems* (Dallas: Foundation for Thought and Ethics, 2008); Guillermo

Gonzalez and Jay W. Richards, *The Privileged Planet: How Our Place in the Cosmos Is Designed for Discovery* (Washington, DC: Regnery, 2004).

8. Wish-fulfillment does not a valid argument make.

9. Dawkins, *God Delusion*, 31.

10. At least part of Eve's fault was that she uncritically accepted Satan's explanation of God's refusal to let her eat from the Tree of the Knowledge of Good and Evil. She didn't ask who Satan was or why he was suddenly supposed to be an authority about God. If she had done any checking at all, she would have discovered that Satan had been kicked out of heaven, that his current address was far from God's, and that he was widely regarded as a liar and the father of lies (John 8:44).

11. Cornel West, "On My Intellectual Vocation," in *The Cornel West Reader* (New York: Basic Civitas, 1999), 33. Originally published in George Yancy, ed., *African American Philosophers: 17 Conversations* (London: Routledge, 1998), 32–48.

12. Ibid.

13. See http://www.channel4.com/culture/microsites/C/can_you_believe_it/debates/rootofevil .html (accessed May 22, 2008).

14. Richard Dawkins, "Is Science a Religion?" *The Humanist* 57 (Jan./Feb. 1997): 26.

15. Quoted from *Hitler's Table Talk* (1941–1943), presented in Alan Bullock's *Hitler: A Study in Tyranny*, rev. ed. (New York: Harper & Row, 1964), 672. I e-mailed Dawkins on January 13, 2006: "Had you seen Hitler's quote before you came up with yours or did you come up with it independently?" He replied to me the same day: "You ask whether I was aware of the Hitler quote when I made my own statement. The answer is no, but I have become aware of it more recently in the course of investigating Hitler's religious beliefs." He then immediately defended his own atheistic worldview, remarking that it is "ludicrous" to suggest "that Hitler, Stalin and Mao were motivated by atheism in committing their atrocities." It seems, then, that Dawkins was unsurprised to learn that he was echoing Hitler.

16. The type of theodicy I am proposing thus falls under *philosophical theology*. Philosophical theology begins with theological data and tries to make sense of them philosophically. In the case at hand, it tries to make philosophical sense of the biblical data about evil, sin, and suffering. A different type of theodicy falls under *philosophy of religion*. Looking to universally accessible data rather than to specifically theological data, philosophy of religion tries to understand, in general philosophical terms, how a God who is good and powerful can coexist with evil. A prime goal of this type of theodicy is to answer critics who claim that the problem of evil is insurmountable for Christian theism, making it collapse into logical absurdity. For an example of this type of theodicy, see Peter van Inwagen, *The Problem of Evil* (Oxford: Oxford University Press, 2006).

17. In Rom 12:2, the apostle Paul wrote, "Be not conformed to this world, but be ye transformed by the renewing of your mind, that ye may prove what is that good and acceptable and perfect will of God." Nineteen hundred years later, J. Gresham Machen described what happens when Christians do not take Paul's words here to heart: "False ideas are the greatest obstacles to the Gospel. We may preach with all the fervor of a reformer and yet succeed only in winning a straggler here and there, if we permit the whole collective thought of the nation or of the world to be controlled by ideas which, by the resistless force of logic, prevent Christianity from being regarded as anything more than a harmless delusion." Quoted from J. Gresham Machen, *What Is Christianity?* (Grand Rapids, Mich.: Eerdmans, 1951), 162.

18. Missionaries approaching a completely unreached people group understand this point implicitly. See, for instance, Don Richardson, *Peace Child*, 4th ed. (Ventura, Calif.: Regal Books, 2005). Here Richardson describes the Sawi people of New Guinea, who placed a premium on deceit and treachery. Yet they had one inviolable principle, that the peace offering of a child exchanged between warring factions must at all costs be honored. This presented an opening for the gospel by identifying Jesus Christ as God's "peace child" to humanity. As a consequence, the Sawi people converted in overwhelming numbers to Christ.

19. Richard Dawkins, *River out of Eden* (New York: HarperCollins, 1996), 133.

20. John Milton, *Paradise Lost* I.22–26. For the complete works of John Milton, see http://www.luminarium.org/sevenlit/milton/miltbib.htm (accessed December 29, 2008).

21. Epictetus, *Discourses* I.6, in Epictetus, *Discourses and Enchiridion*, trans. T. W. Higginson (New York: Walter J. Black, 1946), 17. Compare William Law's remark: "Would you know who is the greatest saint in the world? . . . It is he who is always thankful to God, who wills everything that God willeth, who receives everything as an instance of God's goodness and has a heart always ready to praise God for it." From *A Serious Call to a Devout and Holy Life*, ch. 15, available online at http://www.worldinvisible.com/library/law/seriouscall/scch15.htm (accessed March 29, 2003).

22. Edward T. Oakes, "Edward T. Oakes and His Critics: An Exchange," *First Things* 112 (April 2001): available online at http://www.firstthings.com/article.php3?id_article=2168 (accessed June 3, 2008).

23. Augustine, *Enchiridion* (trans. A. C. Outler), ch. 27. See http://www.ccel.org/ccel/augustine/enchiridion.txt (accessed March 15, 2007).

24. Oakes, "His Critics."

25. See, for instance, process theologian Charles Hartshorne's *Omnipotence and Other Theological Mistakes* (Albany, N.Y.: SUNY Press, 1983). In classical Christian theology, autonomy was never a feature of the world. Rather, as Georges Florovsky summarized the teachings of the Church Fathers on creation, the world exhibits an "absolute creatureliness and non-self-sufficiency." See Georges Florovsky, "Creation and Creaturehood," in William A. Dembski, Wayne J. Downs, and Fr. Justin B. A. Frederick, eds., *The Patristic Understanding of Creation: An Anthology of Writings from the Church Fathers on Creation and Design* (Riesel, Tex.: Erasmus, 2008), 552.

26. A particularly striking example in contemporary theological reflection of this shift to an ultimate reality beyond God may be found in James E. Huchingson, *Pandemonium Tremendum: Chaos and Mystery in the Life of God* (Cleveland: Pilgrim, 2001).

27. A full-blown theological determinism, for instance, would trace the ultimate origin of evil to God himself (biblical passages used to support such a view include Isa 45:7, Lam 3:38, Rom 9:11–13, Exod 14:4, and 1 Kgs 24:1). Within such a determinism, God is not the origin of evil in the passive sense of creating the conditions in which evil can occur spontaneously; rather, God is actively decreeing the very means by which the evil occurs. Within Christian theology, there is a stream of thought flowing from Paul to Augustine to Calvin that accepts such a determinism.

28. *Catholic Encyclopedia*, s.v. "evil," available online at http://www.newadvent.org/cathen/05649a.htm (accessed March 15, 2007). In support of this passage, the *Catholic Encyclopedia* cites Dionysius the Areopagite and Augustine. "Moral evil" here is what I've been calling "personal evil"; "physical evil" here is what I've been calling "natural evil."

Chapter 1

1. See Shaw's preface to his play *Major Barbara*, where he recommends renaming Christianity "Crosstianity." George Bernard Shaw, *Major Barbara* (1905; reprinted Whitefish, Mont.: Kessinger, 2004).

2. Catherine Aslanoff, Paul Meyendorff, and Andrew Tregubov, *The Incarnate God: The Feasts of Jesus Christ and the Virgin Mary* (Crestwood, N.Y.: St. Vladimir's Seminary Press, 1994), II:152.

3. James Carroll, *Constantine's Sword: The Church and the Jews—A History* (New York: Mariner, 2001).

4. Quoted in John Barry, *The Great Influenza: The Epic Story of the Deadliest Plague in History* (New York: Penguin, 2004), 273.

5. See Gregory of Nazianzus on Apollinarianism, ca. 380, in Alister McGrath, ed., *The Christian Theology Reader*, 3rd ed. (Oxford: Blackwell, 2007), 269–70.

6. David J. Bartholomew, *God, Chance and Purpose: Can God Have It Both Ways?* (Cambridge: Cambridge University Press, 2008), 229.

7. The full verse (in the King James Version) reads, "And all that dwell upon the earth shall worship him [i.e., the beast], whose names are not written in the book of life of the Lamb slain from the foundation of the world." The Greek, which is not as sensitive to word-order as English, puts "from the foundation of the world" right after "the Lamb slain." Some translations (e.g., the New Revised Standard Version), however, associate "from the foundation of the world" with those "whose names are not written in the book of life." Here is the NRSV translation of this verse: "And all the inhabitants of the earth will worship it [i.e., the beast], everyone whose name has not been written from the foundation of the world in the book of life of the Lamb that was slaughtered." The KJV provides the more natural translation. Translators who follow the other word order are probably trying to maintain consistency with Rev 17:8, which does, in the Greek, juxtapose "from the foundation of the world" with those whose names were "not written in the book of life." But doesn't this parallel passage raise at least a doubt about the reading and translation of Rev 13:8 that I am advocating? No, because the idea of Christ as the Lamb slain from the foundation of the world is found unequivocally elsewhere in Scripture. For instance, 1 Pet 1:19–20 describes Christian believers as redeemed "with the precious blood of Christ, as of a lamb without blemish and without spot: who verily was foreordained before the foundation of the world, but was manifest in these last times for you."

8. *The Living God: A Catechism*, trans. (from French) Olga Dunlop (Crestwood, N.Y.: St. Vladimir's Seminary Press, 1989), I:187.

9. Bertrand Russell, *Problems of Philosophy* (Oxford: Oxford University Press, 1912), ch. 5.

10. In *The City of God* (v. 9) Augustine even to far as to state that any being that does not know the future is not God. The relevant passage is available online at http://www.newadvent.org/fathers/120105.htm (accessed November 27, 2008).

11. *Aristotle's Nichomachean Ethics*, trans. Hippocrates G. Apostle (Grinnell, Iowa: Peripatetic, 1984), VIII.9, 1159a 6–7, page 149.

12. "Evidently, then [divine thought] thinks of that which is most divine and precious, and it does not change; for change would be change for the worse, and this would be already a movement. . . . Therefore it must be of itself that the divine thought thinks (since it is the most excellent of things), and its thinking is a thinking on thinking." Aristotle, *Metaphysics*,

in Richard McKeon, ed., *The Basic Works of Aristotle* (New York: Random House, 1941), 1074b 26–33, page 885.

13. On humility, pride, and virtue in Luther's thought, see Paul Althaus, *The Theology of Martin Luther*, trans. R. C. Schultz (Minneapolis: Fortress, 1966), 148.

14. Timothy Keller, *The Reason for God: Belief in an Age of Skepticism* (New York: Dutton, 2008), 30.

15. Ibid., 28.

16. Ibid., 30.

17. For an extensive list of celebrity atheists, see http://www.celebatheists.com (accessed January 13, 2009).

18. G. K. Chesterton, *Orthodoxy*, in *Collected Works of G. K. Chesterton*, vol. 1 (San Francisco: Ignatius, 1986), 243.

19. The physics community is much taken these days with the idea of a multiverse—an ensemble of universes that makes real anything that's physically possible. The known universe that we inhabit is therefore just one of a gazillion other universes that constitute the multiverse. In the multiverse, universes with physical laws like ours but wildly different histories are just as real as ours. Thus, the multiverse contains a universe exactly like ours except that in it, after years of devotion and charity, Mother Teresa on her eightieth birthday suddenly becomes an ax-murderer. The multiverse is not a creation—it involves no self-limitation or inclusion/exclusion in Chesterton's sense (see the previous note). For a helpful critique of the multiverse, see Stephen M. Barr, *Modern Physics and Ancient Faith* (Notre Dame, Ind.: University of Notre Dame Press, 2003), ch. 17.

20. The arson metaphor has scriptural precedent: "Behold, how great a matter a little fire kindleth! And the tongue *is* a fire, a world of iniquity: so is the tongue among our members, that it defileth the whole body, and setteth on fire the course of nature; and it is set on fire of hell" (Jas 3:5–6).

Chapter 2

1. Elliott Sober also feels the force of this problem: "It is often claimed that some evils exist because human beings have free will and sometimes freely choose actions that are wrong. Free will is supposed to be such a wonderful thing that a benevolent God would have given us this great benefit even though it brought with it a considerable cost. Like a number of other philosophers, I don't see why having free will rules out always freely choosing to do the right thing. If a sinner can have free will, why can't a saint?" Quoted from his *Evidence and Evolution: The Logic Behind the Science* (Cambridge: Cambridge University Press, 2008), 166.

2. Maximus the Confessor, *The Four Hundred Chapters on Love* I:5 and I:7, in *Maximus Confessor: Selected Writings* (New York: Paulist, 1985), 36.

3. Traditional Christian theology regards the redemption of Christ as not just overturning the negative consequences of the Fall but also bringing about good that would not have been possible apart from the Fall. But the good here is due to God's active role in redemption and not to the Fall as such. The Fall, apart from redemption, is within traditional theology the ruin of humanity.

4. Patricia Williams, *Doing Without Adam and Eve: Sociobiology and Original Sin* (Minneapolis, Minn.: Fortress, 2001).

5. C. S. Lewis, *Miracles: A Preliminary Study*, rev. ed. (1960; reprinted San Francisco: Harper, 2001), 125.

6. John Hick, *Evil and the God of Love*, rev. ed. (New York: Harper & Row, 1977), 253–61. Hick, in formulating this theodicy, looks to the church father Irenaeus for inspiration. While I find much to commend this theodicy, the metaphor of the world as a school for soul-making entails more difficulties than it resolves.

7. John Polkinghorne, "God's Action in the World," 1990 J. K. Russell Fellowship Lecture, available online at http://www.starcourse.org/jcp/action.html (accessed November 18, 2008). Polkinghorne repeated this anecdote in the fall of 2002 at the Parchman Lectures, sponsored by Baylor University's Truett Seminary (September 30 and October 1, 2002).

8. Thomas Aquinas writes, "O fortunate fault, which merited so great a redeemer" (*Summa Theologiae* III.1.3(3)). In his *Enchiridion* (27), Augustine writes, "God judged it better to bring good out of evil than to allow no evil to exist." And in Rom 5:20 NIV, Paul writes, "Where sin increased, grace increased all the more."

9. Aristotle's *Metaphysics* opens with "All men by nature desire to know." See Aristotle, *Metaphysics*, in Richard McKeon, ed., *The Basic Works of Aristotle* (New York: Random House, 1941), 980a 1, page 689.

Chapter 3

1. For process theism, especially as it relates to our concerns with evil, see David Ray Griffin, *God, Power, and Evil: A Process Theodicy* (Louisville, Ky.: Westminster John Knox Press, 2004), ch. 18. For open theism, see Gregory A. Boyd, *God of the Possible: A Biblical Introduction to the Open View of God* (Grand Rapids, Mich.: Baker, 2000).

2. Harold Kushner, *When Bad Things Happen to Good People* (New York: Avon, 1981), 134.

3. Gary Stern, *Can God Intervene? How Religion Explains Natural Disasters* (Westport, Conn.: Praeger, 2007), 115–16.

4. A long-standing theme in Campolo's writings is divine renunciation of power. See Anthony Campolo, *The Power Delusion* (Wheaton, Ill.: Victor, 1983).

5. Stern, *Can God Intervene?* 46.

6. See, for instance, Francis A. Schaeffer, *Genesis in Space and Time: The Flow of Biblical History* (Downers Grove, Ill.: InterVarsity, 1972). Schaeffer, however, did not insist on a recent 6,000-year creation.

7. C. S. Lewis, *The Problem of Pain* (New York: Macmillan, 1962), 133.

8. John Polkinghorne, "Eschatology: Some questions and Some Insights from Science," in J. Polkinghorne and M. Welker, eds., *The End of the World and the Ends of God: Science and Theology on Eschatology* (Harrisburg, Penn.: Trinity Press International, 2000), 41.

9. Quoted by Patricia Williams, "Can Christianity Get Along Without Adam and Eve?" *Research News & Opportunities in Science and Theology* 3(3) (November 2002): 20.

10. Patrick Miller, "Judgment and Joy," in J. Polkinghorne and M. Welker, eds., *The End of the World and the Ends of God: Science and Theology on Eschatology* (Harrisburg, Penn.: Trinity Press International, 2000), 161.

11.   Denis Alexander, *Creation or Evolution: Do We Have to Choose?* (Oxford: Monarch, 2008), 270–71.

12.   Jürgen Moltmann, "Is There Life After Death?" in J. Polkinghorne and M. Welker, eds., *The End of the World and the Ends of God: Science and Theology on Eschatology* (Harrisburg, Penn.: Trinity Press International, 2000), 241.

13.   Lewis, *Problem of Pain*, 134–35.

14.   Ibid., 134.

15.   For biblical citations, see Hugh Ross and Kenneth Samples, "The Bible and UFOs," in H. Ross, K. R. Samples, and M. Clark, eds., *Lights in the Sky and Little Green Men: A Rational Christian Look at UFOs and Extraterrestrials* (Colorado Springs: NavPress, 2002), 159–66.

16.   Gregory A. Boyd, *Satan and the Problem of Evil: Constructing a Trinitarian Warfare Theodicy* (Downers Grove, Ill.: InterVarsity, 2001).

17.   Ibid., ch. 9.

18.   See Michael Crichton's Caltech Michelin lecture titled "Aliens Cause Global Warming," delivered January 17, 2003 and available online at http://www.crichton-official.com/speeches/speeches_quote04.html (accessed April 19, 2006).

19.   See Noam Chomsky, *Language and Mind*, enlarged edition (New York: Harcourt Brace Jovanovich, 1972); Mortimer Adler, *The Difference of Man and the Difference It Makes*, with introduction by D. W. Hudson (1967; reprinted New York: Fordham University Press, 1993); William Dembski and Jonathan Wells, *The Design of Life: Discovering Signs of Intelligence in Biological Systems* (Dallas: Foundation for Thought and Ethics, 2008), ch. 1.

20.   Bruce S. Thornton, *Plagues of the Mind: The New Epidemic of False Knowledge* (Wilmington, Del.: ISI, 1999), 96.

21.   Carl Sagan, *Pale Blue Dot: A Vision of the Human Future in Space* (New York: Ballantine, 1994), 7.

22.   Blaise Pascal, *Pensées*, no. 348, trans. W. F. Trotter, in R. M. Hutchins, ed., *Great Books of the Western World* (Chicago: Encyclopedia Britannica, 1952), 234.

23.   Julian of Norwich, *Showings*, ed. and trans. E. College and J. Walsh, in *The Classics of Western Spirituality* (New York: Paulist Press, 1988), 131–32.

24.   G. K. Chesterton, *Orthodoxy*, in *Collected Works of G. K. Chesterton* (San Francisco: Ignatius, 1986), I:264–65.

25.   Guillermo Gonzalez and Jay W. Richards, *The Privileged Planet: How Our Place in the Cosmos Is Designed for Discovery* (Washington, D.C.: Regnery, 2004). In the same spirit, see the essays in Henry Margenau and Roy Varghese, eds., *Cosmos, Bios, and Theos* (LaSalle, Ill.: Open Court, 1992).

Chapter 4

1.   This section was largely inspired by John Stott's *The Cross of Christ* (Downers Grove, Ill.: InterVarsity, 1986) and, in particular, his assimilation there of Saint Anselm's *Cur Deus Homo?*

2.   Ibid., 87. Compare http://www.ronaldbrucemeyer.com/rants/1213almanac.htm (accessed May 11, 2006), which places the quote a decade earlier in response to an attack of paralysis.

3.   Not only Scripture but also history shows Pelagianism to be wrong. There is little, if any, evidence that, all by ourselves, we suddenly resolve to lead virtuous lives and begin to do so. When it does happen, it almost always results from a spiritual transformation, most plausibly attributable to divine intervention (grace).

4.   We condone things when we overlook them because we don't think they're all that bad. Condonation is not forgiveness. Forgiveness occurs when a grave evil has been perpetrated against us, we recognize its gravity, and yet we decide to drop the charges against the perpetrator in order to preserve the relationship.

5.   The theodicy developed in this book does not depend on any particular theory of the atonement (e.g., ransom, Christus Victor, satisfaction, penal substitution, or moral influence). Rather, it stresses that regardless of our theory of the atonement, we must understand sin. Specifically, we must understand the nature and extent of our sin, its ramifications for the whole of creation, and the cost that Christ paid to deal with it.

6.   Redemption is usually at a fixed price. The pawn shop owner, for instance, is not free to decide that the item has increased (or decreased) in value since the ticket was issued and that the redeemer should therefore pay more (or less). The fixed price for our redemption was the Cross.

Chapter 5

1.   See, for instance, Henry Morris, *Scientific Creationism* (San Diego, Calif.: Creation-Life, 1974), 208, 211, 226, 229, 243, 245. Other scriptural passages that young-earth creationists cite to argue for death as a consequence of human sin include Gen 3:14–19; Rom 8:18–25; and 1 Cor 15:20–23. Commenting on these Genesis and Romans passages, Henry Morris argues that the Fall altered the second law of thermodynamics and thereby extended God's curse of humanity to the whole physical creation. See his *The Biblical Basis for Modern Science* (Green Forest, Ark.: Master, 2002), 181. Compare as well Ken Ham, ed., *The New Answers Book* (Green Forest, Ark.: Master, 2006), 53–54, 263–65; and Jonathan Sarfati, *Refuting Compromise* (Green Forest, Ark.: Master, 2004), 195–224.

2.   All these dates are conventional within the mainstream scientific literature. See William Dembski and Jonathan Wells, *The Design of Life: Discovering Signs of Intelligence in Biological Systems* (Dallas: Foundation for Thought and Ethics, 2008), chs. 3 and 8.

3.   Russell Moore, "A Creationist Watches *Animal Planet*," *The Southern Seminary Magazine (The TIE)* 74(2) (Summer 2006): 11, available online at http://www.sbts.edu/pdf/tie/2006Summer.pdf (accessed May 27, 2008).

4.   One might contend that the Old Testament saints were not really saved at the time of their earthly lives and that God reserved them in some sort of limbo until Christ should appear and save them at the Cross. The problem with this argument is that it fails to respect the holiness of God: all the Old Testament saints were sinners, fell short of God's holiness, and thus apart from Christ's salvation were subject to divine judgment. And yet during their earthly lives, they all were the beneficiaries of divine favor. That favor, derived from the Cross, was applied retroactively to their benefit.

5.   Helen Roseveare, *Living Faith* (Minneapolis, Minn.: Bethany, 1980), 44–45. I learned of this example from J. P. Moreland's *Kingdom Triangle: Recover the Christian Mind,*

Renovate the Soul, Restore the Spirit's Power (Grand Rapids, Mich.: Zondervan, 2007), ch. 1.

6. William A. Dembski, Wayne J. Downs, and Fr. Justin B. A. Frederick, eds., *The Patristic Understanding of Creation: An Anthology of Writings from the Church Fathers on Creation and Design* (Riesel, Tex.: Erasmus, 2008), 90.

7. Origen, *Contra Celsum* (*Against Celsus*) 1.19. For the quote, see Dembski et al., *Patristic Understanding of Creation*, 136.

8. Augustine, "Of the Falseness of the History Which Allots Many Thousand Years to the World's Past," *De Civitate Dei* (*The City of God*) xii:10. For the quote, see Dembski et al., *Patristic Understanding of Creation*, 481.

9. Thomas Aquinas, *Summa Theologiae* I:91:2. The entire *Summa* is available online at http://www.newadvent.org/summa (accessed May 27, 2008).

10. Mark Ryland, "Thomistic Evolutionism as an Interlocutor in the Evolution Debate," presented November 4, 2006 in Nashville at the American Maritain Association Thirtieth Annual Meeting, cited at http://www.jacquesmaritain.org/program.pdf (accessed December 1, 2008). Ryland heads the Institute for the Study of Nature (http://www.isnature .org).

11. Aquinas, *Summa*, I:74:3.

12. Aquinas, *Summa*, I:61:3.

13. Ibid. Aquinas here is quoting Jerome's *Commentary on the Epistle to Titus*. Note that Jerome here calculated the age of the physical universe on the basis of the Septuagint and that almost a thousand years had passed from his time to that of Aquinas. In any case, Aquinas would not have questioned that the earth was under 10,000 years old.

14. See Luther's lectures on the first five chapters of Genesis in Jaroslav Pelikan, ed., *Luther's Works* (St. Louis: Concordia, 1958), I:3.

15. Ibid., 6.

16. John Calvin, *Institutes of the Christian Religion*, ed. J. T. McNeill (Philadelphia: Westminster Press, 1960), 2:925.

17. John Calvin, *Commentary on Genesis* (Edinburgh: Banner of Truth, 1984), 105.

18. R. C. Sproul, *Truths We Confess: A Layman's Guide to the Westminster Confession of Faith, Volume 1: The Triune God* (Phillipsburg, N.J.: P&R, 2006), 127–28.

19. My friend and colleague Jack Collins, an Old Testament scholar, thinks I may be overstating the role of science in encouraging people to turn away from a young earth. As he put it to me in an e-mail (January 28, 2009), "Not everyone who rejects the 24-hour day reading of Genesis 1 does so for the sake of science alone. My own reading of these days as God's workdays has an important precedent in Herman Bavinck, who was skeptical of geology in the late 19th century. That is, I have literary and exegetical reasons for my position. Further, at the same time as the sciences have concluded on the antiquity of the earth, texts from the ancient Near East have become available, and some of these provide helpful genre classifications for Genesis 1–11. Also, linguistic study of Hebrew and other ancient Semitic languages has taken a step up as well, and this in turn affects how we think we should read Genesis. So there are more things (or more sciences) going on than just the natural sciences." See his book *Genesis 1–4: A Linguistic, Literary, and Theological Commentary* (Phillipsburg, N.J.: P&R, 2006). Nonetheless, it's hard to imagine how these other things

could turn people from the 24-hour day reading of Genesis except for the challenge posed by the natural sciences. If science is not the whole reason for questioning the traditional reading, it is the reason for the other reasons.

20. Sproul, *Truths We Confess*, 120.

Chapter 6

1. See the essay titled "Young Earth Creationism" by Paul Nelson and John Mark Reynolds in J. P. Moreland and John Mark Reynolds, eds., *Three Views on Creation and Evolution* (Grand Rapids, Mich.: Zondervan, 1999), 73.

2. See, for instance, Don DeYoung, *Thousands . . . Not Billions: Challenging an Icon of Evolution, Questioning the Age of the Earth* (Green Forest, Ark.: Master, 2005); Jonathan Sarfati, *Refuting Compromise: A Biblical and Scientific Refutation of "Progressive Creationism" (Billions of Years) As Popularized by Astronomer Hugh Ross* (Green Forest, Ark.: Master, 2004); John Morris, *The Young Earth: The Real History of the Earth—Past, Present, and Future* (Green Forest, Ark.: Master, 2007); Walter T. Brown, *In the Beginning: Compelling Evidence for Creation and the Flood*, 7th ed. (Phoenix, Ariz.: Center for Scientific Creation, 2001); Kurt Wise, *Faith, Form and Time: What the Bible Teaches and Science Confirms About Creation and the Age of the Universe* (Nashville: B&H, 2002).

3. E.g., Henry M. Morris, ed., *Scientific Creationism* (San Diego, Calif.: Creation-Life, 1974), ch. 5.

4. See, for instance, Mark Isaak, *The Counter-Creationism Handbook* (Berkeley, Calif.: University of California Press, 2007), 130–31 (polystrate fossils) and 160–67 (sedimentation). See also Don Lindsay's "'Polystrate' Fossils," at http://www.don-lindsay -archive.org/creation/polystrate.html (accessed January 14, 2008).

5. DeYoung, *Thousands . . . Not Billions*, 180. Italics in the original. In a similar vein, John Morris remarks, "let me not leave the impression that radioisotope dating has been overturned. It has been called into question, flaws in its foundation exposed, and its results shown to be inconsistent. In short, it is in trouble, but it is still a formidable concept in the minds of many. Much research needs to be done and is being done at ICR and elsewhere." Quoted from his book *The Young Earth*, 63.

6. Georges Florovsky, "Creation and Creaturehood," in William A. Dembski, Wayne J. Downs, and Fr. Justin B. A. Frederick, eds., *The Patristic Understanding of Creation: An Anthology of Writings from the Church Fathers on Creation and Design* (Riesel, Tex.: Erasmus Press, 2008), 552.

7. I am indebted to Greg Smith for this insight. Smith suggests that Genesis 1 be read covenantally in that it introduces the covenant name *Yahweh* in Gen 2:4 as well as the specific covenant or treaty language used in the unfolding of the creation week. The phrase repeated in Hebrew, "and God saw that it was good," employs treaty terminology that was quite common in the ancient Near East. In the ancient world, covenants are described as "good" provided they produce desired results. Covenants are validated and confirmed as "true" when these desired results are "seen" (i.e., visually confirmed). Smith suggests that this repeated phrase signals God's kairological activity in creation by which the problem of the Fall is both anticipated and responded to covenantally. Adam and Eve will have a place to go and experience their exile from the Garden, just as Israel experiences exile from the Promised Land, both at Kadesh-Barnea and after the destruction of Jerusalem in 586 BC. This covenantal understanding of Genesis 1 reveals the constancy of God's activity toward both his creation and his chosen people. Moreover, other biblical authors present it as a timeless theological truth.

Jeremiah, for example, grounds the hope of God's future covenantal activity toward Judah's faithful remnant on the firmness of God's covenantal activity: "This is what the LORD says: 'If I have not established my covenant with day and night and the *fixed laws* of heaven and earth, then I will reject the descendants of Jacob and David my servant and will not choose one of his sons to rule over the descendants of Abraham, Isaac and Jacob'" (Jer 33:25–26, NIV, emphasis mine). See Greg Smith, "Can a Good Creation Be Bad and Good at the Same Time? Another Look at Bill Dembski's 'Christian Theodicy in Light of Modern Science,'" paper presented at the Evangelical Theological Society, Providence, R.I. (November 2008). See also Greg Smith, *The Testing of Our Faith: A Pentateuchal Theology of Testing* (Ph.D. dissertation., The Southern Baptist Theological Seminary, Louisville, Ky., 2005), 40–46.

8. Edward T. Oakes, "Edward T. Oakes and His Critics: An Exchange," *First Things* 112 (April 2001): available online at http://www.firstthings.com/article.php3?id_article=2168 (accessed June 3, 2008).

9. See, for instance, Guillermo Gonzalez and Jay W. Richards, *The Privileged Planet: How Our Place in the Cosmos Is Designed for Discovery* (Washington, D.C.: Regnery, 2004), 22–26.

10. See, for instance, Michael Oard, "Do Greenland Ice Cores Show Over One Hundred Thousand Years of Annual Layers?" *[Answers in Genesis] Technical Journal* 15(3) (December 2001): 39–42, available online at http://www.answersingenesis.org/tj/v15/i3/greenland.asp (accessed January 10, 2008).

11. See Kurt Wise, *Faith, Form and Time*, 193.

12. Terry Mortenson, "Christian Theodicy in Light of Genesis and Modern Science: A Young-Earth Creationist Response to William Dembski," paper presented at the Evangelical Theological Society, San Diego, Calif. (November 15, 2007).

13. A presuppositional apologist might jump in here and contend that one can't simply bracket, or lay to one side, the truth of Scripture, as I seem to be suggesting, since the truth of Scripture must be presupposed to understand any truths whatsoever, including the truths of geology for dating the earth. But this objection quickly runs aground. At issue is not the truth of Scripture but how properly to interpret certain controversial portions of it. My argument for the theological acceptability of an old earth is independent of the brand of apologetics one adopts (presuppositional, reformed, evidential, classical, etc.).

14. F. F. Bruce, *Commentary on the Book of the Acts* (Grand Rapids, Mich.: Eerdmans, 1977), 18.

15. Trevor Bryce, *The Kingdom of the Hittites,* 2nd edition (New York: Oxford University Press, 2005).

16. For the origin of human writing, see Denise Schmandt-Besserat, *How Writing Came About*, abridged edition (Austin, Tex.: University of Texas Press, 1997).

17. See the doll displays at the Oriental Institute, which is located on the campus of the University of Chicago, http://oi.uchicago.edu (accessed May 12, 2006).

18. Henry M. Morris, *Many Infallible Proofs: Evidences for the Christian Faith*, revised and expanded (Green Forest, Ark.: Master, 1996); Morris, *Scientific Creationism.*

Chapter 7

1.   Philip H. Gosse, *Omphalos: An Attempt to Untie the Geological Knot* (London: John Van Voorst, 1857).

2.   D. Russell Humphreys, *Starlight and Time: Solving the Puzzle of Distant Starlight in a Young Universe* (Green Forest, Ark.: Master, 1994), 37.

3.   Henry M. Morris, ed., *Scientific Creationism* (San Diego, Calif.: Creation-Life, 1974), 210.

4.   See Barry Setterfield and Trevor Norman, "The Atomic Constants, Light, and Time," research report, August 1987, available online at http://www.setterfield.org/report/report .html (accessed January 11, 2008).

5.   See Guillermo Gonzalez and Jay W. Richards, *The Privileged Planet: How Our Place in the Cosmos Is Designed for Discovery* (Washington, D.C.: Regnery, 2004), ch. 10.

6.   Ibid., 198–99. There Gonzalez and Richards define nuclear resonance as "a range of energies that greatly increases the chances of interaction between a nucleus and another particle—for example, the capture of a proton or a neutron. An energy resonance in a nucleus will accelerate reactions if the colliding particles have just the right kinetic energy. Resonances tend to be narrow, so even slight changes in their location would lead to enormous changes in the reaction rates." They then describe how carbon-12's nuclear resonance allows it to be formed in sufficient quantities during stellar burning to make the universe life-permitting.

7.   Don Batten (ed.), Ken Ham, Jonathan Sarfati, and Carl Wieland, "How Can We See Distant Stars in a Young Universe?" available at http://www.answersingenesis.org/docs/405 .asp (accessed January 11, 2008).

8.   Humphreys, *Starlight and Time*, 13.

9.   Edward Fackerell, "Analysis of 'Starlight and Time,'" typescript, available online at http:// anzachristianscholarship.org/starlight.pdf (accessed January 11, 2008).

10.   Ibid.

11.   Samuel R. Conner and Don N. Page, "*Starlight and Time* is the Big Bang," *CEN Technical Journal* 12(2) (1998): 174–94, available online at http://www.trueorigin.org/rh _connpage1.pdf (accessed January 11, 2008).

Chapter 8

1.   Thus, to the question, "What do the Scriptures principally teach?" the Westminster Shorter Catechism answers, "The Scriptures principally teach what man is to believe concerning God and what duty God requires of man." See The Westminster Shorter Catechism, q. 3, available online at http://www.creeds.net/reformed/Westminster/shorter_catechism.html (accessed November 28, 2008).

2.   Stephen Jay Gould, *Rocks of Ages: Science and Religion in the Fullness of Life* (New York: Ballantine, 1999), 6.

3.   According to Nancy Pearcey, this false dichotomy between fact and value is the reason we live in a post-Christian culture. See Nancy Pearcey, *Total Truth: Liberating Christianity from Its Cultural Captivity* (Wheaton, Ill.: Crossway, 2004).

4. Karl Barth, *Church Dogmatics: The Doctrine of Creation* III/3, ed. G. W. Bromiley and T. F. Torrance, trans. G. W. Bromiley and R. J. Ehrlich (Edinburgh: T. & T. Clark, 1957), 290.

5. Karl Barth, *Church Dogmatics: The Doctrine of the Word of God* I/1, ed. G. W. Bromiley and T. F. Torrance, trans. G. W. Bromiley and T. F. Torrance (Edinburgh: T. & T. Clark, 1955). Barth even went further, denying all forms of apologetics, thus claiming that our intellects are incapable of reasoning to any valid knowledge of God.

6. Richard Dawkins, *The Blind Watchmaker: Why the Evidence of Evolution Reveals a Universe Without Design* (New York: Norton, 1986), 6.

7. See Alister McGrath, *Dawkins' God: Genes, Memes, and the Meaning of Life* (Oxford: Blackwell, 2005).

8. See Andrea Frova and Mariapiera Marenzana, *Thus Spoke Galileo: The Great Scientist's Ideas and Their Relevance to the Present Day*, trans. James H. McManus (Oxford: Oxford University Press, 2006), 233–34.

9. The need for theories to match up with observational data has been known since the time of the ancient Greeks, who described this problem in terms of "saving the phenomena." In other words, the task of science (known back then as "natural philosophy") was to match up scientific theories with the phenomena (or appearances) of nature. Physicist Pierre Duhem even wrote a book on this topic: Pierre Duhem, *To Save the Phenomena: An Essay on the Idea of Physical Theory from Plato to Galileo*, trans. E. Dolan and C. Maschler (Chicago: University of Chicago Press, 1969). He also wrote another book focused on theory choice in science and how different theories may be empirically indistinguishable when accounting for the same observational data (hence the "underdetermination" of theory by data): Pierre Duhem, *The Aim and Structure of Physical Theory*, trans. P. P. Wiener (Princeton: Princeton University Press, 1954). The point to realize is that the Catholic Church, in examining Galileo, knew all of this.

10. Richard Dawkins, *The God Delusion* (New York: Houghton Mifflin, 2006), 285.

11. John F. Ashton, ed., *In Six Days: Why Fifty Scientists Choose to Believe in Creation* (Green Forest, Ark.: Master, 2001), 355. Kurt Wise's chapter in this book is also available online at http://creationontheweb.com/content/view/4044 (accessed June 3, 2008).

12. Charles Hodge, *Systematic Theology* (reprinted Grand Rapids, Mich.: Eerdmans, 1981), I:171. Emphasis added.

13. All of this is beautifully recounted in chapter 11, "The Revisionist History of the Copernican Revolution," in Guillermo Gonzalez and Jay W. Richards, *The Privileged Planet: How Our Place in the Cosmos Is Designed for Discovery* (Washington, D.C.: Regnery, 2004).

Chapter 9

1. Hugh Ross, *Creation and Time: A Biblical and Scientific Perspective on the Creation-Date Controversy* (Colorado Springs: NavPress, 1994), 68.

2. Ross asks rhetorically, "Could it be that God's purposes are somehow fulfilled through our experiencing the 'random, wasteful inefficiencies' of the natural realm He created?" Ibid., 88.

3. Mark S. Whorton, *Peril in Paradise: Theology, Science, and the Age of the Earth* (Waynesboro, Ga.: Authentic Media, 2005), 151.

4.   Theistic evolutionists are guilty of the same—see chapter 21.

5.   David Snoke, "Why Were Dangerous Animals Created?" *Perspectives on Science and Christian Faith* 56(2) (2004): 125, available online at http://www.asa3.org/ASA/ PSCF/2004/PSCF6–04Snoke.pdf (accessed January 10, 2006).

6.   Ibid., 119–20. To argue his case, Snoke lists passages of Scripture that celebrate carnivores and carnivorousness (especially from Job 39–41). Jack Collins, approaching the problem of natural evil as an exegete, suggests that animal death as such need not be evil. See his *Genesis 1–4: A Linguistic, Literary, and Theological Commentary* (Phillipsburg, N.J.: P&R, 2006), 165. But animal death and suffering as it exists now and as it appears to have existed throughout the fossil record bespeak a cruelty and perverseness that only exacerbates the problem of evil (see chapters 20 and 21). What would the non-evil death of, for instance, large mammals look like in a non-fallen world? We haven't a clue. Nor does the Bible anywhere grant the assumption underlying this question, namely, that the death of such animals could result from anything other than evil. Once evil is here, large flamboyant carnivores elicit a certain admiration. But let us ever bear in mind the image of the messianic reign in Isa 11:6: "The wolf also shall dwell with the lamb, and the leopard shall lie down with the kid; and the calf and the young lion and the fatling together; and a little child shall lead them." It would seem that Scripture glories less in carnivorousness than in its eradication.

7.   Snoke, "Dangerous Animals," 117.

8.   For a fuller treatment of Snoke's views, see his *A Biblical Case for an Old Earth* (Grand Rapids, Mich.: Baker, 2006).

Chapter 10

1.   Beavers actualize by chewing down small trees, damming water courses, and building massive lodges. They don't have what we call a language, though the instincts to behave as they do are imprinted somehow, and the genes responsible and the resulting neural networks can function as a language in a rudimentary way. All beavers build roughly the same type of structure because of the sharp limitation this system of information transfer places on individual intelligence.

2.   George J. Thompson, *Verbal Judo: The Gentle Art of Persuasion* (New York: HarperCollins, 2004), 129.

3.   Claude Shannon and Warren Weaver, *The Mathematical Theory of Communication* (Urbana, Ill.: University of Illinois Press, 1949), 34.

4.   Hence the importance of the "royal" imagery for God in Scripture. A royal son accounts his father greater than himself, but in another sense they meet as equals.

5.   Compare Isa 40:8, which contrasts the eternality of God's Word with the temporality of its manifestations: "The grass withereth, the flower fadeth: but the word of our God shall stand for ever."

6.   Vera Pless, *Introduction to the Theory of Error-Correcting Codes*, 3rd ed. (New York: Wiley-Interscience, 1998).

7.   Compare Leslie Zeigler, "Christianity or Feminism?" in William A. Dembski and Jay Wesley Richards, eds., *Unapologetic Apologetics* (Downers Grove, Ill.: InterVarsity, 2001), 179–86.

8. According to Noam Chomsky, "When we study human language, we are approaching what some might call the 'human essence,' the distinctive qualities of mind that are, so far as we know, unique to man and that are inseparable from any critical phase of human existence, personal or social. . . . Having mastered a language, one is able to understand an indefinite number of expressions that are new to one's experience, that bear no simple physical resemblance and are in no simple way analogous to the expressions that constitute one's linguistic experience; and one is able, with greater or less facility, to produce such expressions on an appropriate occasion, despite their novelty and independently of detectable stimulus configurations, and to be understood by others who share this still mysterious ability. The normal use of language is, in this sense, a creative activity. This creative aspect of normal language use is one fundamental factor that distinguishes human language from any known system of animal communication." Quoted from "Form and Meaning in Natural Languages," in *Language and Mind*, enlarged edition (New York: Harcourt, Brace, Jovanovich, 1972), 100.

9. See Wheeler's autobiography: John A. Wheeler and Kenneth W. Ford, *Geons, Black Holes, and Quantum Foam: A Life in Physics* (New York: Norton, 1999), 63–64.

10. Ibid., 64.

11. Ibid.

12. See, for instance, Keith Devlin, *Logic and Information* (Cambridge: Cambridge University Press, 1991), 2; Hans Christian von Baeyer, *Information: The New Language of Science* (Cambridge, Mass.: Harvard University Press, 2004); Roy Frieden, *Physics from Fisher Information: A Unification* (Cambridge: Cambridge University Press, 1998); and Paul Davies, "Bit Before It?" *New Scientist* 161 (January 30, 1999): 3.

Chapter 11

1. Fred Dretske, *Knowledge and the Flow of Information* (Cambridge, Mass.: MIT Press, 1981), 26. Carl Jung makes essentially the same point in developing his parallel notion of synchronicity, characterizing it as an acausal connecting principle. See his book *Synchronicity*, trans. R. F. C. Hull (Princeton: Princeton University Press, 1973).

2. Ibid. Note that in repeating the quote, I substituted "source" for *s* and "receiver" for *r*.

3. My remarks on transposition draw heavily from C. S. Lewis, "Transposition," in *The Weight of Glory and Other Addresses* (New York: Collier, 1980), 54–73. I'm grateful to Jake Akins for drawing my attention to this essay.

4. I've never been able to find a reference to Blackwell's super supercomputer. It may simply be an urban legend floating among mathematicians.

5. Ludwig Wittgenstein, *Remarks on the Foundations of Mathematics*, rev. ed., ed. G. H. von Wright, R. Rhees, and G. E. M. Anscombe, trans. G. E. M. Anscombe (Cambridge, Mass.: MIT Press, 1983), 95, 143, 155.

Chapter 12

1. Marvin Vincent, *Vincent's Word Studies in the New Testament* (Peabody, Mass.: Hendrickson, 1984), s.v. "John 1:1–5."

2. In this etymological study of *logos* and its cognates as well as in other word studies later this book (especially with the *chronos* vs. *kairos* distinction in Part IV), my approach is not that of *historical linguistics*, which tries to understand the precise way these words were employed in ancient texts. Instead, I'm engaged in what might be called *conceptual*

improvisation, taking these words and their historical usage as a springboard for generating true insights into fundamental realities. The concepts and distinctions developed are useful and real even if they are not tethered as tightly to their linguistic roots as professional linguists might like.

3. Creation is not the neurotic, forced self-revelation offered on the psychoanalyst's couch. Nor is it the superficial self-revelation of idle chitchat.

4. Erich Fromm, *The Art of Loving* (New York: Harper, 1974), 18–19. Compare Acts 20:35, "Remember the words of the Lord Jesus, how he said, It is more blessed to give than to receive." Compare also Heb 7:7, "Without all contradiction the less is blessed of the better."

5. Christos Yannaras, *Elements of Faith: An Introduction to Orthodox Theology* (Edinburgh: T&T Clark, 1991), 44–45.

6. Creation is a sacred activity. For deep connections between the creation of the world and the construction of the Jewish temple (thus picturing the cosmos as a sanctuary), see G. K. Beale, *The Erosion of Inerrancy in Evangelicalism: Responding to New Challenges to Biblical Authority* (Wheaton, Ill.: Crossway, 2008), chs. 6 and 7, which are both titled "Can Old Testament Cosmology Be Reconciled with Modern Scientific Cosmology?" For divine rest in creation and temple construction, see 184–90.

Chapter 13

1. Humans exercise the ability to invent and modify language. Consider American Sign Language, for example, or the creoles that develop when children from a variety of places are thrown together in an encampment where their parents are mutually incomprehensible. The evolution of the English language is a remarkable story too. It was pulled back from the brink of extinction by a single writer, Chaucer. Eliezer Ben-Yehudah resurrected Hebrew and made it the language of Israel. None of this is Darwinian evolution in any important sense. It is evolution based on intelligent decisions by people who want to communicate in a particular way. That is how languages evolve.

2. The phrase "reimagining God" dates to the mid 1990s—see Johanna W. H. Van Wijk-Bos, *Reimagining God: The Case for Scriptural Diversity* (Louisville, Ky.: Westminster John Knox, 1995). The idea of changing or evolving conceptions of God remains much the rage in theological circles. One tongue-in-cheek Web page even boasts having assembled a "a crack team of 'metaphysical engineers' who have devised a new computer-modelling virtual environment in which to test the plausibility of different conceptions of God." See http://www.philosophersnet.com/games/whatisgod.htm (accessed December 10, 2008).

3. For an overview of this literature as well as a critique, see Mary A. Kassian, *The Feminist Mistake: The Radical Impact of Feminism on Church and Culture* (Wheaton, Ill.: Crossway, 2005).

4. Janet Martin Soskice, *The Kindness of God: Metaphor, Gender, and Religious Language* (New York: Oxford University Press, 2008), 68.

5. Ibid. The most important thing people who are repelled by the idea of God as father need is precisely the image of a good father. All of us need a father, someone to tell us who we are, to bless us for who we are, to send us on our way to be the best we can be, to be there for us as long as possible, and to be a good example. Bad fathers who do not do those things don't change that fact any more than bad mothers who don't feed and teach their children don't change the fact that children need to be fed and taught.

6. For more on why the traditional metaphors of God are just fine and don't need to be revised to suit the contemporary fashion (Is process theology, for instance, really improving our understanding of God by describing him as a "lure"?), see C. S. Lewis, *Miracles: A Preliminary Study*, rev. ed. (1960; reprinted San Francisco: Harper, 2001), ch. 10.

7. This is the most widely used translation of Einstein's dictum. It appears in Antonina Vallentin, *The Drama of Albert Einstein*, trans. Moura Budberg (New York: Doubleday, 1954), 39. When it first appeared in English in 1936 with the *Journal of the Franklin Institute*, it was translated by Jean Piccard as "The eternal mystery of the world is its comprehensibility." See Albert Einstein, "Physics and Reality," *Journal of the Franklin Institute* 221 (1936): 351.

8. G. K. Chesterton, *Orthodoxy*, in *Collected Works of G. K. Chesterton* (San Francisco: Ignatius, 1986), I:236, emphasis in original.

9. C. S. Lewis developed this line of argument in chapter 3 ("The Cardinal Difficulty of Naturalism") of *Miracles*. Victor Reppert devoted a whole book to it: *C. S. Lewis's Dangerous Idea: In Defense of the Argument from Reason* (Downers Grove, Ill.: InterVarsity, 2003). Alvin Plantinga formulated a technical probabilistic (Bayesian) version of it in *Warranted Christian Belief* (Oxford: Oxford University Press, 2000), ch. 7.

10. Because communication is also widely studied in the social sciences (e.g., in departments of speech, rhetoric, and communication), communication theory in the technical engineering sense described here is now usually called simply information theory. See Thomas M. Cover and Joy A. Thomas, *Elements of Information Theory*, 2nd ed. (New York: Wiley, 2006).

11. For instance, Lerner and Trigg's massive encyclopedia of physics, which was published in the early 1990s, contains no entry or index reference to "communication" or "information"—see Rita G. Lerner and George L. Trigg, *Encyclopedia of Physics*, 2nd ed. (New York: VCH Publishers, 1991).

12. Paul Davies, "Bit Before It?" *New Scientist* (January 30, 1999): 3.

Chapter 14

1. Stephen R. Covey, *The Seven Habits of Highly Effective People* (New York: Simon & Schuster, 1989), 99. Emphasis in the original.

2. Ibid.

3. Ibid.

4. G. K. Chesterton, *Orthodoxy*, in *Collected Works of G. K. Chesterton* (San Francisco: Ignatius, 1986), I:281–82.

5. See http://www.musicweb-international.com/classRev/2006/May06/points_North_cameo2036 .htm (accessed August 8, 2008).

6. Which is not to limit the freedom of creation. The world presents us with live options, and we retain the capacity to imagine things otherwise.

7. Posted by Esther Battle, http://www.cartalk.com/content/timekill/lamejokes/car.html (accessed November 28, 2008).

8. J. Jay Dana, "The Religion of Geology," *Bibliotheca Sacra* 10 (1853): 521. Dana in this essay reviews Edward Hitchcock's *The Religion of Geology and Its Connected Sciences*

(Boston: Phillips, Sampson & Co., 1851). Hitchcock held that even though natural evil predated humans, human sin was the reason for natural evil. Hitchcock was a leading American geologist whose books were quite popular and widely used as college texts. As early as 1846, Dana had articulated a retroactive view of the Fall: J. Jay Dana, "On the Relations between Religion and Geology," *Biblical Repository and Classical Review* 26 (1846): 296–320. I'm indebted to historian and philosopher of science Michael Keas for drawing my attention to the thought of the nineteeth-century biblical geologists.

9.   Conrad Wright, "The Religion of Geology," *The New England Quarterly* 14(2) (June 1941): 347. Emphasis added. The quote in this passage is from Edward Hitchcock, *Religion of Geology*, 104.

10. Nicolaas A. Rupke, "Geology and Paleontology," in Gary Ferngren, ed., *Science and Religion: A Historical Introduction* (Baltimore: Johns Hopkins University Press, 2002), 187.

11. See Charles Hodge, *Systematic Theology* (reprinted Grand Rapids, Mich.: Eerdmans, 1981), I:570–74. These pages, in a subsection titled "Geology and the Bible" and part of a larger section titled "Objections to the Mosaic Account of the Creation," fail even to address the problem of natural evil predating human sin. Hodge's *Systematic Theology* was widely employed in American theological education. One may speculate what the history of creationism in the United States would have been if the biblical geologist's retroactive view of the Fall had been widely disseminated through the work of Hodge.

Chapter 15

1.   The Templeton Foundation sponsored this event: http://www.templeton.org/humble _approach_initiative/Complexity_Information_Design (accessed September 18, 2008). Niels Gregersen edited the symposium proceedings: *From Complexity to Life: On the Emergence of Life and Meaning* (New York: Oxford University Press, 2002).

2.   Davies's worry is essentially the Cartesian worry about mind-body dualism: how does a nonphysical mental cause have a physical effect?

3.   For this exchange, see Daniel F. Styer, *The Strange World of Quantum Mechnics* (Cambridge: Cambridge University Press, 2000), 128. See also Walter Isaacson, *Einstein: His Life and Universe* (New York: Simon & Schuster, 2007), 326.

4.   God does as he likes. According to Dan 4:35, God "doeth according to his will in the army of heaven, and among the inhabitants of the earth: and none can stay his hand, or say unto him, What doest thou?"

5.   Brown University biologist Kenneth Miller calls himself an "orthodox Catholic" and an "orthodox Darwinian." Throughout his book *Finding Darwin's God* (New York: HarperCollins, 1999), he insists that God's activity in natural history (though not in salvation history) be consistent with natural law. When I e-mailed arch-atheist Richard Dawkins to ask whether he had a problem with the prayer that opened Miller's January 3, 2006 lecture on evolution at Case Western Reserve University, he took no offense. In a January 13, 2006 e-mail to me, he remarked, "It is most kind of you to send me the url of Kenneth Miller's splendid lecture at Case Western University [i.e., mms://mv-helix1.cwru.edu/a/2006/biology/intelligent_design_384kbps_01_03_2006_1.wmv]. I lost no time in listening to the entire lecture, and the Q and A afterwards. I am almost embarrassed to admit that, in the privacy of my room, I stood and applauded when the lecture came to an end. . . . I would dearly love to get my hands on a higher resolution copy of the film so that I can, with permission of course, make it more widely available in Britain. Complete with the opening prayer, which is important (especially Kenneth Miller's sanctioning of it)

for dispelling the widespread and pernicious underestimate of the support that evolution enjoys among theologically sophisticated Christians, from the late Pope on. I shall in any case now add the url of Miller's lecture to my forthcoming book, *The God Delusion*, now nearing completion." God may be a delusion for Dawkins, but he is happy to praise religious believers whose God moves no particles.

6. Norbert Wiener, *Cybernetics*, 2nd ed. (Cambridge, Mass.: MIT Press, 1961), 132.

7. Interestingly, given the imprecision inherent in all our measurements, there is no way ever to establish determinism with finality.

8. See my article "Randomness by Design," *Nous* 25(1) (1991): 75–106.

9. Augustine, *The Literal Meaning of Genesis*, trans. J. H. Taylor, *Ancient Christian Writers*, 2 vols. (New York: Paulist, 1982), 1: 90, 141–42. Augustine writes here of "seminal principles" and "reason-principles" and "implanted causal reasons."

10. Gottfried Wilhelm Leibniz, *Theodicy: Essays on the Goodness of God and the Freedom of Man and the Origin of Evil*, trans. E. M. Huggard (La Salle, Ill.: Open Court, 1985).

11. Charles Babbage, *The Ninth Bridgewater Treatise* (London: Murray, 1836).

12. See the following two articles by Michael Polanyi: "Life Transcending Physics and Chemistry," *Chemical and Engineering News* 45 (August 1967): 54–66; and "Life's Irreducible Structure," *Science* 113 (1968): 1308–12.

13. Go to http://video.google.com/videoplay?docid=-6006084025483872237 or else http://www.youtube.com/watch?v=rYabfifhEPE (accessed January 31, 2009).

14. By the way, I'm no fan of middle knowledge. I simply present it here as an option. Philosophically, I object to middle knowledge because it hinges on assigning determinate truthvalues to counterfactual conditionals, a property these conditionals can't reasonably be said to possess. *If John F. Kennedy hadn't been assassinated, he would have been reelected in 1964.* Is this counterfactual conditional true? Given Kennedy's popularity, it seems likely that he would have been reelected. Given his sexual indiscretions, a scandal might have prevented him from being reelected.

The standard possible-worlds semantics for these conditionals (see David Lewis, *Counterfactuals* [Cambridge, Mass.: Harvard University Press, 1973]) depends on a similarity metric on possible worlds: the counterfactual *if A, then B* is true if in the worlds closest to ours where A is true B is also true. Such measurements of closeness among possible worlds, however, fail to respect the multidimensionality of similarity—along which dimension(s) do we gauge similarity? Cf. Amos Tversky, "Features of Similarity," *Psychological Review* 84 (1977): 327–52.

On the assumption that humans have libertarian free will, how does God figure out what we would do in a given circumstance? Sure, God will know our range of options. But if Kennedy hadn't been assassinated, how does God know all the free actions of voters as they cast or refrain from casting their ballots for JFK? Does God determine the action of the voters? That would defeat the whole point of middle knowledge, which is to avoid the hard theological determinism of Calvinism. But if God has no determinative role in human action (and many passages of Scripture suggest that he does, e.g., Prov 21:1), is God's knowledge of the action of free agents in particular circumstances simply a surd? In other words, it simply is the case, with nothing further making it true, that free agents act in one and only one way in a given circumstance. While there may be no logical contradiction in treating middle knowledge as a surd, that hardly commends it.

Theologically, I object to middle knowledge because it seems to compromise grace. The big selling point of middle knowledge for theodicy is that it portrays God as doing everything he can to break the grip of evil over fallen creatures. If God has middle knowledge, God knows what a given creature would do in every conceivable circumstance. Thus, if God is also truly loving, he will employ his middle knowledge to arrange circumstances so that the creature derives maximal benefit.

Here's the difficulty: the problem of evil is so insidious that the free will of some free creatures will never shake it. Many free creatures, if we are to believe Scripture, will use their freedom to embrace evil and consign themselves to hell. What starts out as a way of killing two birds with one stone—God appears to get a theodicy and we humans appear to get free will—thus winds up providing neither. If middle knowledge is correct, for free creatures that perpetually abuse their freedom, under no conceivable circumstance will such creatures turn from evil to good—no matter how much of God's grace gets applied to turn the tide of evil in their lives.

But think what this means. Here is a creature incapable of being touched by God's grace, a creature so completely trapped that try what God may, that creature will never escape evil. Call this a free creature if you will, but this free creature of the Arminians is functionally equivalent to the reprobate creature of the Calvinists. (Arminians stress the ability of humans to respond to God's grace. Calvinists stress the sovereignty of God and the inability of humans to do anything to further their salvation apart from God's grace.) Both creatures have been determined to remain in evil, one for the noble-sounding reason that the creature's free will unremittingly chooses evil, the other for the ignoble-sounding reason that God, for the sake of his glory, chose the creature to remain interminably in evil. It seems absurd to think that there can be genuine creaturely freedom where grace does not even have the possibility of breaking through.

Karl Barth summarizes the theological problem with middle knowledge as follows: "Where grace is not extolled, there can only be sin. There is no third possibility. But the doctrine of the *scientia media* [i.e., middle knowledge] is not an extolling of grace. It will not deny it, but it hedges it round with so many reservations and limitations that it is only too clear that there is in it no love for grace as grace. And because there is no love, there is hatred of it." Quoted from Karl Barth, *Church Dogmatics: The Doctrine of God*, Volume II/1, ed. G. W. Bromiley and T. F. Torrance, trans. G. W. Bromiley (Edinburgh: T. & T. Clark, 1957), 586.

15.   Joseph's brothers, after the death of their father Jacob, worry that Joseph will do them harm for selling him into slavery. Joseph's reply to his brothers provides a classic illustration of divine concurrence: "Even though you intended to do harm to me, God intended it for good, in order to preserve a numerous people, as he is doing today" (Gen 50:20 NRSV).

16.   Compare Leibniz's idea of a "preestablished harmony" in his *Theodicy* as well as in "The Controversy between Leibniz and Clarke, 1715–1716," in Gottfried Wilhelm Leibniz, *Philosophical Papers and Letters*, ed. L. E. Loemker, 2nd ed. (Dordrecht: Reidel, 1976), 710–15.

Chapter 16

1.   See Christos Yannaras, *Elements of Faith: An Introduction to Orthodox Theology* (Edinburgh: T&T Clark, 1991), 40. Yannaras writes, "The world in its entirety and in its every detail is an effected *word* (*logos*), a personal creative activity of God. According to the account of Genesis, God created everything only by his word: 'He spoke, and it came to be' (Ps. 33:9 NIV). The word of God does not come to an end, but is hypostasized in an effected event, 'immediately becoming nature.' As the human reason of a poet constitutes a new reality, which is the poem, outside of himself but at the same time a consequence and

manifestation of his own reason, so also the word of God is given effect dynamically 'in the ground and formation of creation.'"

2.　For the scholastic perspective on the order of creation, see Thomas Aquinas, *Basic Writings of Saint Thomas Aquinas: God and the Order of Creation*, ed. Anton Pegis (Indianapolis: Hackett, 1997). Compare the order of divine decrees in Reformed theology—see, for instance, Oliver D. Crisp, *Jonathan Edwards and the Metaphysics of Sin* (Aldershot, UK: Ashgate, 2005), ch. 1.

3.　See Peter M. Hess, "Natural History," in Gary Ferngren, ed., *Science and Religion: A Historical Introduction* (Baltimore: Johns Hopkins University Press, 2002), 195–207.

4.　James Barr, *Biblical Words for Time* (Naperville, Ill.: A. R. Allenson, 1962), 20–46.

5.　William F. Arndt and F. Wilbur Gingrich, *A Greek-English Lexicon of the New Testament and Other Early Christian Literature*, 2nd ed. (Chicago: University of Chicago Press, 1979), 394–95.

6.　See http://www.holy-trinity.org/liturgics/sokolov-deacon.html (accessed May 11, 2006), which gives the notes to deacons of the Eastern Orthodox liturgy.

7.　Available online at http://www.religion-online.org/showchapter.asp?title=2310&C=2308 (accessed May 11, 2006). See also the opening of Tillich's *A History of Christian Thought* (New York: Touchstone, 1972) as well as volume 3 of his *Systematic Theology* (Chicago: University of Chicago Press, 1967).

8.　Lee Irons and Meredith G. Kline, in their contribution to *The Genesis Debate*, essentially reinvent the *chronos-kairos* distinction, distinguishing a "lower-register" cosmology, which is the realm of the visible, from an "upper-register" cosmology, which is the realm of the invisible. As they put it: "The two-register cosmology of Scripture [consists] of the upper (invisible) and lower (visible) registers. . . . [The] two-register cosmology explains the significance of the nonliteral nature of the time indicators in Genesis 1 within the overall cosmological teaching of Scripture. . . . Although some critics might be tempted to dismiss two-register cosmology as a speculative construct, in reality the terms *upper register* and *lower register* are useful terms for the two realms that compose the created order. The upper register is the invisible dwelling place of God and His holy angels, that is, heaven. The lower register is called 'earth,' but includes the whole visible cosmos from the planet Earth to the star-studded sky (Col. 1:16)." See their essay "The Framework View" in David G. Hagopian, ed., *The Genesis Debate: Three Views on the Days of Creation* (Mission Viejo, Calif.: Crux, 2001), 236–37.

Chapter 17

1.　C. S. Lewis, *Miracles: A Preliminary Study*, rev. ed. (1960; reprinted San Francisco: Harper, 2001), 291–92. Lewis adds, "The following question may be asked: If we can reasonably pray for an event which must in fact have happened or failed to happen several hours ago, why can we not pray for an event which we know *not* to have happened? e.g. pray for the safety of someone who, as we know, was killed yesterday. What makes the difference is precisely our knowledge. The known event states God's will. It is psychologically impossible to pray for what we know to be unobtainable; and if it were possible the prayer would sin against the duty of submission to God's known will" (292–93).

2.　The context of this remark is the death of Einstein's longtime friend Michele Besso, written in condolence to Besso's sister and son: "Now he has departed from this strange world a little ahead of me [Einstein died four weeks later]. That means nothing. People like us, who believe in physics, know that the distinction between past, present, and future is only a stubbornly persistent illusion." Quoted in Freeman J. Dyson, *Disturbing the Universe* (New York: Basic Books, 1979), 193. Stephen Hawking makes this quote the basis of an Einstein anthology: Stephen Hawking, ed., *A Stubbornly Persistent Illusion: The Essential Scientific Works of Albert Einstein* (Philadelphia: Running Press, 2007).

3.   According to Lewis, "One of its causes [i.e., causes of an event in the past] is your present prayer. Thus something does really depend on my choice. My free act contributes to the cosmic shape. That contribution is made in eternity or 'before all worlds'; but my consciousness of contributing reaches me at a particular point in the time-series." Quoted from *Miracles*, 292. Past-directed prayer continues to be a subject of philosophical inquiry. See, for instance, chapter 11, titled "Praying for Things to Have Happened," in Thomas Flint, *Divine Providence: The Molinist Account* (Ithaca, N.Y.: Cornell University Press, 1998); and Kevin Timpe, "Prayers for the Past," *Religious Studies* 41 (2005): 305–22.

4.   For a nice popular treatment of Newcomb's Paradox, see William Poundstone, *Labyrinths of Reason: Paradox, Puzzles, and the Frailty of Knowledge* (New York: Doubleday, 1988), ch. 12. Newcomb himself seems never to have formally written up the paradox named in his honor.

5.   Robert Nozick, "Newcomb's Problem and Two Principles of Choice," in N. Rescher, ed., *Essays in Honor of Carl G. Hempel,* Synthese Library (Dordrecht, Holland: D. Reidel, 1969), 115.

6.   William Lane Craig, "Divine Foreknowledge and Newcomb's Paradox," *Philosophia* 17 (1987): 331–50, available online at http://www.leaderu.com/offices/billcraig/docs/newcomb.html (accessed January 12, 2006).

7.   Craig, "Divine Foreknowledge."

8.   For instance, in *The City of God* (v. 9) Augustine writes, "For one who is not prescient of all future things is not God." Available online at http://www.newadvent.org/fathers/120105.htm (accessed November 27, 2008).

9.   For instance, appeals to quantum indeterminacy to undercut divine foreknowledge are highly dubious—as though a deity that creates a world operating by quantum mechanical principles should be limited by those principles.

Chapter 18

1.   C. S. Lewis, *Miracles: A Preliminary Study*, rev. ed. (1960; reprinted San Francisco: Harper, 2001), 284.

2.   Divine causality, as operating by an intentional-semantic logic, is thus *orthogonal* to physical causality, as operating by the causal-temporal logic. Orthogonality here is a technical term introduced by the philosopher of science Ernest Nagel. (See Ernest Nagel, "Teleology Revisited," in C. Allen, M. Bekoff, and G. Lauder, eds., *Nature's Purposes* [1977; reprinted Cambridge, Mass.: Bradford/MIT Press, 1998], 211.) Orthogonality refers to the joint action of a teleological and physical cause that together implement a given outcome but for which the teleological cause is irreducible to the physical cause.

    Obviously, when God orders the creation, he achieves purposes that cannot be redescribed in purely physical terms. For a failure of orthogonality, compare the case of a pendulum, whose "goal" or "*telos*," we might say, is to seek a stable equilibrium, and yet whose restoring force (i.e., the force that attempts to restore equilibrium) is directly proportional to the displacement force. The displacement force here covaries precisely with the restoring force and thereby accounts for it. Orthogonality was for Nagel so important that he refused to ascribe goal-directedness to processes for which teleological causes were not orthogonal to physical causes.

Many authors acknowledge the importance of orthogonality, albeit by using different terminologies. Jacques Monod used the term *gratuity* to describe the relationship between chemistry and the function of biomacromolecules. See Jacques Monod, *Chance and Necessity* (New York: Vintage, 1972). Michael Polanyi described biological systems as constrained by "boundary conditions" that transcend the laws of physics and chemistry. See Michael Polanyi, "Life's Irreducible Structure," *Science* 113 (1968): 1308–12. See also James Barham, "Biofunctional Realism and the Problem of Teleology," *Evolution and Cognition* 6 (1) (2000): 2–34.

3. C. S. Lewis writes: "Naturalistic assumptions, beggings of the question such as that which I noted on the first page of this book, will meet you on every side—even from the pens of clergymen. . . . It comes partly from what we may call a 'hangover'. We all have Naturalism in our bones and even conversion does not at once work the infection out of our system. Its assumptions rush back upon the mind the moment vigilance is relaxed." Quoted from *Miracles*, 267–68.

4. C. S. Lewis, "Transposition," in *The Weight of Glory and Other Addresses* (New York: Collier, 1980), 71–72.

5. For this "up from under" root meaning of our English word *evil,* see *Webster's New World College Dictionary,* 4th ed. (Cleveland, Ohio: Wiley, 2008), 493, s.v. "evil." I'm indebted to Bill Newby for drawing my attention to this etymology.

6. Many exegetes follow John Calvin in denying that such passages refer to Satan. Thus, in his commentary on Isaiah, Calvin says this about Isa 14:12: "The exposition of this passage, which some have given, as if it referred to Satan, has arisen from ignorance; for the context plainly shows that these statements must be understood in reference to the king of the Babylonians. But when passages of Scripture are taken up at random, and no attention is paid to the context, we need not wonder that mistakes of this kind frequently arise. Yet it was an instance of very gross ignorance, to imagine that Lucifer was the king of devils, and that the Prophet gave him this name. But as these inventions have no probability whatever, let us pass by them as useless fables." John Calvin, *Commentary on Isaiah,* trans. John King (Charleston, S.C.: Forgotten Books, 2007), I:404.

Jan Ridderbos, in likewise addressing Isa 14:12, thinks that Calvin is correct exegetically but may have gone a bit too far theologically in distancing this passage from Satan: "Church fathers such as Jerome and Tertullian took this verse to refer to the devil, hence the name Lucifer (morning star) given to him. Luther and Calvin both reject this notion as a gross error, and in a sense rightly. Still, there is an element of truth in the idea: by his self-deification Babylon's king is the imitator of the devil and the type of the Antichrist (Dan. 11:36; 2 Thess. 2:4); therefore his humiliation also is an example of Satan's fall from the position of power that he has usurped (cf. Luke 10:18; Rev. 12:9)." Quoted from Jan Ridderbos, *The Bible Student's Commentary: Isaiah,* trans. John Vriend (Grand Rapids, Mich.: Regency, 1985), 142. Similar observations apply, mutatis mutandis, to Ezekiel 28.

My own view is that Ridderbos's "element of truth" about the "self-deification" described in Isaiah 14 and Ezekiel 28 refers preeminently to Satan and then derivatively to whatever figures in human history Isaiah and Ezekiel may have had in mind. In interpreting these passages, we need to avoid a false choice between Satanically inspired historical figures and Satan himself. If Satan is real, then the motions described in these passages, even if exemplified by humans and intended by the biblical authors to describe humans, derive their primary inspiration from Satan. Hence, to interpret these passages as describing Satan seems entirely appropriate, even if context would suggest a more mundane interpretation. I therefore think the Church Fathers, who saw in these passages clear references to Satan, were closer to the truth than some of the more recent exegetes, who focus so narrowly on context that they miss the broader theological import of these passages.

To see that the Church Fathers overwhelmingly regarded Isa 14:12–15 and Ezek 28:12–19 as referring to Satan, see Steven A. McKinion, ed., *Isaiah 1–39*, in *Ancient Christian Commentary on Scripture, Old Testament*, ed. Thomas C. Oden (Downers Grove, Ill.: InterVarsity, 2004), X:121–24; and Kenneth Stevenson and Michael Glerup, eds., *Ezekiel, Daniel*, in *Ancient Christian Commentary*, XIII:93–97. Augustine, Ambrose, Origen, and Jerome saw in these passages Satan as the principal actor. Note that Thomas Oden's *Ancient Christian Commentary* series strives to provide for each book of the Bible a representative sample from the writings of the Church Fathers on it. Arguably, this series is the best resource currently available for understanding the mind of the early Church.

7.   Alexander Schmemann, *For the Life of the World* (Crestwood, N.Y.: St. Vladimir's Press, 1988), 100.

8.   Our secular elite include not only Enlightenment rationalists but also postmodernists. Postmodernists are only too happy to attack faith in the name of science, especially in the name of Darwinian evolution. Take Richard Rorty, who until his death was America's best known postmodernist (he called himself a neo-pragmatist). "Keeping faith with Darwin," according to Rorty, means realizing that "our species, its faculties and its current scientific and moral languages, are as much products of chance as are tectonic plates and mutated viruses." And Rorty was all for keeping faith with Darwin: "The idea that one species of organism is, unlike all the others, oriented not just toward its own increased prosperity but toward Truth, is as un-Darwinian as the idea that every human being has a built-in moral compass—a conscience that swings free of both social history and individual luck." Quoted from Richard Rorty, "Untruth and Consequences," a review of *Killing Time* by Paul Feyerabend, in *The New Republic* (July 31, 1995): 32–36.

Rorty took as a main inspiration the American pragmatist John Dewey. According to Dewey, such was the prestige of the design argument that "by the late eighteenth century it was, as approved by the sciences of organic life, the central point of theistic and idealistic philosophy." Yet Darwin upset all that. Dewey continued, "The Darwinian principle of natural selection cut straight under this philosophy. If all organic adaptations are due simply to constant variation and the elimination of those variations which are harmful in the struggle for existence that is brought about by excessive reproduction, *there is no call for a prior intelligent causal force to plan and preordain them.*" Quoted from John Dewey, *The Influence of Darwin on Philosophy and Other Essays* (New York: Henry Holt, 1910), 11–12, emphasis added. Thus Dewey saw science, and Darwinism in particular, as eliminating the need for any intelligence behind the world.

9.   Leslie Zeigler, "Christianity or Feminism?" in W. A. Dembski and J. W. Richards, eds., *Unapologetic Apologetics: Meeting the Challenges of Theological Studies* (Downers Grove, Ill.: InterVarsity, 2001), 181.

10.   *Phaedo* 98d, in Plato, *The Collected Dialogues of Plato, Including the Letters*, ed. E. Hamilton and H. Cairns (Princeton: Princeton University Press, 1961), 80.

11.   *Philebus* 28d, in *Collected Dialogues of Plato*, 1106.

Chapter 19

1.   David Bohm, *Wholeness and the Implicate Order* (London: Routledge & Kegan Paul, 1980).

2.   For chaos theory and nonlinear dynamics, see Leonard Smith, *Chaos: A Very Short Introduction* (Oxford: Oxford University Press, 2007).

3. Compare Thomas Aquinas's view of divine causation as summarized by William Carroll: "divine causality and creaturely causality function at fundamentally different levels. In the *Summa contra Gentiles*, Aquinas remarks that 'the same effect is not attributed to a natural cause and to divine power in such a way that it is partly done by God, and partly by the natural agent; rather, it is wholly done by both, according to a different way, just as the same effect is wholly attributed to the instrument and also wholly to the principal agent.' [III 70.8] It is not the case of partial or co-causes with each contributing a separate element to produce the effect. God, as Creator, transcends the order of created causes in such a way that He is their enabling origin. [As Brian Shanley notes,] the 'same God who transcends the created order is also intimately and immanently present within that order as upholding all causes in their causing, including the human will.' For Aquinas 'the differing metaphysical levels of primary and secondary causation require us to say that any created effect comes totally and immediately from God as the transcendent primary cause and totally and immediately from the creature as secondary cause.'" Quoted from Carroll's essay "Creation, Evolution, and Thomas Aquinas," available online at http://www.catholiceducation .org/articles/science/sc0035.html (accessed September 22, 2006).

Chapter 20

1. David G. Hagopian, *The Genesis Debate: Three Views on the Days of Creation* (Mission Viejo, Calif.: Crux Press, 2001).

2. Note that in Deuteronomy 5, where the Decalogue is repeated, Sabbath observance is justified in terms of God's deliverance of Israel from slavery in Egypt.

3. "But if the angelic mind can grasp simultaneously all that the sacred text sets down separately in an ordered arrangement according to causal connection, were not all these things also made simultaneously, the firmament itself, the waters gathered together and the bare land that appeared, the plants and trees that sprang forth, the lights and stars that were established, the living creatures in the water and on the earth? . . . In this narrative of creation Holy Scripture has said of the Creator that He completed His works in six days; and elsewhere, without contradicting this, it has been written of the same Creator that He created all things together. It follows, therefore, that He, who created all things together, simultaneously created these six days, or seven, or rather the one day six or seven times repeated. Why, then, was there any need for six distinct days to be set forth in the narrative one after the other? The reason is that those who cannot understand the meaning of the text, *He created all things together*, cannot arrive at the meaning of Scripture unless the narrative proceeds slowly step by step." Augustine, *The Literal Meaning of Genesis*, iv.33, in William A. Dembski, Wayne J. Downs, and Fr. Justin B. A. Frederick, eds., *The Patristic Understanding of Creation: An Anthology of Writings from the Church Fathers on Creation and Design* (Riesel, Tex.: Erasmus Press, 2008), 430–31.

4. See Benjamin Wiker and Jonathan Witt, *A Meaningful Universe: How the Arts and Sciences Reveal the Genius of Nature* (Downers Grove, Ill.: InterVarsity, 2006), especially ch. 4. See also Mark Steiner, *The Applicability of Mathematics as a Philosophical Problem* (Cambridge, Mass.: Harvard University Press, 1999).

5. Contemporary theology tends to revel in divine inscrutability—that nothing can really be known of God or legitimately ascribed to him. Compare this attitude to the following statement by the prophet Jeremiah: "Thus saith the LORD, Let not the wise man glory in his wisdom, neither let the mighty man glory in his might, let not the rich man glory in his riches: But let him that glorieth glory in this, that he understandeth and knoweth me, that I am the LORD which exercise lovingkindness, judgment, and righteousness, in the earth: for in these things I delight, saith the LORD" (Jer 9:23–24).

The view presented here is thus at odds with extreme forms of "negative theology" in which the knowledge of God consists in what can (and on this view must) be denied of the deity. Rudolf Otto's Mysterium Tremendum is a case in point. The problem with a purely negative theology is that it is self-referentially incoherent. G. K. Chesterton made this point as follows: "We do not know enough about the unknown to know that it is unknowable." (See G. J. Marlin, R. P. Rabatin, and J. L. Swan, eds., *The Quotable Chesterton* [Garden City, N.Y.: Image, 1987], 336. The original source is Chesterton's 1910 biography of William Blake.)

Christian orthodoxy has always balanced an apophatic theology with a kataphatic theology. Apophatic theology recognizes that none of our concepts can fully encompass God and thus approaches the knowledge of God via negations. Kataphatic theology, on the other hand, recognizes that negation, if pushed too far, becomes a positive affirmation of divine inscrutability; it therefore emphasizes the need for positive affirmations about God that are accurate as far as they go but can only go so far.

6. Some scholars see God as bringing physical reality into being in Gen 1:1 and then interpret the days of creation as God organizing this brute unformed physical reality (described in Gen 1:2 as "formless and void"). Nothing in my kairological reading of Genesis 1 is fundamentally changed on this view. There are, however, exegetical reasons for preferring the approach I am taking, which identifies the origin of physical reality with the creation of light on day 1. See, for instance, Marguerite Shuster's sermon on Genesis in Paul K. Jewett, ed., *God, Creation, and Revelation: A Neo-Evangelical Theology* (Grand Rapids: Eerdmans, 1991), 506–12.

7. Thomas Dubay, *The Evidential Power of Beauty: Science and Theology Meet* (San Francisco: Ignatius, 1999), 83.

8. See John Polkinghorne, *Science and Providence: God's Interaction with the World* (West Conshohocken, Penn.: Templeton Foundation, 2005), 10–13.

9. Note that God's providential will falls under what previously we called *general providence* and that God's active will falls under what previously we called *particular providence*. See the introduction to this book.

10. Polkinghorne, *Science and Providence*, 11.

11. See, for instance, Stephen Oppenheimer, *The Real Eve: Modern Man's Journey Out of Africa* (New York: Carroll and Graf, 2003). Evolutionists see speciation as occurring through reproductive isolation, with a small subpopulation breaking away from an original population and, once reproductively isolated, undergoing substantial evolutionary change. The smaller the breakaway subpopulation, the less averaging of existing traits and the greater the evolutionary potential. The ideal circumstance for speciation is therefore reproductive isolation of a single breeding-pair—an Adam and an Eve. For more on speciation, as well as a critique, see William Dembski and Jonathan Wells, *The Design of Life: Discovering Signs of Intelligence in Biological Systems* (Dallas: Foundation for Thought and Ethics, 2008), ch. 4. Compare also Fazale Rana and Hugh Ross, *Who Was Adam? A Creation Model Approach to the Origin of Man* (Colorado Springs: NavPress, 2005), ch. 4. Rana and Ross are old-earth creationists who in that book present genetic evidence for the descent of modern humans from a single male-female pair.

12. Denis Alexander, *Creation or Evolution: Do We Have to Choose?* (Oxford: Monarch, 2008), 270–71.

13. Quoted in Gerald Bray, ed., *Romans*, in *Ancient Christian Commentary on Scripture, New Testament*, ed. Thomas C. Oden (Downers Grove, Ill.: InterVarsity, 1998), VI:224.

14. From "In Firefighting, What Is a Backfire?" at http://www.wisegeek.com/in-firefighting -what-is-a-backfire.htm (accessed December 30, 2008). Italics added.

15. I'm indebted to Greg Smith for this backfire analogy.

16. Steve Lohr, "Swedes Scuttle Cruise for Young Delinquents," *New York Times* (June 6, 1989): http://query.nytimes.com/gst/fullpage.html?res=950DE4DD1730F935A35755C0 A96F948260 (accessed November 11, 2008).

17. Ibid. Perhaps the Swedish government should reconsider instituting such cruises, only this time by pitting Swedish prisoners against Somali pirates.

18. Charles Darwin, *The Correspondence of Charles Darwin* 8, 1860 (Cambridge: Cambridge University Press, 1993), 224.

19. For the connection between the bacterial flagellum and type-three secretory system, see William Dembski and Jonathan Wells, *The Design of Life: Discovering Signs of Intelligence in Biological Systems* (Dallas: Foundation for Thought and Ethics, 2008), ch. 6.

20. John R. Lucas, *Freedom and Grace* (London: SPCK, 1976), 9.

21. See Eugene Maly, "Introduction to the Pentateuch," in Raymond Brown, Joseph Fitzmyer, and Roland Murphy, eds., *Jerome Biblical Commentary* (Englewood Cliffs, N.J.: Prentice-Hall, 1968), 1:3–4.

22. The Matrix presents a version of what philosophers call a "brain in a vat." Such a brain is disembodied and put in a vat where it is fed experiences. Robert Nozick developed this idea at length in what he called "the experience machine." See Robert Nozick, *Anarchy, State, and Utopia* (New York: Basic, 1974), 42–45.

23. Writing with emphasis (the italics are his), Robert Nozick asks, "*What else can matter to us, other than how our lives feel from the inside?*" Ibid., 43.

24. Physicist Don Page, in responding to this understanding of Eden, remarks, "Your picture of the Garden of Eden being phenomenologically the same whether it were in a perfect world or in a fallen world was very interesting. I could not resist thinking of the metaphor of [Hugh] Everett's relative states [for quantum mechanics], so that given a state for a subsystem (in this case the Garden), the surroundings could be in a relative state that is a superposition of perfect and fallen. Then one could imagine that in the part of the evolution of the Garden in which Adam and Eve chose sin, that part could have a relative state that is the fallen world, whereas the relative state to the component of the evolution of the Garden in which Adam and Eve did not choose sin could be a perfect world. . . . Now I don't suppose that if your picture is literally true, with both the perfect and the fallen world actually existing, that they are likely to be such quantum superpositions (since they might not be within the same Hilbert space, or maybe the perfect world has something different from QM [i.e., quantum mechanics]), but I couldn't resist thinking of this analogy. It might help some quantum physicists, though I doubt that it would help the general public for whom you are writing." Personal communication sent in an e-mail dated January 31, 2009.

25. "According to Islam, when Allah created the first human beings, Adam and Eve, He placed them in the Garden of Eden, which was in heaven. The story of the first humans is similar to the one in the Bible, yet the Bible describes the location of the Garden of Eden as an area in modern-day Iraq, rather than a place in heaven. The Qur'an describes how Satan (Iblis) beguiled Adam and Eve into eating the forbidden fruit in the Garden, thus disobeying Allah. Then, according to Islam, Adam, Eve, and Satan were cast down to the world Allah had created, because of their disobedience. Since this point Allah and Satan have been in a

tug-of-war trying to persuade humans to follow their ways." Quoted from Abraham Sarker, *Understand My Muslim People* (Newberg, Oreg.: Barclay, 2004), 219.

26. Saint Francis of Assisi's well-known "Canticle to Brother Sun and Sister Moon" ends "Praised be You, my Lord through Sister Death, / from whom no-one living can escape. / Woe to those who die in mortal sin! / Blessed are they She finds doing Your Will. / No second death can do them harm. / Praise and bless my Lord and give Him thanks, / And serve Him with great humility." Available online, along with other prayers of Saint Francis, at http://www.yenra.com/catholic/prayers/francisofassisi.html (accessed January 19, 2009).

27. Philip Yancey and Paul Brand, *In His Image* (Grand Rapids, Mich.: Zondervan, 1984), 22.

28. Moral sensibilities in animals, as when senior animals discipline junior animals in a group, properly belong to "what is" rather than "what should be." Such senior animals may properly be said to experience anger and such junior animals to experience discomfort and perhaps even guilt, but the consciousness that "all's not right with the world" or "I should be a better person" is, I submit, uniquely human. Concern with "what should be" requires the ability to distance oneself from one's experience in an act of self-transcendence. Animals give no evidence of this ability.

Chapter 21

1. Denis Alexander writes, "Being an anatomically modern human was necessary but not sufficient for being spiritually alive." Quoted from *Creation or Evolution: Do We Have to Choose?* (Oxford: Monarch, 2008), 237.

2. Anyone familiar with my work on intelligent design will know where I stand on this question. See, for instance, my books *Intelligent Design: The Bridge between Science and Theology* (Downers Grove, Ill.: InterVarsity, 1999); *The Design Revolution: Answering the Toughest Questions about Intelligent Design* (Downers Grove, Ill.: InterVarsity, 2004); and (with coauthor Sean McDowell) *Understanding Intelligent Design: Everything You Need to Know in Plain Language* (Eugene, Oreg.: Harvest House 2008).

3. Alexander, *Creation or Evolution*, 292.

4. Jerry Coyne, "Don't Know Much Biology," June 6, 2007, available online at http://www .edge.org/3rd_culture/coyne07/coyne07_index.html (accessed November 13, 2008).

5. See the articles in Warren S. Brown, Nancey Murphy, and H. Newton Malony, *Whatever Happened to the Soul? Scientific and Theological Portraits of Human Nature* (Minneapolis: Augsburg Fortress, 1998). Compare Peter Van Inwagen, *Material Beings* (Ithaca, N.Y.: Cornell University Press, 1990).

6. Mario Beauregard and Denyse O'Leary, *The Spiritual Brain: A Neuroscientist's Case for the Existence of the Soul* (San Francisco: HarperOne, 2007); Jeffrey Schwartz and Sharon Begley, *The Mind and the Brain: Neuroplasticity and the Power of Mental Force* (New York: Regan, 2002).

7. See Nancey Murphy, "Nonreductive Physicalism: Philosophical Issues," in Brown et al., *Whatever Happened to the Soul?*, 127–48.

8. "Humans are also unique in ways that defy evolutionary explanation and point to our spiritual nature. This includes the existence of the Moral Law (the knowledge of right and wrong) and the search for God that characterizes all human cultures throughout history." Francis Collins, *The Language of God: A Scientist Presents Evidence for Belief* (New York: Free Press, 2006), 200.

9. Charles Darwin, *The Descent of Man and Selection in Relation to Sex*, 2nd ed. (London: John Murray, 1882), 126.

10. Karl W. Giberson, *Saving Darwin: How to Be a Christian and Believe in Evolution* (San Francisco: HarperOne, 2008), 13. Emphasis in the original.

11. William Dembski and Jonathan Wells, *The Design of Life: Discovering Signs of Intelligence in Biological Systems* (Dallas: Foundation for Thought and Ethics, 2008), ch. 1, which is on human origins.

12. This is, of course, a vast topic, and the references to Giberson's and my own work only scratch the surface. The evolutionary literature overwhelmingly argues against human uniqueness. For the other side, see Mortimer Adler's book cited in the next note as well as the following: Benjamin Wiker, *Moral Darwinism: How We Became Hedonists* (Downers Grove, Ill.: InterVarsity, 2002); C. Stephen Evans, *Preserving the Person: A Look at Human Sciences* (Vancouver, B.C.: Regent College Publishing, 1994); David Berlinski, *The Devil's Delusion: Atheism and Its Scientific Pretensions* (New York: Crown Forum, 2008).

13. For the distinction between a difference in kind and a difference in degree, especially as it applies to human uniqueness, see Mortimer Adler, *The Difference of Man and the Difference It Makes* (New York: Fordham University Press, 1993). This book, though originally published in 1967, is must reading for anyone concerned with the problem of human uniqueness. It opens with a thought experiment about what would happen if it were possible to cross a human and an ape.

    Forty years later, Richard Dawkins proposed breaking the species barrier with "a successful hybridization between a human and a chimpanzee." (See his brief article "Breaking the Species Barrier," January 2009, at http://www.edge.org/q2009/q09_16.html, accessed January 17, 2009.) Dawkins continues, "Even if the hybrid were infertile like a mule, the shock waves that would be sent through society would be salutary. This is why a distinguished biologist described this possibility as the most immoral scientific experiment he could imagine: it would change everything!"

    Dawkins views such an experiment not as immoral but, if successful, as liberating: "Our ethics and our politics assume, largely without question or serious discussion, that the division between human and 'animal' is absolute." A "humanzee" would, for Dawkins, refute human uniqueness and thereby destroy the entire Judeo-Christian ethical system based on it—a prospect he relishes. Are theistic evolutionists like Giberson prepared to follow Dawkins down this path? Absent human uniqueness, why not?

14. Giberson, *Saving Darwin*, 12. C. S. Lewis appreciated—and rejected—Giberson's point. According to Lewis, the skeptic of traditional theological doctrines "naturally listens with impatience to our solutions of particular difficulties and our defences against particular objections. The more ingenious we are in such solutions and defences the more perverse we seem to him. . . . I have come to regard that attitude as a total misunderstanding." C. S. Lewis, *Miracles: A Preliminary Study*, rev. ed. (1960; reprinted San Francisco: Harper, 2001), 109–10.

15. Giberson might demur that he is merely redefining or reconceptualizing the Fall in a way that preserves what historically has been most important about it. But Christian orthodoxy's understanding of the Fall is unrecognizable in his reconceptualization of it.

16. Giberson, *Saving Darwin*, 12.

17. For this line of reasoning taken to its logical conclusion, see Gaymon Bennett, Martinez J. Hewlett, Ted Peters, and Robert John Russell, eds., *The Evolution of Evil* (Göttingen, Germany: Vandenhoeck & Ruprecht, 2008).

18. Ayala seems concerned to preserve God's honor only when promoting Darwinian evolution. All quotes in this and the previous paragraph are from Francisco Ayala, *Darwin's Gift to Science and Religion* (Washington, D.C.: Joseph Henry, 2007), 159–60.

19. C. Robert Mesle, *Process Theology: A Basic Introduction* (St. Louis: Chalice, 1993), 62.

20. The subtitle of Giberson's *Saving Darwin* makes precisely this point: *How to Be a Christian and Believe in Evolution*.

21. Charles Darwin, *On the Origin of Species*, facsimile 1st ed. (1859; reprinted Cambridge, Mass.: Harvard University Press, 1964), 76, 79, 129, 490.

22. Ibid., 490.

23. Darwin, *Descent of Man*, 156. This passage is identical in both the 1871 first edition and the 1882 second edition of *The Descent of Man*.

24. Alexander, *Creation or Evolution*, 282.

25. Robert Wright, *Nonzero: The Logic of Human Destiny* (New York: Pantheon, 2000).

26. Cooperation can also be against the cruelties of inanimate nature, as when a fungus and an alga cooperate to produce a lichen, the first stage of plant colonization of a rock face. See Lynn Margulis and Dorion Sagan, *Acquiring Genomes: A Theory of the Origins of Species* (New York: Basic, 2002), 13–14.

27. Darwin, *Origin of Species*, 489.

28. Ibid., 490.

29. Alexander, *Creation or Evolution*, 282.

30. Unlike Darwin, who tried to minimize evolution's cruelty, some Darwinists positively revel in it. Take the annual Darwin Awards. According to Wendy Northcutt, author of the Darwin Award books, these are given posthumously to individuals who "ensure the long-term survival of our species by removing themselves from the gene pool in a sublimely idiotic fashion." (Quoted from the front cover of her book *The Darwin Awards II: Unnatural Selection* [New York: Plume, 2003]). In these books Northcutt details in case after case the misfortunes of people who died. Yes, the circumstances of their deaths are ridiculous. But I know of no other view, religious or secular, that inspires its adherents to celebrate the deaths of people they regard as stupid. Why is Darwin's name associated with these awards? Could it be because the name fits? Can anyone imagine Albert Einstein or Martin Luther King Jr. or Michelangelo lending their names to such an award?

    Traditional religious believers are not alone in faulting evolution for cruelty. Take New Age writer Lynne McTaggart: "Our self-image grew even bleaker with the work of Charles Darwin. His theory of evolution—tweaked slightly now by the neo-Darwinists—is of a life that is random, predatory, purposeless and solitary. Be the best or don't survive. You are no more than an evolutionary accident. The vast checkerboard biological heritage of your ancestors is stripped down to one central facet: survival. Eat or be eaten. The essence of your humanity is a genetic terrorist, efficiently disposing of any weaker links. Life is not about sharing and interdependence. Life is about winning, getting there first. And if you do manage to survive, you are on your own at the top of the evolutionary tree." Quoted from *The Field: The Quest for the Secret Force of the Universe*, updated edition (New York: HarperCollins, 2008), xxiv–xxv. Granted, this statement is a bit of a caricature. But why does evolution inspire such caricatures?

31.   With or without evolution, a suitably imperfect world could be perfectly redemptive. In-
       deed, it could provide the perfect vehicle for God's perfect love. The Cross springs first
       to mind, in this regard. But the possibilities for finding perfection within imperfection are
       ongoing and widespread if we have but eyes to see. For a moving illustration, see the story
       recounted by Wayne Dyer on pages 45–47 of his book *The Power of Intention* (Carlsbad,
       Calif.: Hay House, 2004).

Chapter 22

1.   Phyllis Trible, *Texts of Terror: Literary-Feminist Readings of Biblical Narratives* (Min-
       neapolis: Augsburg Fortress, 1984).

2.   With regard to the four Old Testament women that Phyllis Trible considers in *Texts of Ter-
       ror*, in no case was the terror they experienced ordered or approved by God. Abraham's
       family mistreated Hagar, but her mistreatment cannot be ascribed to God. Happily, Hagar
       made out all right in the end: in God's providence, her son Ishmael became the father of
       twelve tribes, just as Isaac did. The rape of Tamar was a straightforward case of David's not
       keeping his sons under control, which resulted in the bloody rebellion of Absalom and goes
       well beyond Tamar's rape. As for the unnamed, dismembered woman in Judges 19, where
       does the text suggest that God had anything to do with what happened? The whole point
       of the book of Judges is that all did what was right in their own eyes. As for Jephthah's
       daughter, did God say he wanted Jephthah to sacrifice his daughter? Unlike the religions
       surrounding the Israelites, the Torah made no provision for human sacrifice.

       Notwithstanding, doubts about God's goodness can arise even when Scripture does not
       present God as approving certain acts. In an e-mail to me dated January 31, 2009, Don
       Page noted, "I certainly agree that much of the horror in the Old Testament is not attributed
       to God, but it often does bother me that the inspired writers do not seem to rebuke what
       we would now regard as horrible practices, such as Lot's giving his virgin daughters to
       be raped to save his male guests [Gen 19:8]. The silence of these parts of the Bible on the
       immorality of such sexist practices is rather disturbing, often more what I would expect
       from something just a product of the age than from divine inspiration." Given that (1) God
       inspired the Bible, (2) the Bible consistently rebukes many practices (e.g., idolatry), (3) Lot
       later, while drunk, impregnated both his daughters (Gen 9:30–36), and (4) 2 Pet 2:7 refers
       to "just Lot" (i.e., claims that Lot was a righteous man), it might seem that God turns a
       blind eye to certain forms of wickedness. Although I personally don't believe this, like my
       friend and colleague Don, I feel the force of this objection.

3.   See respectively Charles Darwin's *On the Origin of Species*, facsimile 1st ed. (1859; re-
       printed Cambridge, Mass.: Harvard University Press, 1964), 129; and Alfred Lord Tenny-
       son's, "In Memoriam A. H. H.," in Karen Hodder, ed., *The Works of Alfred Lord Tennyson*
       (1850; reprinted Hertfordshire, U.K.: Wordsworth Editions, 2008), 339.

4.   For a fascinating and accessible introduction to immunology, see Lauren Sompayrac, *How
       the Immune System Works*, 2nd ed. (Malden, Mass.: Blackwell, 2003).

5.   It is perhaps not coincidental that the Tree of Life was positioned at the center of the Gar-
       den and that the tree on which Christ was crucified was positioned at Jerusalem, effectively
       the center of the Promised Land. In *Genesis Unbound* (Sisters, Oreg.: Multnomah, 1996),
       John Sailhamer offers an interesting argument identifying the Garden with the Promised
       Land.

6.   Boethius, *The Consolation of Philosophy*, in *Loeb Classical Library* (Cambridge, Mass.:
       Harvard University Press, 1973), 153.

Chapter 23

1. "Nunc patimur longae pacis mala, saevior armis luxuria incubuit victumque ulciscitur orbem." Juvenal, *Satires*, VI.292, translated by G. G. Ramsay, available online at http://www.fordham.edu/halsall/ancient/juvenal-satvi.html (accessed January 1, 2009).

2. Alexander Schmemann, *For the Life of the World* (Crestwood, N.Y.: St. Vladimir's Press, 1988), 100.

3. Martin Luther, *The Bondage of the Will*, trans. J. I. Packer and O. R. Johnston (Grand Rapids, Mich.: Revell/Baker, 1990).

4. No doubt, such an assertion will sound strange to postmodern ears. We live in odd times when people need reminding that obedience to God constitutes a virtue.

5. Romans 8:28 teaches that God works all things out for good for those who love God and are called according to his purpose. It does not follow that God is working things out for evil for those who don't love God and are not called according to his purpose. God, as love, is always working things out for good; only those who persist in rebelling against God do not appreciate his efforts in this regard. Indeed, since the highest good is God himself, God's greatest act of love for people is to move them toward himself. The wicked, who want nothing to do with God, experience this movement as evil, but that's their problem. God loves the just and the unjust; only the unjust do not see God's love as love.

6. Bernard Malamud, *The Fixer* (New York: Farrar, Straus, and Giroux, 1966), 30.

7. Ibid., 317.

8. For the psychology underlying the "decoy effect," see Itamar Simonson and Amos Tversky, "Choice in Context: Tradeoff Contrast and Extremeness Aversion," *Journal of Marketing Research* 29 (August 1992): 281–95.

9. Viktor Frankl, *Man's Search for Meaning* (Boston: Beacon, 1959).

10. John Cassian, *On the Eight Vices*, in G. E. H. Palmer, Philip Sherrard, and Kallistos Ware, eds., *The Philokalia* (London: Faber and Faber, 1979), I:83.

11. Bernie S. Siegel, *Peace, Love, and Healing* (New York: Harper & Row, 1989), 212.

12. Denyse O'Leary, in a personal communication, takes this further: "Evil men are always busy." Indeed, only the busy can be evil. Was not the serpent busy when he stuck his nose in Eve's business? No wonder that God's judgment is directed at idle words (Matt 12:36).

13. William Blake, "Jerusalem: The Emanation of the Giant Albion," 1804, available online at http://www.preteristarchive.com/Books/1804_blake_jerusalem.html (accessed November 27, 2008).

14. Harold Kushner, *When Bad Things Happen to Good People* (New York: HarperCollins, 1981), 133. One wonders what Aaron would say. Would he wish all the good undone so that he could have a few decades of life in this world, especially when he is—according to his father's faith—in the glorious kingdom of *melech ha'olam* (King of the Universe)?

Chapter 24

1. This chapter is the work of Jana Dembski.

2. Tertullian, *Against Marcion* (circa 208) II.16. The translation is by Andreas Andreopoulos in his article "The Icon of God and the Mirror of the Soul: Exploring the Origins of Iconography in Patristic Writing," typescript, available online at http://repositories.cdlib

.org/cgi/viewcontent.cgi?article=1234&context=cmrs/comitatus (accessed November 27, 2008).

3. Augustine, *Confessions,* trans. F. J. Sheed (1943; reprinted Indianapolis: Hackett, 1993), 35.

4. Dante Alighieri, *The Divine Comedy,* "Paradiso," canto X, trans. Henry Wadsworth Longfellow, available online at http://www.everypoet.com/archive/poetry/dante/dante_contents.htm (accessed June 18, 2009).

5. W. H. Auden, "Lullaby," *Another Time* (New York: Random House, 1940), 41.

6. Epictetus, *Discourses* I.6, in Epictetus, *Discourses and Enchiridion,* trans. T. W. Higginson (New York: Walter J. Black, 1946), 17.

7. William Cowper, "God Moves in a Mysterious Way," in *The Lutheran Hymnal* (St. Louis: Concordia, 1941), 514.

8. John Updike, "Archangel," in *Pigeon Feathers* (New York: Ballantine, 1959), 169–71.

9. Augustine, *Confessions,* trans. R. S. Pine-Coffin (New York: Penguin, 1961), 240.

10. Ibid., 232.

11. The Westminster Shorter Catechism, q. 1. Available online at http://www.creeds.net/reformed/Westminster/shorter_catechism.html (accessed November 28, 2008).

12. Aristotle, *Nichomachean Ethics* VI.7, 1141b 3–9, in Richard McKeon, ed., *The Basic Works of Aristotle* (New York: Random House, 1941), 1028.

13. Erich Neumann, *Creative Man: Five Essays by Erich Neumann* (Princeton: Princeton University Press, 1979), 140.

14. Wallace Stevens, "The Idea of Order at Key West," in George Perkins et al., eds., *The American Tradition in Literature* (New York: Random House, 1956), 1316– 17.

15. Ibid.

16. Thomas Aquinas, *Questiones Disputatae de Veritate,* in Timothy McDermott, ed. and trans., *Thomas Aquinas: Selected Philosophical Writings* (Oxford: Oxford University Press, 1993), 54.

NAME INDEX

SUBJECT INDEX

SCRIPTURE INDEX